RESPECTABILITY AND THE LONDON POOR, 1780–1870: THE VALUE OF VIRTUE

Perspectives in Economic and Social History

Series Editors: Andrew August
Jari Eloranta

Titles in this Series

RESPECTABILITY AND THE LONDON POOR, 1780–1870: THE VALUE OF VIRTUE

BY

Lynn MacKay

Routledge
Taylor & Francis Group

LONDON AND NEW YORK

First published 2013 by Pickering & Chatto (Publishers) Limited

Published 2016 by Routledge
2 Park Square, Milton Park, Abingdon, Oxfordshire OX14 4RN
711 Third Avenue, New York, NY 10017, USA

First issued in paperback 2015

Routledge is an imprint of the Taylor & Francis Group, an informa business

© Taylor & Francis 2013
© Lynn MacKay 2013

BRITISH LIBRARY CATALOGUING IN PUBLICATION DATA

MacKay, Lynn, author.
Respectability and the London poor, 1780–1870: the value of virtue. –
(Perspectives in economic and social history)
1. Poor – England – London – History – 18th century. 2. Poor – England –
London – History – 19th century. 3. London (England) – Social conditions
– 18th century. 4. London (England) – Social conditions – 19th century. 5.
London (England) – Economic conditions – 18th century. 6. London (England)
– Economic conditions – 19th century.
I. Title II. Series
305.5'69'09421-dc23

ISBN-13: 978-1-138-66187-5 (pbk)
ISBN-13: 978-1-8489-3281-4 (hbk)
Typeset by Pickering & Chatto (Publishers) Limited

CONTENTS

This book is dedicated to my mother, Patricia Doreen Magee MacKay, whose support has been unwavering, and who never once asked me why I hadn't stayed at the Treasury Board.

ACKNOWLEDGEMENTS

Early stages of this project were funded by the Social Science and Humanities Research Council of Canada, and I was also fortunate to receive research grants from Trent and Brandon Universities. I am grateful for this support. I owe a debt of thanks to many people for their advice and assistance, most obviously to Nick Rogers, who supervised the original research and who provided quite the best introduction to the historical profession. Doug Hay was generous with his time and made many incisive comments on my work. Joan Sangster was untiring in finding ways to keep me employed during the hiring drought after I finished my PhD, for which I am still grateful. Audience members and anonymous reviewers asked thoughtful and thought-provoking questions of the papers and articles that were part of the development of this project, and I thank them.

I should also like to thank the staff of the Westminster Public Archives, the British Library, the London Metropolitan Archives and the National Archives for their assistance and patience. I owe a particular debt of gratitude to my colleagues in the History Department at Brandon, David Winter, Jim Naylor and Patti Harms, and to Jessica Sheetz-Nguyen and Tish Langlois. Finally, my family has been supportive of this project for far longer than should have been necessary, and I am grateful.

LIST OF FIGURES AND TABLES

INTRODUCTION

Historians are agreed that in the last two hundred years there has been a transformation in social relations: in the late eighteenth century, life was lived largely in public outside the home, and this was especially the case in plebeian neighbourhoods in cities. Neighbours depended upon one another in the struggle to make ends meet, lending, borrowing and sometimes simply giving and receiving assistance; subsistence was a collective endeavour. Reputation in the neighbourhood was crucial, and neighbours judged one another constantly; being thought respectable was the key to various kinds of assistance. The focus was generally very short-term; the ability to get through the next week was often the crucial concern. Finally, there was a greater tolerance of violence, both interpersonal and against animals. Since the eighteenth century, home has become a sanctuary and a main locus of leisure time. Families no longer regularly rely on neighbours in trying to maintain subsistence: men and women are meant to make ends meet through their own good efforts. Respectability has been redefined and no longer rests primarily on the judgement of neighbours. The focus has become much more long-term, and violence is thought shameful and is frequently hidden, especially if it occurs within the family. As well as the widespread agreement that such shifts have occurred, there has also been consensus that in the nineteenth century the middle and upper classes promoted such shifts, especially for plebeian women and men, and that demands for the adoption of new codes of behaviour and habits of mind were couched in moral terms. It was thought necessary, in short, for plebeian men and women to undergo a moral reformation.

There has been much less agreement concerning the timing of such shifts, however. Robert Shoemaker, one of the most trenchant, and certainly one of the most prolific historians focusing on these changes, has argued in a series of articles and in his book, *The London Mob*,[1] that by the end of the eighteenth century there had been significant changes in plebeian behaviour. He says street disputes, both physical and verbal, lessened over the course of the eighteenth century, and the importance of reputation diminished. Shoemaker links these shifts to new notions of masculinity and femininity that downplayed violence for the former and encouraged passivity for the latter; to the growth of politeness – especially significant for the middle and upper classes; and to an increasing desire for privacy that lessened the significance of the streets for sociability. Most of all, however, Shoemaker posits the changing relationship between the individual and the community as the crucial factor in lessening interpersonal conflict and violence. He says that for all but the very poorest,

> What one said or did in public, or what others said about you, became less important than what happened behind closed doors, or indeed one's own individual self-exam-ination. Increasingly, the individual was able to shape his or her own reputation without reference to the wider public ...
>
>   A more modern notion of the individual developed ... in which identity was determined by the inner, 'true' self, regardless of public opinion.[2]

Shoemaker concludes that as distinctions between the public and private spheres became more rigid, reputation less important and the neighbourhood ability to police it less efficacious, the street crowd 'lost its central place in London public life', so that 'By the end of the eighteenth century the age of the mob was over'.[3] Underlying these shifts was urban growth, which, according to Shoemaker, 'radi-cally altered patterns of public social interaction in eighteenth-century London. Owing to the rapid pace of population growth, economic change and social mobility, a new kind of urban environment was created in which relationships formed in neighbourhoods and on the streets became less important than those forged in less public contexts'.[4]

In concentrating on various kinds of street activities occurring throughout the century, Shoemaker brings his readers close to the tenor of plebeian life.[5] He also insists, quite rightly, that plebeian Londoners were not mere passive recipi-ents of new cultural notions and values trickling down from on high.[6] That said, however, there are some fundamental problems with the trajectory he describes. First, for all he insists that all classes contributed to shaping the cultural shifts he identifies, it is often not clear in the book which class Shoemaker is discuss-ing – generic Londoners appear regularly. Nor, as Nick Rogers has noted, does Shoemaker adequately explain the plebeian agency he posits. As Rogers points out, 'Gestures toward the decline of neighbourhood and its consequent effect upon public reputations remain gestures. To make the case a richer social geog-raphy of London is required'.[7] Finally, the evidence does not seem to bear out claims that these shifts had taken place for most plebeian people by the end of the eighteenth century.

John Carter Wood has studied particular aspects of these shifts, and the timeframe he posits differs from Shoemaker's. Focusing especially on plebeian violence in nineteenth-century England, Carter Wood charts the ways in which two dominant mentalities of violence interacted through the century: what he terms the 'civilizing' (language idealizing 'rationality and self-restraint') and the 'customary' ('Originating in an older social context, legitimating direct physical confrontation, appealing to less restrained notions of propriety'[8]). According to Carter Wood these mentalities became identified respectively with the middle and working classes, although by the 1870s, he says, all but the roughest sections of the working class had 'adopted various elements of Victorian respectability',[9] resulting in a wide penetration of the 'civilising' ethos, as Jon Lawrence put it in his review of the book.[10] Lawrence criticizes Carter Wood for being overly schematic, particularly in overemphasizing the hegemony of the civilizing mentality in the middle class. For all its sensitivity to customary culture and the importance of spatiality, Carter Wood's book inadequately explores the ambivalences, adaptations and instances of resistance in various sectors of plebeian London to what been called the middle-class civilizing mission.[11] One of his most important influences is the work of Norbert Elias,[12] whose notion that social change begins at the top of society and then trickles out and down through subordinate ranks seems to deny agency to the majority and does not adequately recognize that adoption, co-option, adaptation or rejection of new codes of behaviour may result at least in part from factors internal to subordinate classes. In Elias's version of change, when the majority does reject elite discourses, it seemingly becomes little more than a retrograde force blocking the path to civilization. This diminishes the humanity of the majority and runs counter to the whole impetus of social history in the past four or five decades. For all these reasons, then, Elias's analysis seems rather a poisoned chalice for historians, in spite of the nuanced attempts by people like Carter Wood to use it.[13]

A third period on offer for the transition from customary codes of behaviour is the decade of the 1930s. During this ten-year span more than a million families moved from inner-city neighbourhoods to the glory of home ownership in the suburbs. A recent BBC Four documentary, relying on the work of Martin Pugh and Richard Overy among others, echoed the claims historians have made for the late eighteenth century and the 1870s: in the 1930s 'Daily life became centred on the home and family rather than on the street and the extended community'.[14] Indeed, salient features of the customary neighbourhood were still to be found in some 1950s neighbourhoods – Willmott and Young's examination of Bethnal Green being the best-known study of these – and Philip Abrams's work on even later decades still found in places a 'densely woven world of kin, neighbours, friends and co-workers, highly localised and strongly caring within the confines of quite tightly defined relationships'.[15]

Clearly there is no consensus concerning the timing of this shift that in the long run all agree took place. This study argues that in many sectors of plebeian London, customary forms of thought and behaviour persisted far longer than often supposed; that neighbourhood reputation upon which respectability rested remained crucial; that collective resources for maintaining subsistence remained popular and necessary; that a short-term focus remained the norm; and that violence remained accepted. There was, in fact, no single date at which a transformation in social relations can be said to have occurred for plebeian London as a whole. At different times, different sectors adopted, adapted, resisted, manipulated or rejected various strands of the new discourse extolling privacy and individual responsibility. In order to make sense of this very complex situation, a systematic framework of analysis is helpful, since it is in the nature of cultural transformations to be complicated. While making no claim to chart the transition being examined to its fruition, this study hopefully will help establish a more systematic approach to understanding such change.

To this end, four factors have been identified that helped customary culture remain resilient: spatiality, economic uncertainty, the extent and nature of the social safety net, and finally, the lack of mobility. The importance of spatiality has, until recent years, perhaps been under-appreciated by historians. As Edward Soja has noted, geography became marginalized in critical social thought in the nineteenth century, and space came to be seen 'as dead, fixed, undialectical, immobile, while time was seen to be filled with richness, fecundity, life, dialectic'. Throughout his work, Soja has opposed 'space blinkering historicism',[16] as he calls it, but he also notes that while space helps shape social beings, people also make and remake physical spaces.[17] The spatial configuration of neighbourhoods – the type of housing and its arrangement along streets, courts, yards and alleys – was crucial in promoting or discouraging the kind of private, self-sufficient family life being touted by middle- and upper-class reformers in the nineteenth century. As will be seen, the spatiality of plebeian neighbourhoods in central London was not conducive to the new demands. When economic uncertainty is widespread, especially when resulting from fairly long-term patterns and structures of employment, people frequently hesitate to embrace discourses that may well make subsistence more difficult to maintain, or which cannot deliver on what they promise. As David Green has shown, economic security in many of the trades found in the central part of the capital was decreasing during this period, making cultural experimentation yet more risky for many plebeian Londoners.[18] The chief instrument of state social assistance at this time was the poor law. During the nineteenth century, both this system and philanthropy were reformulated to reflect and achieve priorities and values the middle and upper classes thought necessary. Both changed in ways that limited their usefulness to plebeian Londoners. As Martin Bulmer has observed, 'Self-help networks at the local level were a realistic response to low incomes, economic adversity and unpredictable domestic crisis. In the absence of state support for the relief in the home of illness, old age or unemployment, the "safety net" for most families was the neighbourhood itself'.[19]

The final factor, lack of mobility, resulted from the absence of widely accessible cheap public transportation before the last quarter of the nineteenth century. Even with its establishment, however, plebeian women and men were still often tied to the neighbourhoods of central London. Men had to be able to work on very short notice when a job turned up; women needed to be able to access credit at shops where they were known. As George Sims said of the central London poor in 1883, 'There are thousands of these families who would go away into the suburbs, where we want to get them, if only the difficulty of travelling expenses to and fro could be conquered. They herd together all in closely packed quarters because they must be where they can get to the dock, the yard, the wharf, and the warehouses without expense'.[20] Acting together, these factors combined to help the web of customary cultural responses remain resilient and plausible for many plebeian Londoners between 1780 and 1870. Given that the last of these factors – cheap public transportation – in the time period of this study is important through its absence, the focus of examination will be on the first three. Identifying factors that permitted customary cultural practices to retain their appeal does not mean they wholly determined such preferences. Rather, such factors should be seen as creating conditions of plausibility: helping to convince people that particular behaviours and priorities – particular discourses – offered practical help and the greatest chance of success in the business of maintaining life.

Saying that different sectors of plebeian London dealt with the new notions of social relations at different times is not to deny the existence of class. Rather, neighbourliness of the sort that will be discussed in this study played a crucial role in the development of class, although admittedly, it was not a necessary and sufficient condition automatically producing class solidarities. The argument of this book builds on the work of Catharina Lis and Hugo Soly, and David Green. As Lis and Soly acknowledge, neighbourliness, and the street life in which it was embedded, could provide 'mutual support and consolidation' that might diffuse the potential for class conflict, encouraging people to endure conditions better resisted. Moreover, given that plebeian London was composed of innumerable strata often shading one into another, whose occupants assiduously defended their status, neighbourliness could easily lead to intra-class conflict and dissention. Nevertheless, Lis and Soly also point out that 'the vitality and conviviality of much working-class street life could cement a sense of shared identity and common interests among the … class', and this in turn had the potential to promote class solidarity. Thus, neighbourliness could be a crucial enabling factor: as Lis and Soly note, 'Cultural practices like gossip, blame, public ridicule and street demonstrations remained focused on preventing forms of internal differentiations that could harm solidarity'.[21] Neighbourliness also made it possible to raise street crowds quickly in order to address a variety of grievances – actions that cannot simply be dismissed as pre-political mob fury, as Edward Thompson and a host of followers have shown. Rather, in environments in which alternative forms of action were difficult and limited, crowd tactics, as James C. Scott has insisted, did not reflect popular incapacity for more 'advanced' forms of action, but were the result of conscious, realistic assessments of political constraints.[22] Neighbourliness also played a role in more formal responses to authorities and employers. Whether or not it is seen as a kind of precursor to mature class consciousness does not negate the role of neighbourliness as a continuous enabling factor. Among male artisans, the most politicized sector of the working class, solidarity to be sure centred on the workplace, but as Green has shown, it also 'meshed imperceptibly with working-class residential communities. The pub, house of call, friendly society and trade unions were primarily local institutions that reinforced the close spatial links between workplace and home'.[23] For casual workers, propinquity was also crucial. These workers had to be known by employers and to be close at hand to take up any work opportunities that arose. Consequently, while they moved often, these people rarely moved out of a neighbourhood. As Green has noted, 'structures of information and assistance were highly localized and reinforced the role of the neighbourhood in working-class life' so that 'the working-class community overlapped closely with that of the workplace'.[24] Green concludes that propinquity

> provided a local setting for the construction of dense, social networks in which neighbours and fellow-workers were one and the same. Those who offended against the trade, by refusing to join the union, for example, or acting as a blackleg, ran the risk of alienating both workmates and neighbours alike.
>
> This pattern of residential propinquity had much to do with the solidarity of working-class communities, and specifically with the close associational life of artisans.[25]

A multiplicity of identities within plebeian London was available as people defined themselves and their status against one another. Nevertheless, a number of features of the discourse on customary popular culture were shared by various plebeian aggregates, and there was at times an awareness of common interests – or at least an identification of common enemies – that could transcend particular plebeian collectivities. Class, in short, was a Janus-faced concept, in one direction facing outward, calibrating relations with other classes, and in the process helping continuously to shape and reshape a shared plebeian identity based on neighbourhood and work solidarities. Facing the other direction, inward within labouring communities, class was a finely graduated hierarchy that could lead to roiling discontent and acrimony between and among plebeian people. The notion that class does not possess a unitary definition borrows from the insights of David Cannadine, but rejects his insistence on the greater valency of the hierarchic: that is, the social world of Britain as a whole encompassing 'a carefully graded ordering of rank and dignity, in which each layer melded and merged almost imperceptibly into the next', being 'a seamless web'.[26] This kind of privileging seems necessarily to eviscerate class as a meaningful analytic concept. Rather, in understanding class it is necessary to attempt to maintain a Janiform counterpoise, in this case to see plebeian Londoners as copemates in both its contronymic meanings: at once as partners and as antagonists.

In positing this understanding it is necessary to consider the relationship between language and class. Certainly, in the wake of the linguistic turn the importance of language has to be acknowledged, but this does not mean that it wholly produces class. The moral reform discourse was available throughout the nineteenth century, but for much of the period it met with dogged resistance, or at best provisional and temporary acquiescence from a number of plebeian collectivities. Not until structural factors like the labour market, the spatial arrangements of housing and neighbourhoods, a more useful social safety net and cheap public transit had been reconfigured did the discourses of moral individualism gain currency. As Eley and Nield observed,

> Poststructuralism has been at its most productive when forcing us to confront the complex machineries of meaning through which poverty comes to be understood, all the complex modalities of its social and cultural construction ... That we now need to approach poverty as a discursive formation is for us beyond dispute. However, that does not exhaust all the registers of possible or necessary approach.
>
> For example, can the poststructuralist register deal sufficiently with the question of how people enter the condition of being poor, with the processes that produce and reproduce poverty as well as those that discursively secure such a condition of being? ...
>
> Discourse may provide the limits of our ability to talk about things, but discursive constructions cannot exhaust the world's field of precultural or noncultural settings and actualities.[27]

This study explores the plausibilities structured by language, but also those emanating from non-cultural settings, insisting on the retention of 'the more structuralist register of analysis' that characterized social history.[28]

Before turning to the focus and context of this study, it is necessary to explicate several central terms: 'respectability', 'resistance' and 'the poor'. Respectability is a slippery notion and has been interpreted variously by historians. It has not often been seen, however, as a plebeian resource to be deployed against the upper classes – as a weapon of the weak, to use Scott's evocative phrase. Certainly, in trying to explain why plebeian men and women chose to adopt a respectable way of life, a number of historians have focused on its relationship to class and status, asking whether it promoted or weakened class solidarity. Both Geoffrey Best and F. M. L. Thompson, for instance, insisted that notions of respectability cut across class boundaries, promoting greater consensus in nineteenth-century society. Other historians like Geoffrey Crossick and R. Q. Gray disagreed, arguing that respectability did not promote greater consensus throughout society, but took on particular class inflections and somewhat different meanings – that skilled workers, in particular, moulded and adapted it to a traditional artisanal culture. Respectability helped to define a particular identity for these workers and to further the collective aspirations of this group. Still other historians like Neville Kirk and J. Robert Wegs have shown that respectability existed beyond the rarefied climes of the skilled worker – that it was widespread throughout the working class.[29] Kirk argued that in the 1840s respectability, which he saw as indigenous to the working class and not imposed from above, promoted class consciousness. After the political defeats of the 1840s and the growth of greater economic stability, however, Kirk came to believe that this changed, that respectability became 'a point of division which worked against class solidarity'. Indeed, he thought that by the 1860s the main cultural division in the working class was between the rough and the respectable.[30] In much of this work, the focus was on the working class itself – or segments thereof – and much less on the role plebeian respectability actually played in the process of relating to other classes.

These various interpretations of respectability share another underlying assumption: they are predicated upon a fairly clear-cut definition of this notion. Most historians have agreed that the respectable working man did not rely on charity, poor relief or patronage, but made ends meet through his wages and through friendly society or union support. He was independent, and increasingly in the second half of the nineteenth century he was expected to be the sole financial support of his family. His focus, as far as possible, was on the long-term maintenance of independence. Individual initiative in achieving subsistence rather than reliance on traditional neighbourhood-based communal resources was a cardinal tenet of his respectability. The respectable worker's wife withdrew from gossipy street-centred neighbourhood life, with its female borrowing networks and reliance on credit and pawning to make ends meet. Feminist historians have shown that for these women, their ability to provide a well-maintained home for their families and to raise well-behaved and well-turned-out children with proper prospects were crucial centres of their self-respect.[31] The respectable pursued self-improvement, reading worthwhile texts and increasingly favouring rational recreation and sobriety by the late decades of the century. They were readily recognizable, moreover, through their style of dress and the cleanliness of their homes, indoors and out.

While respectability as discussed thus far may seem straightforward, a number of historians have shown the notion to be fraught with ambiguity. As Jennifer Davis pointed out, the division between the rough and the respectable was not hard, fast and categorical, but elusive and contingent upon perceived perceptions – the 'rough', the 'casual poor', or towards the end of the century, the 'residuum' – however named, the so-called disreputable were, in fact, an ideological construct rather than an identifiable group with objective reality.[32] Indeed, it is revealing that upper-class contemporaries and historians alike have often had difficulty in differentiating the rough from the respectable.[33]

The assumptions underlying the understanding of respectability have also been called into question by other historians who have depicted the plebeian adoption of respectability as an instrument for pragmatic gain: a façade of appearance and behaviour adopted strategically in order to gain access to various kinds of assistance. As Peter Bailey argued, individuals may have donned and doffed a respectable persona depending upon the circumstances in which they found themselves. Respectability became less an internalized code of values and behaviour than a social role individuals could deploy – or not – in the fluid urban world of the mid-nineteenth century. Often, as Bailey indicated, it was used strategically to impress philanthropists. Iain McCalman further muddied the water by demonstrating the ease with which some early nineteenth-century plebeian radicals combined respectability in some areas of their lives with pornography, drunkenness, and even blackmail and fraud.[34] Behaviour could be, as was, compartmentalized, a notion further complicating this study.

One of the central issues here is the extent to which rough or respectable values were internalized. Arguments that respectability promoted or undermined class solidarity assume implicitly that the discourse was sincerely held. Clearly, as Davis, Bailey and McCalman have shown, this cannot be assumed unproblematically. The difficulty seems irresolvable, since historians writing long after the period in question cannot know with certainty the degree to which belief in the tenets of respectability was sincere, however much they may try to empathize with these historical actors. Indeed, claims that it promoted or weakened class solidarity are ultimately speculative, since they assume a transparent relationship between behaviour and belief. Bailey provided a plausible alternate reading of the evidence, although his interpretation is still beset by the same problem: belief – or lack thereof – cannot simply be read off or inferred from behaviour. One way out of this impasse is to see behaviour – in this case respectable behaviour – as situational: the best we can do is to explore it within the contested terrain in which it operated. This means exploring respectability where possible in the context of what Mary Jo Maynes has termed 'the whole-life perspective', since people act 'on the basis of the sense they make of a particular experience within the context of a lifetime'.[35] To this end, autobiographies and partial institutional biographies of workhouse inmates have been used repeatedly throughout this study.

In examining the ways in which respectability was deployed in the lives of plebeian women and men, it is also necessary to rethink the nature of resistance and accommodation. In doing so, the work of a number of anthropologists and sociologists is helpful. Scott pointed out that elites are largely responsible for formulating what he calls the public transcript – of which respectability was a part. By public transcript he means the openly accepted version of relations between the dominant and their subordinates. It is the version of social relations as the elite wishes them to be seen, but there are limitations on the elite. In order to legitimate its rule in the eyes of its subordinates, the elite must act according to the tenets of the public transcript, or at least represent its actions as falling within the purview of this transcript. Scott also says that elites and their subordinates each possess hidden transcripts, which take place away from the public stage. In their hidden transcripts subordinates can express to one another the anger and resentment against the elite that it would be too dangerous to voice publicly. Hidden transcripts of the subordinate also contain veiled or anonymous acts of resistance – Scott gives poaching and tax evasion as two common examples.[36] The relationship between public and hidden transcripts, moreover, is a site of constant struggle: subordinates constantly test limits to see what they can get away with; elites strive to impose and maintain their versions of public transcripts. The situation is not as cut and dried as it might at first seem, for subordinates may well choose to criticize the dominant if the latter, in their behaviour, are perceived to fall short of the standards set out in the public transcript. As Scott has pointed out, such criticisms were difficult to deflect because 'they begin by adopting the ideological terms of reference of the elite'.[37]

Marc Steinberg, relying on the ideas of the Bakhtin circle, has explored this kind of situation in some depth. In his analyses of the uses the Spitalfields weavers made of the ideology of political economy, he notes that ideological struggle does not mean that one worldview is pitted against another. Rather, such struggle was 'a conflict on the boundaries, that is, those areas in this dominant ideology where definitions of the moral, just, and possible were open to contention'.[38] Steinberg says this because no dominant ideology is ever totally hegemonic. There are always spaces within the ideology where alternative or even subversive meanings can be produced, and since hegemony is constructed through actions as well as words, experience can provide a vantage through which to 'challenge the reasonableness of the ruling ideology'.[39] By ideology, Steinberg means 'the collective production of shared moral meanings for the conduct of social life, critique and change'.[40]

For both Scott and Steinberg, resistance is a constant process, even when plebeian people were not directly and overtly challenging the dominant discourse. This broader notion of resistance has also been explored in two themed issues of the *International Journal of Historical Archaeology*[41] – as Bill Frazer put it, 'Resistance is carried out not only by explicitly contesting and subverting, but also by circumventing and, nearer to a practical consciousness, simply ignoring domination'. Frazer insists that wherever power differentials have existed, so too has resistance: 'to accept the presence of inequality and domination in the past means understanding that resistance, as the other half of a dialectical relation of power, did also [exist]'.[42] Respectability, in the hands of some plebeian women and men, was just such a site of agency and resistance. To be sure, as a number of historians have observed, it was used to denote status and to ensure access to various kinds of assistance, but these were only some of the ways in which it was useful. It was also used to resist the upper classes and to fight for rights, foci that are less often discussed. Simon Cordery's insistence that friendly societies used respectability to gain freedom from middle-class control is an instance where this kind of use has been recognized. Cordery argued that respectability was a resource for friendly societies that used it 'initially to gain legal protection and later to defend public-house meetings from middle-class censure'. Just as plebeian institutions were able to use it 'to forge an arena of autonomy for working-class mutualism (the pursuit of collective social security)',[43] so too, at an individual level, respectability functioned as an important weapon.

As noted earlier, the vernacular population of London was divided into a multiplicity of strata whose boundaries were often ill-defined, although that between skilled and unskilled workers was considered significant and generally recognized. This study pays particular attention to the most vulnerable in London's plebeian communities: the poor. The inexactness of the terms 'poor' and 'poverty' is problematic, however. For example, in the early nineteenth century, the contemporary police magistrate Patrick Colquhoun, whose works were widely read and approved, saw poverty as a social necessity that benefited society as a whole, since it was a goad causing people to work. Labour, he believed, was the source of wealth and prosperity. Thus, for Colquhoun, poverty was 'the state and condition in society where the individual has no surplus labour in store and consequently, no property but what is derived from the constant exercise of industry in the various occupations of life ... the state of everyone who must labour for subsistence'.[44] Indigence, on the other hand, was a calamity, and he defined it as 'the condition of society which implies want, misery and distress ... the state of anyone who is destitute of the means of subsistence and is unable to procure it to the extent nature requires'.[45] This kind of distinction, while common during the period, was imprecise, since the boundaries between the two states were often amorphous. Nor can hard and fast distinctions between artisans and labourers easily be drawn. Aside from problems of occupational nomenclature, people often changed jobs, and within one family there could be a variety of skill and wage levels. Moreover, while many skilled artisans lived above the subsistence level, earning more than required for their everyday needs, many other artisans fell into destitution due to illness, accident, deskilling or trade depression. Labourers who earned less and worked less regularly were even more liable to be destitute at some time in their lives. Historians have regularly pointed out the vulnerability of plebeian Londoners generally: increasing difficulties in a number of trades, as well as illness, recession, seasonality, age, family size or, conversely, death in the family were just some of the factors that could tip people into destitution at various points in the life cycle.[46] Rather than attempting to impose rigid definitions of poverty and the poor at the outset, measures identifying the at-risk and the most vulnerable will be explored in the course of the study. For these reasons, the 'poor' who are the subject of this study are those people who lived close to the subsistence level, as well as those who actually applied for parish and charitable relief.

The manner in which poverty has been understood, the causes assigned for it, and the solutions proposed to it have all varied with time and place. Similarly, the ways in which the poor understood their situation, their cultural priorities, and the constrained and limited options they preferred in making ends meet have also shifted over time. Indeed, in England by the 1780s, the strains in the conventional eighteenth-century conceptual language of poverty had become increasingly apparent as poor relief levels escalated dramatically, and new discourses in economics and criminality gained a hearing among the middle and upper classes. Poor relief costs rose from £1.5 million in 1775 to more than £4 million in 1800, peaking at almost £7.9 million in 1818 for England and Wales. By the 1820s costs had fallen, but gradually crept up to reach £7 million once more in 1832. Thereafter, even though the population virtually doubled, this benchmark was not achieved again until 1868.[47] This increase in the level of poverty was puzzling and disturbing to the affluent, and it engendered an extended debate on the nature and treatment of the problem. After Britain joined the French Revolutionary Wars in 1793, the debate was intensified by fears for social stability due to high food prices and the seeming incursion of Jacobin ideas. Such fears remained high in the years immediately following the end of the wars, flared again in the period around the passage of the New Poor Law in 1834, and then again with the coming of economic depression and Chartism in the 1840s. In London the 1860s were also very difficult, due in part to the fallout from the Overend & Gurney collapse. Shock waves 'coursed through the London economy ... hastening the demise of Thames shipbuilding and dragging hundreds into the mire of bankruptcy'.[48]

The timeframe of this study, 1780 to 1870, was chosen for several reasons: most obviously, it bookends the conventional period of industrialization. The 1780s also saw growing disillusionment with the Old Poor Law and increasing calls for the moral regeneration of the poor. Sustained population growth was beginning, while the crime wave after the American war increased worries about the efficacy of punishment and convinced many of the need to reform the system. By the 1860s London was undergoing a crisis in the relief of poverty. Kidd calls it a 'watershed' decade in which a sense of urban crisis 'provided the inescapable backdrop to most discussion of society's response to poverty for the rest of the century'.[49] By the 1870s Britain's economy seemed to be entering a new phase with the onset of a prolonged depression. The decade also saw the adoption of new forms of municipal improvement schemes that led to extensive slum clearance: projects that greatly intensified housing problems in London's central districts.

Overall, this was a period during which calls for the moral regeneration of the poor became ever more clamorous and concern for metropolitan living conditions grew exponentially. The urban poor were seen as deeply problematic due to their massed numbers, and this was especially the case for London. Population in Britain was exploding during the period. Already 6.5 million for England and Wales in 1751, it had climbed to 8.3 million in 1791, and to just under 9 million ten years later. By 1821 it stood at 12 million, by the mid-century at just about 18 million and by 1871 at nearly 23 million.[50] By the end of the eighteenth century almost one-third of the English lived in towns of 2,500 or more, and of these 2.5 million people, almost 1 million lived in London alone,[51] making the capital city by far the largest conurbation in Britain – and indeed Europe. By 1811 London's population of slightly less than 1,400,000 was almost double the 650,000 figure given in 1751.[52] By 1851 almost 2.4 million people lived in the capital and by 1871 a little less than 3.3 million.[53] As London expanded, its economic role also began to alter. Regional markets were increasingly integrated into national and international markets, and London became the centre of this new activity. A large proportion of the country's imports and exports passed through the capital – especially goods traded with Europe and the East and West Indies.[54] London also became the reigning international banking and financial centre, ousting Amsterdam as Europe's premier money market and in the process attracting foreign investment.[55] The capital came to be a site for much of the experimentation in the forms of relief afforded to the needy, both public and private,[56] and certainly many of the reformers involved in the *fin de siècle* debate were residents of the capital. While these reasons make the capital a particularly apposite focus for examination, its very size also makes it unmanageable for the kinds of close analysis needed in this study. To that end, where appropriate, the parish of St Martin in the Fields and the City of Westminster will form the foci of examination. For much of the period, a wealth of documentation has survived for St Martin's – workhouse and settlement records, as well as rate books and vestry minutes. Since less historical work focusing on the West End has been undertaken – particularly for the period under examination – this will add to our knowledge of the dimensions of London poverty.

St Martin's was one of the oldest and largest parishes in Westminster, containing some 305 acres, although not all of this land was inhabited. Green Park, more than half of both the Queen's Gardens, and St James's Park fell within the parish boundaries. The Haymarket, Cockspur Street, Charing Cross and Whitehall formed the western perimeter of inhabited neighbourhoods (see Figure

2.1).[57] Its population stood at some 26,000 in the late eighteenth century, making it a small city in and of itself, and while it was one of the wealthiest, the parish also contained areas of real and wretched poverty the equal of anything to be found in the East End. Indeed, Dickens's judgement of Westminster certainly held for St Martin's:

> As the brightest lights cast the deepest shadows, so are the splendours and luxuries of the West End found in juxtaposition with the most deplorable manifestations of human wretchedness and depravity. There is no part of the metropolis which presents a more chequered aspect, both physical and moral, than Westminster. The most lordly streets are frequently but a mask for the squalid districts which lie behind them.[58]

Because of high rents, and fuel and labour costs, London was a city of small workshops, and remained so throughout the period of industrialization – although Green has rightly emphasized the importance of large firms in certain sectors.[59] The pattern of small firms held in Westminster, which overall was one of the wealthiest areas in the metropolis. As the administrative and legal centre, it attracted the rich and powerful, whose presence in turn brought a number of luxury trades. Jewellers and coach-makers were especially prominent in St Martin's, and other skilled craftsmen also set up their workshops in the vicinity. As Green has pointed out for Mayfair, one of the most affluent neighbourhoods in London's West End, 'the wealthy comprised 10 per cent of the population whilst the remaining 90 per cent consisted of those who served their needs: artisans and retailers who made and sold luxury goods, servants who catered for the daily needs of the family, and builders and decorators who repaired their houses'.[60] Indeed, as Richard Dennis has noted, the rich required a veritable army of service workers: 'builders, cabinetmakers, upholsterers, painters, plumbers, gasfitters, coachmen, ostlers, gardeners, cleaners, cooks, messengers, errand boys, newspaper vendors, butchers, bakers, grocers and greengrocers, fishmongers, delivery boys, dressmakers, tailors, haberdashers, laundresses ... few of whom were *resident* domestic servants living in the homes of the rich'.[61] This service-consumption economy serving a rich clientele, while distinctive to Westminster, was not the whole story, however, for beggars, prostitutes and casual workers also flocked to the area so full of 'sites of possible earnings'.[62]

Like most other parts of central London – in contrast to the suburbs – St Martin's was not experiencing rapid growth during this period. According to the census of 1801,[63] there were 25,752 people living in 2,791 houses in the parish. By 1831 both population and the number of inhabited houses fell to 23,732 and 2,252 respectively. The population decrease – 4,282 persons – was blamed specifically on the Strand improvements (including Trafalgar Square, begun in 1829).[64] By 1861 a population of 22,636 lived in 2,283 houses. The Garrick Street improvements were completed in this year, driving 'through crowded working-class neighbourhoods'.[65] Thus, the parish was experiencing a slow demographic decline, in contrast to London as a whole, which doubled its population in the forty years between 1801 and 1841. Unlike the situation in a number of central metropolitan parishes, however, this decline did not result in drastically higher density levels. According to the various census data, an average of 9.2 people lived in a house in St Martin's in 1801.[66] By 1811 this had risen to 9.5 per house, and in 1821 to a zenith of 10.6 per house. In 1831 the density level began to fall slightly, reaching 10.5 people per house. Ten years later the density level fell even further to 9.8, but then in 1851 rose to 10.7 before sinking again in 1861 to 9.9 – an overall rise from the beginning of the period of 0.7 people per house.

If population growth and density levels were fairly stable during the period, St Martin's inhabitants also shared some characteristics that remained tolerably constant as well. In the first place, women outnumbered men in the parish throughout these years, although overall they never formed more than 53 per cent of the population. Younger women were especially numerous. In 1822 women between twenty and thirty years of age formed 56 per cent of that age group in Westminster. By 1861 the percentages respectively had fallen to 52 and 51 per cent. As will be seen later, this skewing, which was especially apparent in prime employment years, spelled trouble for women, since the trades open to them invariably suffered from labour surpluses. In 1841, the first census that gives evidence of birthplace, nearly half of St Martin's inhabitants – 48 per cent – had been born outside the county. This was not a new phenomenon, however, since London had long been a mecca for migrants.[67] In keeping with another general London pattern, there were proportionally more adults in St Martin's than was the case in the country at large: 67 per cent of the parish inhabitants were over twenty in 1841. Again, this was not a new development in a city long infamous for its high infant mortality rates.[68]

With respect to class make-up, L. D. Schwarz estimates that for the metropolis as a whole, only 2 to 3 per cent of the population was upper class (which he defined as families whose incomes were £200 or more per annum). The 'middling classes', with incomes between £80 and £130, formed another 16 to 21 per cent, while the working population consisted of the remaining 75 per cent.[69] With respect to the latter, Schwarz says that approximately 8 per cent were self-employed artisans in Westminster, and that generally speaking, artisans (self-employed or otherwise) formed approximately 35 per cent of the working population. Conversely, he says, 'two-thirds of the working population and half of the entire adult male population were unskilled or semi-skilled'. This was very likely the picture for St Martin's, with one exception.[70] Westminster was one of the wealthier areas of London, and it is likely that the percentage of St Martin's population in the upper class was higher than 3 per cent. Indeed, in the poll books for the 1802 and 1818 Westminster elections, 5 and 6 per cent of the voters identified their occupation as 'gentleman'. While there is no indication of their income, it is probably not unreasonable to assume that the upper class, as Schwarz defined it, consisted of approximately 5 per cent of St Martin's population.

The study has been organized as follows: Chapter 1 explores the contours of customary culture in plebeian London. It focuses especially on those features and resources that assisted in the ongoing battle to achieve subsistence. As such, this necessarily means that some important components of customary culture will suffer relative neglect in this study. Leisure pastimes, for example, will frequently appear in what follows, but will not in themselves be a major focus of study, although, to be sure, the solidarities established at the public house, in gambling dens or at the theatre were undoubtedly helpful in obtaining assistance from neighbours and co-workers. While this study was in its final stages of preparation, Rosalind Crone's monograph on leisure in nineteenth-century London, *Violent Victorians*, was published. In some respects, the argument in Crone's book is similar to the one being made here: both studies claim that customary culture persisted longer than has often been supposed, although clearly this culture was adapted to the urban environment. They differ, however, in how respectability is understood. Crone uses this term as a shorthand for the constellation of values and behaviours being promoted from above. Here, as seen earlier, respectability is understood as a process: a site of ongoing negotiation. In spite of this very real difference, this study will hopefully add to the rich and complex understanding of nineteenth-century plebeian culture that Crone has presented.

If leisure is not a central focus in this study, neither will prostitution, begging or theft be examined systematically, although all will be discussed at various points. The demarcation line between those practising prostitution, begging and theft on the one hand, and the rest of plebeian London on the other, was nowhere as hard and fast as sometimes supposed. Part-time prostitution necessitated by economic hardship was not rare, as Mayhew's needlewomen attested; begging did not necessarily lead to irredeemable moral pollution, as contemporaries frequently supposed; and the distinction between finding an item and stealing it could be rather grey and blurred in a society in which virtually anything – even dog excrement – could have recycle value.[71] Chapter 2 focuses on the physical spaces of late eighteenth-century London and especially of St Martin in the Fields, seeking to identify the courts, yards and alleys where the poor lived and the impact the built environment had on social relations. Chapter 3 explores employment for both men and women. While the same kinds of work remained prominent in central London between 1780 and 1850, conditions in a number of trades became more precarious. Chapter 4 focuses on formal kinds of assistance, principally on poor relief, since recipients can be tracked over time, although philanthropy will be considered as well. The last chapter focuses on two case studies that show how the factors explored in this book presented opportunities or exerted pressures on a woman from a relatively secure artisanal family and on a group who came to define the disreputable: the costermongers. This chapter seeks to counteract a danger of this kind of study, slippage into a crude binary opposition: customary versus modern, collective versus individual. What historians label as 'customary' was not static, but was rather subject to mutation. The urban customary culture that will be discussed in this book was an adaptation of the culture women and men brought with them to London from their natal villages.[72] It was gauged to meet the needs of a new environment, and depending upon local constraints and pressures, could vary. Within the capital itself, as the environment changed, culture could be adjusted. Anna Clark has shown, for example, that when journeymen artisans could no longer reasonably expect to become masters, they narrowed their definition of respectability to a focus on trade skill. At the same time, they devised new rituals and practices centring on drinking and membership in male clubs that strengthened fraternal solidarities, but resulted in more misogynist behaviour.[73] Conversely, new cultural discourses or parts thereof could be incorporated into existing ones. The permutations of culture and the social relations attendant upon it were many and varied.

1 BORROWING A WARM

The lineaments of customary culture shaped and were shaped by the lives of plebeian Londoners. Although some historians like Keith Thomas have noted of the capital generally that 'the growing anonymity of daily life set people free from the constant invigilation and moral surveillance which was such a feature of smaller communities,'[1] this was less the case in plebeian neighbourhoods. The spatial arrangements of houses virtually guaranteed that neighbours would be closely aware of one another's activities. Privacy was difficult, and much of the time impossible: even intimate bits of one's life were open to comment and judgement. The pressures to conform socially may have been slackening generally, but communal supervision of morality and behaviour were still the norm in central neighbourhoods. Plebeian Londoners were not isolated, alienated individuals tossed hither and yon in an anonymous sea of humanity, which Thomas certainly recognized when he continued that 'many districts in big cities were essentially little villages, where anonymity was impossible.'[2] Plebeian London was a city of neighbourhoods, and while today this term congers up warm and positive images, the situation was somewhat different during the period of this study. Neighbourhoods were not simply oases of sweetness and light, sustaining and nurturing women and men in an otherwise hostile environment. Rather, they played a more ambivalent role in the lives of Londoners. They were often the locus of tension and discord as well as mutual support. Little was needed to set off acrimonious disputes between neighbours, yet neighbours could also behave with such generosity to one another that upper-class observers were astonished.

The sense of neighbourhood in London did differ from that in small rural villages, where people were known to their neighbours and probably had been for most of their lives. Migration was very high in the capital – at least 8,000 people annually moved to London in the early eighteenth century, and, according to Penelope Corfield, 'since the gross turnover of population was much greater than the net increase, literally tens of thousands of people must have entered and left London each year'. She continues, 'In 1757 it was estimated that "two Thirds of the grown Persons at any Time in *London* came from distant Parts". Dr. Bland's survey of the origins of several thousand adult patients at the Westminster General Dispensary between 1774 and 1781 showed that an even larger proportion, fully 75 per cent, had been born outside the capital.[3] Corfield cautions that Bland's figures may not have been typical for London as a whole, but it is apparent, even though official surveys are lacking, that migration was very high. This situation might seem to undermine claims for the importance of neighbourhood, but mobility was counterbalanced by density, for as Peregrine Horden and Nicholas Purcell have noted, greater surveillance occurred in cities than in more rural enclaves simply because it was harder to find urban locales free of people.[4]

Moreover, once they arrived in the capital, Londoners tended to settle and to remain in particular neighbourhoods. David Green and Alan Parton found that between 1832 and 1862, in St Giles in the Fields, for instance, 40 per cent of people questioned by poor law officials had resided in the parish for more than ten years. More than half had lived in St Giles for at least five years, and in all, two-thirds had lived in the parish for at least two years. These were among the poorest people in a parish notorious for poverty. One would expect them to move frequently as their rent fell into arrears, and high mobility is certainly apparent from the poor relief records.[5] Nevertheless, the vast majority of these moves were short-distance: people tended to move around within their neighbourhoods, but not out of them. Given the lack of public transportation, it was important for men and women to be within walking distance of work. It was also vital to remain in a neighbourhood where one was known, in order to have access to crucial resources needed to maintain subsistence. Green and Parton have pointed out that this proximity 'fostered kinship links and social relations and as a result dense social networks were built up between neighbours, kin and friends within such small enclosed worlds'.[6] In short, residents in a neighbourhood were generally well known to one another; the situation could hardly have been otherwise given the very public nature of life at this time.

Plebeian dwellings were not the self-contained entities that homes are today: virtually no apartments had running water, and food could not be kept for long. This meant that plebeian women had to make frequent forays into the streets – to fetch water from cisterns and standing taps, to buy food and to gossip at the local shop (where most of them were sufficiently well known to run credit tabs), and to lend and borrow items among neighbours. Men, too, spent much of their time outside the family home. While many men worked at home, a number of the most common occupations in London required them to move about. Porters on delivery, dock workers, those engaged in the building trades, and small masters delivering shoes, clothing or furniture to often distant middlemen all regularly travelled about the streets. Moreover, shopkeepers often had front windows completely open to the street which tended to erase the boundaries between indoor and out and private and public.

Local pubs and coffee houses were popular venues for socializing. Indeed, some people spent most of their waking hours in these establishments. Coffee houses were used by some as a 'respectable' address, as Samuel Johnson had been told earlier in the century,[7] and there are references in the Old Bailey Proceedings to people staying in public houses around the clock. The poorest and least reputable used night-cellars – cheap drinking places – as shelters in which to pass the night. The anonymous author of *Low Life or One Half of the World Knows Not How the Other Half Live* described these places at 3 am: 'Night-Cellars about Covent Garden and Charing Cross filled with Mechanicks, some sleeping, others playing at Cards, with dead Beer before them, and Link-Boys giving their attendance.'[8]

The streets in the vicinity of their homes were the playgrounds of poor children, even when there were green spaces in the area. Speaking of the royal parks in Westminster, George Godwin explained, 'only few of the poorest avail themselves of those very public places; and many have remarked with wonder how small a number of children from pent-up places make use of the parks. This is to be partly accounted for by the circumstances that the ill-clad are often looked at with suspicion. Moreover, young children seldom stray far from home'.[9] Even for children, life was largely lived in public, but a highly localized one.

The streets were themselves the site of entertainment, novelty and excitement. Impromptu football matches, fistfights, arguments and rows and the hue and cry could all induce people to move onto the streets, as could ballad sellers, street entertainers, costermongers and street sellers calling out their wares. All of this meant that people did not spend a lot of waking time in their rooms. Moreover, the public nature of life meant that neighbours were very aware of the comings and goings of people. Neighbours watched each other with relish, and at times with disapproval. Invigilation and moral surveillance were constant, which is apparent in a number of defamation cases heard in the consistory courts of the Church of England between 1780 and 1820. It is telling that in two-thirds of the altercations the cases record, the dispute took place in the streets, or in shops or pubs. Defamation was still the province of the church courts, and while the consistory court heard far fewer than had been the norm in the seventeenth and eighteenth centuries, there were still enough in this forty-year period to offer an invaluable window onto neighbourhood life, since witness statements were still submitted in writing.[10]

In one consistory court case, for instance, a witness said a number of neighbours stood at their doors watching the dispute in question.[11] In another, a male witness, while urinating outside a pub, heard a quarrel. He went back into the pub and proposed that all present should go outside to see the row.[12] In a third case, a shopkeeper in Brokers Row near Drury Lane was standing at his door. He observed a competitor across the alley refer a customer to a third shop, and let loose a volley of abuse. The ensuing quarrel attracted as many as twenty people, according to one witness.[13] In yet another instance, a witness claimed that 'a quarrelsome, bad woman' named Mary Shadd caused continual problems so that 'the whole neighbourhood were frequently up in alarm at the uproar'.[14]

In eighteenth-century London, privacy came with affluence. The rooms the labouring classes called home offered scant sanctuary from the greater world, even when they were not shared with strangers. One consistory court witness claimed when in her apartment to be able to hear 'every word spoken by any person in the next house', since the two buildings were so close together.[15] In another case, Jean Graham accused her next-door neighbour, Katherine Rose, of adultery with John Simpson. According to one witness, Graham had angrily claimed 'that looking through a hole in the wainscotting between her apartment and that occupied by the said Mrs. Rose, she had seen her ... sitting upon the said John Simpson's knee and he kissing her and she him, and that at another time looking through the same hole she saw them upon the bed in the very act'. Graham later explained that she had seen Rose's ankles on the foot of the bed and had seen her come out of Simpson's room clad in only her under-petticoat.[16] People in London neighbourhoods knew each other, and they knew their neighbours – sometimes better than they might wish, seemingly. Neighbourhoods were often the locus of tension: neighbours living all along the street watched; they judged, and when they thought necessary, they condemned. Indeed, of twenty-one defamation cases clearly involving labouring-class people between 1780 and 1820, individuals in twelve of them admitted to having overheard or spied on their neighbours. Seven of the twenty-one cases took place between people who lived in the same house, and nine more between people living alongside, across from or within twenty yards of each other. In only two cases did the prosecutor and defendant come from different neighbourhoods.[17]

The quarrels described in these cases could rupture the peace of the neighbourhood, and they arose for a number of reasons. Ostensibly, the defamation that resulted in the consistory court cases being brought always centred on the sexual reputation of a woman. All but two of the prosecutors were female, reflecting the fact that by this period sexual reputation was wholly the province of women.[18] The two men who brought prosecutions did so because their wives had been called whores.[19] The witnesses, on the other hand, were split almost evenly according to sex: thirty-nine men and thirty-eight women gave evidence. In spite of the immediate focus on sexual reputation, it is clear that the argument often had its genesis in matters that had little to do with sexual propriety. Laura Gowing has noted that

> as much as women were the targets of the regulation ... they made themselves the
> agents of its definition. Women used the broad and powerful possibilities of the word
> "whore" in every sort of local and personal conflict. They called other women whores

loosely, with little or no further details, as one weapon in disputes about money, goods or territory; and they told circumstantial stories of actual, rumoured or imagined sexual transgressions.

It seems that women were using the language of slander to perform a function for which men were more likely to look to the official, institutional, and legal spheres.[20]

Although the cause of the disagreement in these cases was often not made clear, eleven of them do seem to adhere to the pattern Gowing has identified. In two instances of defamation, a rental dispute may have been behind the angry name-calling. In 1789, for instance, witnesses said there were rumours that Ann Jarman, the householder, wanted to let Margaret Sanders's apartment to someone else. Another witness claimed that Jarman believed Sanders had defamed her in order to force her (Jarman) to leave the house.[21] In 1816 Catherine Puzey, also a householder, decided to move and wished her tenant, William Meek, to pay her the rent he owed before she left. Unable to get it, she distrained his furniture. Meek believed she distrained too much, and in the aftermath of the ensuing dispute, he claimed that Puzey had called his wife a whore.[22] Disagreements could also arise from domestic living arrangements. On Christmas Day, 1800, for instance, Catherine Jennings was drying some fine linen by her parlour window. Elizabeth Palmer emptied some dirty water from her window above that spilled onto the linen. According to one witness, an incensed Jennings then called Palmer 'a scandalous, dirty woman for dirtying her clothes'. The same witness said Palmer replied, 'you are a damned black looking whore and I'll lay you fast did you not go to be wet nurse to ... Lady Peters'.[23] In another case, a similar scenario was the immediate cause of the defamatory exchange. While Elizabeth Williams and Esther Palmer had been quarrelling for several months and it is unclear what lay behind the protracted dispute, the crucial defamatory insults resulted when Williams shook a tablecloth containing some bones out an upstairs window. Palmer and a friend were walking below, and in the exchange that followed they claimed that Williams said they no better than whores.[24]

Competition in business and personal slights were other causes of confrontations and name-calling. In the case mentioned earlier, Alexander Ross became angry when he saw his neighbour, Mary Nowlan, send a customer to a third broker's shop kept by a Mr Oliver. He called Nowlan 'an Irish Bitch', and as she left to fetch a constable, he called after her, 'There goes that Irish whore with a feather stuck in her arse'. This quarrel may have been part of an ongoing dispute, since the witness had heard rumours that Nowlan had flung a basin of water at Ross's wife.[25] Personal slights also led to heated arguments. Matthew Moss took offence when his cousin's husband 'had looked shyly upon him'. In retaliation, he began to speak of his cousin 'in a very gross and shameful manner', claiming that 'he had been many times been carnally connected with her ... whilst her husband was gone out'. In this particular instance, his listeners seemed unconvinced, one witness saying that Moss 'is a man much accustomed to give his tongue great liberty with too much freedom of persons'.[26]

Defamation could also become a weapon in marital disputes. In 1783 William Taylor, a publican, repeatedly blackened the reputation of Mary Sefton, a friend of his wife's, possibly from jealousy or in an attempt to be hurtful. He became angry if his wife encouraged Sefton to come to their pub, and on at least one occasion, defamed Sefton before witnesses during a quarrel with his wife. Among other abusive things, Taylor said, 'You bitch you, you are as bad as that gallows whore Mother Sefton over the way and I will not stand pimp for either of you'.[27] Another case from the same year can also be seen as a male attempt to put a woman in her place. William Heberley rented lodgings to George Walker, whom he accused of being the sexual partner of Anna Spence. According to a witness, a man named George Oriel came to Heberley's looking for his wife, who had left him. Walker sent for Spence, since he knew her to be a close friend of Mrs Oriel. She came; a quarrel ensued, after which Heberley exclaimed, 'If it were not for that damned whore Mrs. Spence wives would stay with their husbands and husbands with their wives'.[28] In both these cases, men seemed willing to hurl sexual insults at women who had in some way violated their expectations of proper feminine behaviour, and who, in their eyes, were moving beyond their proper sphere. This behaviour seems of a piece with the artisanal misogyny Anna Clark discussed in *The Battle for the Breeches*: men who were determined to keep women in what they thought their proper place.

Indeed, in another case, it is difficult to see the male defendant's behaviour as anything other than sexual bullying. Eleanor Robinson's husband, a sea captain, was away from home. Her next-door neighbour, James Mills, was described as a man of 'a very quarrelsome disposition'. He mounted a concerted campaign against Robinson, calling her a whore and her children bastards whenever he saw her. On one occasion he said, 'You know you are a whore you were drummed out of Tynemouth Barracks'. It is not known what the genesis of this behaviour was – Mills was a pilot, so this bullying may have resulted from a professional disagreement between him and Mr Robinson; it is simply not clear from the witness depositions. What is apparent is the fact that Mrs Robinson was well thought of by her neighbours. The witnesses agreed she was a very industrious woman, bearing a 'very good reputation and character'. Nor did they believe Mills's charges. According to one of the witnesses, she 'brings up her family with great care and attention', and Mills 'must know this but has for a considerable time been in the habit of abusing and defaming her, especially toward the end of April last'. Nevertheless, even though they did not believe the charges, one witness concluded that Robinson's character had suffered since the neighbours had been discussing one of the altercations, saying, 'it was a shame he should have said what he did … of Eleanor Robinson'. Seemingly, simply being talked about, being the focus of gossip – whether or not the insults were believed – was enough to damage a woman's reputation in the estimation of some neighbours. Robinson must have thought so as well, for according to one witness, because of the continual abuse, she was 'almost ashamed to go out and show her face'.[29]

Finally, defamation charges could spring from the motive of revenge. In the case in which Esther Palmer charged Elizabeth Williams with defamation, for instance, it came out that Palmer had already been found guilty of defaming Williams and had just been forced to perform public penance for doing so.[30] Similarly, Elizabeth Jones charged Hester Parker with defamation after Jones and her husband John had been found guilty at the Quarter Sessions of assaulting Parker and sentenced to six days in jail and a £10 fine respectively.[31]

Even though all of these quarrels focused on a woman's sexual reputation, they seemed to arise from a variety of causes. Rental disputes, cheek-by-jowl living arrangements, competition in business, personal animosities, marital tensions and expectations concerning gender roles could all set off the roiling anger that in turn led to venomous confrontations. Defamation charges could also become weapons with which to avenge injuries already suffered. The cause of the dispute was much less likely to be given in cases where women defamed women: in eight such instances, the cause of the dispute was not explained. In four of these cases, it was clear that the disagreement had been ongoing, sometimes for months. This, in itself, seemed to make the defamatory climax explicable to the witnesses. It may be, as Gowing has suggested, that such defamatory exchanges were a fairly normal part of various kinds of disputes between women, and, hence, required less explanation. Males, moreover, were more likely to wield the language of defamation in attempts to make women behave in ways men deemed proper to their sex. In none of the cases in which women were the defamers was it clear that charges of whoredom were being overtly used in this way.

To be sure, expectations that respectable women would guard their sexual reputations constituted a general form of control over female behaviour. Greer Litton Fox's observations concerning the situation today also apply to the late eighteenth and early nineteenth centuries. Litton Fox has pointed out that the value construct of the 'nice girl' is 'both a standard for and a goal of behaviour'. She calls this kind of control normative restriction, and continues:

> The extension of normative control into a broad range of behavioural contexts is possible precisely because normative control operates through the internalization of norms and values and does not depend on the presence or action of external agents. Normative control extends, furthermore, to the coverage of behaviour that is only remotely connected with sex. There seems to be little that a woman does that cannot be used as a test of her niceness and therefore as an opportunity for control.[32]

In her article, Litton Fox points out that the nice girl value construct not only governs sexual behaviour, but also places limitations on where reputable women can go, when they can be in certain places, and the modes by which they travel. The flexible use to which women put sexual insult may, in part, have resulted from the amorphousness of this form of control. They may have felt comfortable using sexual slander as a code through which to denigrate other forms of behaviour that also violated in some way the constellation of values defining the reputable woman. As such, the use of sexual slander was two-edged. At once a code through which women could express their outrage and grievance concerning a range of matters at issue, its usage also reaffirmed the value construct by which female behaviour was restricted and controlled.

Be this as it may, it was, nevertheless, terribly important to the woman and her family that attacks on her sexual reputation be refuted – as seen in the Robinson case, it would not do simply to try to ignore the insults. This was so even when the defamer was not generally believed. In one case, her neighbours knew Agnes Maddeson to be a troublesome woman – one witness claimed to have told her to her face that she was always scandalizing and abusing the neighbours. Nor did they pay attention to Maddeson when she began to abuse Margaret Powley loudly in the street. Nevertheless, one witness still concluded that Powley's character had been injured even though she had not deserved it.[33] Reputation, and hence respectability, were fragile, and the recourse to the consistory courts was a last-chance scenario; prior to this neighbours frequently tried to mend the quarrel informally, or they interceded in ways to allow the vilified woman to defend herself.

Testimony in nine cases revealed that neighbours intervened in these disputes in various ways. Sometimes, when the defamation was not made to the woman's face, they alerted her to the fact that her character was under attack. Ann Groves, for instance, refused to serve the child of a witness in her shop, since she claimed the witness had informed Ann Dinnis of the attacks she (Groves) had been making on her character.[34] In another case, a witness informed Ann White when Robert Bower began to defame her in the street.[35] Neighbours could also warn the defamer of the consequences of the charges being uttered. One witness warned Matthew Moss that he could well be endangering William and Ann Cairns' marriage through his boasts, while another warned him that he and his family would be ruined if he did not soon settle the dispute.[36] Finally, neighbours intervened directly either to bring the defamatory confrontation to a halt or to resolve the dispute. Thus, a witness persuaded Catherine Jennings to return to her apartment in order to end the immediate confrontation with Elizabeth Palmer.[37] In the dispute between Katherine Rose and Jean Graham, the elders of the dissenting sect to which both belonged tried to resolve the argument, but failed.[38] Similarly, in the disagreement between Anna Spence and William Heberley, the neighbours tried to make up the quarrel, but again failed.[39]

Other neighbours – probably those not closest to the disputants – chose not to become directly embroiled in the quarrel. Instead they sought, through neighbourhood gossip and discussion, to establish whether there were any grounds to the claims.[40] Thus, a witness in Cairns against Moss said the claims 'have been the subject of much conversation among many of her [Cairns's] neighbours some of whom have been inclined to believe that she has been criminal from the daring manner in which ... Matthew Moss ... hath so defamed her'.[41] Similarly, in the case between Isabella Child and Martha Lacey, the dispute was 'spoken of by the neighbours who have asked whether there were any grounds for such abuse'.[42] Indeed, as Bernard Capp and Melanie Tebbutt have shown, in studies bracketing this period, the role of gossip, especially women's gossip, was crucial in plebeian neighbourhoods. As Tebbutt observed, 'Gossip expressed the politics of everyday living, and as such was an important vehicle for the informal power which women of the urban poor often exerted over their neighbourhoods'.[43] She continued, 'gossip provided an important dynamic through which the judgements and values of community life were transmuted and refined'[44] and social pressure was brought to bear on individuals. As useful as gossip was in reinforcing perceived moral boundaries, Capp noted, 'it could also prove divisive and disruptive',[45] as was certainly the case in some of the consistory court disputes.

Reputation and respectability, then, were resolutely to be preserved. Often, the neighbours would help the individual defend theirs – or at the very least warn that reputation was in danger. Sometimes they would simply stand by, a kind of neighbourhood jury waiting to pass judgement on the participants in the dispute. Julian Pitt-Rivers has employed the same metaphor to show how crucially important public opinion was. He says that it forms 'a tribunal before which the claims of honour are brought, "the court of reputation" as it has been called, and against its judgements there is no redress. For this reason it is said that public ridicule kills'.[46]

It is possible, moreover, to glean from the consistory court cases the traits these juridical neighbourhoods considered to be characteristic of good and bad women. A good woman was one who was 'quiet and hardworking',[47] 'industrious', bringing up 'her family with great care and attention'.[48] She was 'sober, modest and virtuous', of 'good character and credit',[49] 'honest, inoffensive',[50] 'good tempered',[51] 'kind ... and ... very good natured ... not quarrelsome or litigious'.[52] Finally, the good woman was 'peaceable' and she got on with her neighbours.[53]

Bad women, on the other hand, aside from being adulterous, were described as being 'of a loose turn'[54] – presumably indicating sexual promiscuity. They were violent-tempered,[55] lied and swore,[56] had a 'taunting, irritating manner',[57] and were abusive, causing 'riots' and 'uproar' in the neighbourhood.[58] They were idle and 'drunk about the streets' and had 'no visible way of getting ... [a] ... livelihood'.[59]

Given the very few males who appeared in the consistory court records, either as defendants or prosecutors, it is not possible to construct these kinds of profiles for men. Earlier in the eighteenth century, however, defamation cases heard in the consistory courts had been much more numerous, and male participation much greater. For the period 1650 to 1750, Peter Earle has been able to tease out the characteristics of good and bad men from the cases he examined. Earle found that the neighbourhood respected an individual as a good man if he was just and fair in his business dealings, hardworking, honest and regular in his habits, and kind and respectful to his wife. Men who did not provide for their families, who were lazy and idle, who engaged in debauched conversation, especially with disreputable women – or who consorted with them, who drank too much, or who abused their wives, families and employees beyond what the neighbourhood thought proper, forfeited their good reputations.[60] It is very likely these characteristics still defined the good man during the period of this study.

It is clear, from the consistory court cases, that reputation and respectability were crucially important to plebeian women and men. The question is why this was so. In part, the concern to maintain a good reputation derived from the very real costs that accompanied its loss. These are hinted at in the Jarman against Sanders case. One witness said that Jarman, who kept a haberdashery shop, had been hurt by the defamation among her neighbours and customers.[61] The material costs of unrefuted defamation were made brutally clear in Dinnis against Groves. Even though her employer, Mrs Hayden, had attempted to clear Dinnis's name by questioning Ann Groves, who then apologized for defaming Dinnis, this was not the end of the latter's problems. Groves continued to spread rumours that Dinnis, a servant, was pregnant by her master, Mrs Hayden's brother. Dinnis subsequently told one witness that 'if she did not clear her name, her mistress, Mrs. Hayden, had threatened to discharge her'.[62] The costs of defamation were even grimmer for Ann Goulee. The victim of Mary Shadd, whom the neighbours agreed was troublesome, bad and abusive, Goulee was one day found crying with her two small children in the court where she lived. She told her neighbour that 'her husband had turned her out of the house in consequence of ... Mary Shadd having said she was a whore and refused to let her return'. The witness and her husband intervened, inviting Goulee 'to walk into their House', which she did. The husband went to speak to Mr Goulee, who said 'he would not bed again with his wife until the business was cleared up'. He did not allow his wife to return home for two nights, until he had seen the man with whom supposedly she was having an affair 'and had convinced himself of such charge being untrue by bringing such gentleman and Mrs. Shadd face to face'.[63] An uncontested defamation, then, could result in a loss of employment and financial hardship, or even in marital separation and in the loss of shelter. A slur on one's reputation was not to be taken lightly.

The importance of reputation and the respectability that flowed from it are apparent from the consistory court cases, but can be seen from other kinds of sources as well. William Hart, a cooper who lived from 1776 to 1857, wrote his autobiography, and in it says that as a young man in London, he lodged with a former shop mate. The latter helped him find a small house to rent and lent him a bed until he could afford to buy one of his own. In slack seasons, Hart was repeatedly able to find work through other old shop mates. The fact that he was deeply religious, sober and industrious no doubt gave others confidence in recommending him for work even when they did not know him intimately.[64] Henry Mayhew's interviews with the London poor in the mid-nineteenth century also reflect the importance of reputation. A male tailor, who sublet part of his house, recounted how he had looked after two brothers, his lodgers, for three weeks during the cholera epidemic. To prevent them starving, he was forced to pawn his bed and bedding. This tailor estimated that the two owed him £2 13s. 9d., but had not paid him back. Nevertheless, he said of them, 'I think they're honest young men and would pay me if they could. Maybe they're ashamed to write me – yes, I dare say they are, for they were good young men – though I never had their money, I'll say that of them'.[65] Obviously, the two had been men of good reputation and respectability that even the non-payment of the debt did not change.

Aside from these very practical reasons for cherishing a good reputation, there are also circumstances peculiar to the society of the period which help to account for the importance people placed upon it. Gatrell has explained the seemingly callous behaviour of scaffold crowds who cheered hangings and made the day a festive occasion. He says this behaviour was part of a more general cultural response in which the need to keep face was crucial. He continued that 'what was celebrated most was triumph over life's adversities, and especially getting something for nothing'. Life was seen as an empty joke, which, if it had meaning, 'must lie in keeping face in the here-and-now rather than in the anticipation of its aftermath'.[66] Gatrell concluded of the seemingly callous indifference of the crowd to the victim's death that it was 'a refusal to be defeated, a compulsive cockiness, a vaunting celebration of cleverness. To triumph over affliction, to refuse surrender, to reject mediocrity, and still to mock and laugh was to achieve the main distinction that plebeian life could offer'. Thus, in the scaffold crowds, 'shame and grief ... must not show; face must be kept up'.[67]

If face, or reputation, are assumed to be coextensive to honour and respectability, then Pitt-Rivers helps us to understand more clearly why these predispositions assumed such importance in this society. By 'honour', Pitt-Rivers means 'the value of a person in his own eyes, but also in the eyes of his society. It is his estimation of his own worth, his *claim* to pride, but it is also the acknowledgement of that claim, his excellence recognized by society, his *right* to pride'.[68] He continues that honour can either mean 'a sentiment and a mode of conduct' or it can mean 'the bestowal of honours – the recognition of high status through birth, and I would add, through achievement'.[69] The second form of honour is precisely the kind of recognition that the plebeian Londoners in the late eighteenth and early nineteenth centuries could not hope to attain. As will be seen, life was precarious for the vast majority. Economic uncertainty was the lot of virtually everyone in the labouring classes, from the most skilled to the least. As Iorwerth Prothero has pointed out, 'accident, sickness and old age; loss of time; underemployment; periodic unemployment; a labour surplus' could all bring destitution in their wake, even to the most skilled.[70] The honour that was available to plebeian women and men, then, was that concerning one's mode of conduct. It was this notion of themselves as well-conducted men and women that plebeian Londoners defended with such alacrity. As Keith Thomas has noted for the early modern period, 'a good reputation was valued at every level of society',[71] and this was true even for the most humble and seemingly disreputable. At the same time, the working population was highly stratified and 'its members acutely sensitive to differences in status'.[72] Reputation, moreover, had to be constantly earned in a city, since, due to mobility and migration, there was no finite group judging behaviour through time. According to Horden and Purcell, to be honourable was 'to be seen to be untouched by ... threats, either because other members of the community feel constrained to avoid making them, or because, once made, they are speedily and successfully answered'.[73] All of this meant that the concerns of reputation led to many quarrels and disagreements. It was vitally necessary to keep face and be well thought of, not just to keep self-respect, but to maintain access to the collective resources the neighbourhood could provide – to credit with shops and landlords and to borrowing networks, for example. Certainly, the consistory court deposition statements in defamation cases from this period support the continuing importance of reputation and the prevalence of neighbourly scrutiny in plebeian neighbourhoods.[74]

The predispositions that Gatrell identified operated in two ways in the lives of these women and men. First, the demand that face be maintained – not to admit defeat – meant that people were predisposed to answer challenges of any stripe: they were tetchy and they could be quarrelsome. Second, in this society it meant that challenges to one's self-respect would be particularly unacceptable. These predispositions underlay the consistory court quarrels already explored: it was crucial for both participants to maintain face, so an infraction upon one's dignity or an injury of some sort could not be allowed to pass unnoticed and unremarked. It had to be answered. The response generally escalated the dispute, and in turn required the original instigator to reply in kind. The quarrel continued to spiral upwards as each person sought to maintain face, until at some stage one of the participants was called a whore. At this point, the person defamed had several options. Most of the time, the quarrel was mended informally – often through the mediation of neighbours and friends. Anna Clark has estimated that only 10 per cent of defamatory disputes found their way to the consistory court,[75] the most formal option available to the aggrieved. Nevertheless, it is apparent, in a society given to such touchy regard for individual reputation, that there had to be a way to control and contain the escalation of the many quarrels that resulted. While the consistory court offered an after-the-fact resolution, it could only please one of the disputants, and in drawing in the neighbours as witnesses could rend the neighbourhood's social fabric for months or even years to come.

It is striking, then, that these quarrels have a ritual quality to them. In several cases, the defamatory exchange began when one of the disputants moved into the street, and addressing no one in particular, but the neighbourhood in general, began calling down in a loud voice the person who was the object of their anger. Thus, Robert Bower stopped in the street outside Ann White's house and began calling out, 'here lives a red-haired whore, a whore in New Castle Street'. White was initially unaware of Bower's performance until she was fetched from another part of her house.[76] Agnes Maddeson went out into the street, and addressing no one in particular began to call out loudly: 'Carpenter's wife in Robinson Lane has been kissing with the man and the master has catched them'. Since there was only one carpenter in the lane, it was obvious to all she meant to refer to Margaret Powley, who lived opposite her. The next day Maddeson continued to go out into the street at regular intervals, calling out her charges (during the course of which, apparently, she called Powley a whore).[77]

Ritualized and rule-bound behaviour was apparent as well in other kinds of disputes. Cesar de Saussure's description of a fist fight reveals both this and his own fascinated disapproval:

> The lower populace is of a brutal and insolent nature, and is very quarrelsome. Should two men of this class have a disagreement which they cannot end up amicably, they retire into some quiet place and strip from their waists upwards. Everyone who sees them preparing for a fight surrounds them, not in order to separate them, but on the contrary to enjoy the fight, for it is a great sport to the lookers on, and they judge the blows and also help to enforce certain rules in use for this mode of warfare. The spectators sometimes get so interested that they lay bets on the combatants and form a big circle around them. The two champions shake hands before commencing, and then attack each other courageously with their fists, and sometimes also with their heads, which they use like rams. Should one of the men fall, his opponent may, according to the rules, give him a blow with his fist, but those who have laid their bets on the fallen man generally encourage him to continue till one of the combatants is quite knocked up and says he has had enough.
>
> Would you believe it, I have actually seen women – belonging, it is true, to the scum of the people – fighting in this same manner.[78]

Physical fights were governed by rituals and rules that women also observed when they fought. In 1835 the anonymous gentleman-author of *The Dens of London* disguised himself and entered a low lodging house in St Giles. The occupants were street beggars and generally the poorest of the poor. As such, they were also the people most resistant to the new notions of respectability, and among those considered most disreputable by their social betters. While in the lodging house, the author witnessed a somewhat convoluted dispute, which he described with contemptuous good humour. Two women began to fight; when one went down to the floor, a Scottish sailor intervened, allowing the floored woman to escape. This did not end the fight, however. The woman who had been winning attacked the Scottish sailor; he declined to retaliate, but his wife did not. She challenged her husband's attacker:

> 'Do you think,' she said, 'that he has nobody to take his part, that you strike as if you were not to be struck again? No, No!' she added, 'he is no man who will strike a woman, except she be his own wife; but here, you ___ ___, I am your,' etc. etc.

The first woman instantly accepted the challenge, and the fight commenced:

> No nails, or tugging of hair, was brought into this action, but everything settled in the true old English style of disputing.
>
> These paragons of the tender sex then threw themselves into attitudes that would have done honour to a Mendoza; but Sawney's wife, who was a real Lady Barrymore hussey, proved the master at arms. Tall and boney, she slashed her opponent at arm's length, with the cutting force of a Curtis, and presently ended her share of the fray.

Still, this did not end the fight. The woman who lost the battle was married to a Welshman, whose sense of dignity would not allow him to let the matter rest:

> The Welshman, after having seen his battered spouse taken care of, returned, and going up to the Scotchman, very gravely said,
>
> 'Joe, I believe there is something between you and me. You were always a good 'un, but I cannot allow any man to meddle with my wife.'
>
> 'Say no more,' said the *canny* Scot; 'it's all right. No man never heard me say, nay.'
>
> 'No, never!' shouted the most of the company. 'You were always a trump!'
>
> 'Well, then,' says Taffy, 'let's have this turn over, and we'll be friends yet.'
>
> And with this kind of chivalrous feeling, did these two honourable blackguards prepare to maul each other, zealously encouraged by their friends.[79]

The ritual behaviour – the challenge, the handshake – and the rules governing physical fights served to keep the dispute within certain limits, although clearly such niceties were not always observed. Nevertheless, while the French tourist Pierre Grosley believed that the English certainly fought a lot, he also thought there was disinclination, even in the most violent disturbances, 'for truly great bloodshed'.[80] In the low lodging house, the demands of face certainly led to these disputes: the notion that no man ought physically to interfere with another man's wife meant that the husband had to issue a challenge. The notion that no woman ought to take advantage of this situation in order to attack a man with impunity meant that his wife would defend the family honour. While the competition between individual demands to keep face, moreover, could lead to protracted and convoluted disputes, this society also sought to ensure that mechanisms for resolution or, at the very least, containment of the violence were well established. Thus, the spectators at a fight and the neighbours who witnessed quarrels all tried to ensure that the disputes were conducted along certain lines or that they were resolved informally within the neighbourhood. Clearly they were not always successful, but neighbours frequently were proactive in trying to defuse conflict.[81]

So far, the various ways in which the demands of face lead to tension and conflict within London's neighbourhoods have been explored. As noted at the beginning of this chapter, however, neighbourhoods also played positive roles in the lives of the men and women who lived within them: reputation and respectability were crucial in the sustaining aspects of neighbourhoods. Peter Earle again described, for a slightly earlier period, the various ways in which reputation was important. As he put it,

> The maintenance of character or reputation was an essential safeguard against times of trouble when the opinion of one's neighbours could be literally the difference between life and death. Many a defendant at the Old Bailey won a not guilty verdict from a jury or relative mercy from a judge by the willingness of neighbours to come and speak in court for his or her character
>
> ... Reputation was equally important in less dramatic circumstances. It could make the difference between a job and no job, tick or no tick at the local chandler's shop or alehouse, a pension or free accommodation at the expense of the parish rather than a spell in the workhouse or eviction from the parish for the destitute. Neighbours looked after their own, but they only looked after those of whom they approved.[82]

Being well thought of by one's neighbours meant having access to various kinds of assistance. In addition to the very real benefits Earle has identified, which were still in play in the period of this study, bearing a good reputation in one's neighbourhood also meant having access to a crucial resource in making ends meet: mutuality, which meant that during short-term periods of distress, people could turn to their family, friends and neighbours for assistance. This help was not viewed as charity, since it was given on the clear understanding that it would be reciprocated. When the tables were turned – as almost inevitably they would be in London's uncertain labour market – and the giver required assistance, the expectation was that it would be forthcoming. The fine calculations of mutuality are apparent in the comment of a mid-nineteenth-century navvy, who said of himself and his wife, 'It is not our way, don't you see, to ask anyone to help us, unless it's one of our own sort. We don't mind taking a few shillings from people like ourselves, so we can do the same for them another time; but we never begs of anyone else. It's against our rules.'[83]

References to mutuality abound in the sources throughout the period. Auto-biographies provide numerous instances of this behaviour, and there is evidence from the 1780s to the mid-nineteenth century of women's borrowing networks – indeed, Ellen Ross argued convincingly that they were still vitally important in the period just before World War I.[84] To appreciate the centrality of mutuality, it is necessary to understand the preferences and priorities of plebeian Londoners in making ends meet. The uncertainties and irregularities of work that afflicted these people meant that it made little sense to accede to notions of individual initiative, thrift and foresight. Why save extra money when there was no guarantee it would be adequate protection against coming vicissitudes in the labour market? Even if saving banks had been widely available, what would be the point of deposit-ing money when it was unlikely to remain there long enough to earn interest? Why plan ahead and forego pleasure today when the future was all but uncon-trollable? Not surprisingly, most plebeian Londoners did not save their money and plan ahead in their struggles to maintain subsistence. Rather, they retained a constellation of priorities and preferences centring on mutuality that made good sense given the uncertain economic climate. Plebeian families behaved in ways that reaffirmed their sense of belonging in their communities. Hans Medick has pointed out that these people sought to strengthen 'the bonds of kinship, neigh-bourhood and friendship' as the most reliable form of security.[85] The assistance available from these sources, however, was not unlimited. As David Vincent has noted, neighbours would often provide crucial short-term assistance, while only near kin would be expected to take in a destitute household.[86]

A short-term focus was pervasive in plebeian London. Money at hand, for instance, was to be used in order to make ends meet this week or even through today. Any money left over after these immediate goals had been achieved was invested in ways in which the upper classes had difficulty fathoming:

> [It] could be invested in socio-cultural reproduction, permitting the purchase of prestige and luxury goods and defraying the costs for demonstrative outlay for festi-vals, celebrations and other rituals of interaction. For the small producer money as a means of hoarding reserves was as remote as his chances of long-term accumulation in the face of capitalistic exploitation and surplus extraction. Money income, therefore, found its most 'rational' use in its relatively short-term conversion into the currency of socio-cultural reproduction.[87]

Put simply, people reaffirmed their sense of belonging in their neighbourhoods and their families by spending extra money when they had it on festivals, on their friends at the pub, in giving gifts, on a luxury item like a watch, or in the case of costermongers, a kingsman – a silk neckerchief – that would enhance their status. Such items also served another purpose, for as Melanie Tebbutt has pointed out, workers in London in irregular or seasonal trades had a tradition of buying valuable items as a form of insurance against future lay-offs or financial difficulty, which was actually described as an inverted form of thrift by some commentators. It involved the regular purchase of 'luxury items' like furniture, domestic utensils and ornaments in the summer months which were 'pawned off one by one, in Winter, to help tide over bad times'. While an exceptional depression often meant the permanent disappearance of the family furniture, it had the tangible advantage of providing both a comfortable home and resources against want and starvation.[88]

The amount of money paid to renew the pledge, and finally to redeem the article (if fortunate), was not taken into account. Immediate enjoyment of the article and ready security gained from pawning it were of far more consequence than long-term computations of interest. Since a central goal of plebeian Londoners at this time was the maintenance of an independent position within the community, admonitions to thrift, sobriety and foresight were unpopular for two reasons. First, they would have isolated the plebeian family. By not reaffirming its position within the community through social intercourse, the family would have risked losing necessary social support. Second, for most plebeian women and men, the long-term betterment which adherence to these values was supposed to ensure was simply unreachable, as they well knew. Not until work became regular, and wages rose, could this goal become realistic.

Given these priorities and preferences, it is not surprising that mutuality was well-nigh universal, from the most to the least skilled. As has already been seen, in the 1790s William Hart, a cooper, received various kinds of assistance from neighbours and workmates because they thought well of him. Thomas Carter, born in 1792, was another highly skilled artisan who wrote his autobiography. It is a fuller account than Hart's, and in it, it is possible to see the role mutuality played throughout his life. As Vincent has noted, labouring-class autobiographers tended to be atypical. These writers were 'self-improving' men who adopted 'values and forms of behaviour which were often in direct conflict with both their inherited culture and the practices and outlook of the majority of their class.'[89] Autobiographies like Carter's clearly show the extremely high costs of attempting this – in his case the adoption of extreme thrift and foresight. That mutuality figures so regularly throughout the life of someone like Carter certainly argues for its pervasiveness. That adhering to values like thrift and foresight was so difficult indicates that only an extraordinary few would even try the experiment.

Carter was a tailor who published his autobiography in 1845 when he was fifty-three. He was the epitome of artisanal respectability. He valued education, belonged to a book club and wrote poetry. Carter abhorred swearing, went to church twice on Sundays and (unlike so many in his class) saved his money. In spite of all this thrift and foresight, however, one of the most striking features about his life was its precariousness. Carter was the son of a cellar man. The family, which had been 'comfortable', fell on hard times partly because the father took to drink, and partly due to the inflation during the Napoleonic Wars.[90] In spite of this, the mother, who seemed to be an unusually determined woman, kept the family 'very respectable'. She demanded industriousness from her son, and in his words 'she thought it no argument against my doing anything, that it was usually performed by girls; nor would she at all excuse me from doing it on this ground'.[91]

Carter's mother kept a dame school, from which she contributed two or three shillings a week to the family income.[92] When he was not quite thirteen, Carter went to work as a servant to a woollen draper. Shortly thereafter he became seriously ill, and remained bedridden for five weeks. He was able to depend on his parents (as one would certainly expect), but at a cost to his family. He said, 'My parents did their best to promote both my comfort and my restoration to health; but all they were able to do amounted to but little, on account of their straightened circumstances. These were now made still narrower by the loss of my wages, which, though small, were yet an important addition to their scanty income'.[93] After his illness, his master trained him as a tailor, and in 1810, at age eighteen, Carter went to London. He practised his trade, but was still able to rely on his family – some thirty-two miles away – for support. During one slack period, he returned home for a visit, thus cutting living expenses. This mutuality operated in both directions, however. When his father died in 1817, Carter considered his duty, and concluded that he should 'send some needful help to the living, rather than ... take an expensive journey out of respect for the dead. I therefore remained at my work, and remitted £5 sterling to my widowed mother. It was of course a very seasonable supply, and I felt glad I had been able to send it'.[94] In London, Carter relied on fellow tailors to find work in slow times. On one occasion a co-worker not only provided four or five weeks of work, but shared work space which allowed Carter 'the advantage of being both warmer and at the same time cost less' than if he had had to work alone. This co-worker, whose name Carter could not even recall, had also provided shop-board room, fire and candles at no cost, as well as the actual work.[95]

If, like most plebeian Londoners, Carter faced economic insecurity on a fairly regular basis, and relied on mutuality to ensure subsistence, he was, nevertheless, extraordinary in his adherence to the long view. Carter was extremely determined in trying to ensure his year-round independence by saving as much money as he could, and was willing to adopt draconian measures to ensure that he should. Time and again, his small stock of savings was annihilated by his needs during slack periods. This occurred in spite of a stern adherence to frugality. During these periods, Carter cut back on food, eating a penny roll and half a pint of porter for breakfast, a penny loaf for dinner on the rare occasions he ate at mid-day, and bread, cheese, porter and onions for supper.[96] Had he been married with children, it is unlikely that Carter would have been able to save money, especially in his early years. Certainly, most plebeian Londoners would have found this Sisyphean exercise hardly worth the pursuit.

Carter himself was aware that his allegiance to what has often been termed 'artisanal respectability' was unusual. He said of his co-workers that they were 'civil men', but then added, 'I made myself as much at home with them as the difference between our tastes and habits would allow'.[97] When independence was so precarious, individual initiative was often inadequate to ensure it. Instead, even the staunchest devotees of artisanal respectability were forced to rely on resources like mutuality. In Carter's case, he relied on both his family and fellow workers. Moreover, his being single and his willingness to scale down his cost of living to the level, as he put it, of 'an inmate of a poor-house'[98] when unemployed undoubtedly permitted him to maintain his independence when others would not have been able – or would not have chosen – to do so. Independence based on individual initiative may have been his goal, but in the mid-nineteenth century independence could only be maintained by relying on assistance from others as well.

It is apparent that Carter possessed more determination than was, and is, typical. Moreover, he published his life story in the 1840s when the value of individual initiative was particularly extolled. That mutuality surfaces repeatedly in the books of people who were trying to appear respectable at a time when individual initiative was championed indicates its pervasiveness. This behaviour, moreover, was not limited to those who were best able to give. In the Report on the State of the Handloom Weavers in 1840, W. E. Hickson recounted the statement of a poor silk weaver's wife: 'Often, sir, and often were we obliged, when half-starving, to go without a pennyworth of bread, and buy a pennyworth of coals, or take the children over to a neighbour, to borrow a warm at their fire, or put them early to bed, shivering and crying with cold'.[99] Borrowing a warm may have been the most humble kind of loan on offer, but generosity of this sort was not unusual. To be sure, mutuality could take different forms. It was highly gendered: men's mutuality was more likely to be work-centred – tradesmen finding each other employment during slack seasons or shop mates helping one another in various ways. Women's mutuality, on the other hand, tended to be neighbourhood-based. Married women were expected to manage the family budget, which required considerable skill and financial dexterity, and an important resource in doing so for most wives was the female borrowing network. Since these practices by their very nature were informal, it is difficult to uncover direct evidence of them. One instance where these borrowing patterns do become visible occurs in the Proceedings of the Old Bailey. In these accounts of trials, the accused usually gave statements explaining or defending their actions, and in a number of theft cases – almost all involving women – it is clear that borrowing back and forth had led to the charges. Usually in these cases the items had been borrowed in order to be pawned. This transaction then provided the borrower with much needed ready cash. The understanding was that subsequently the borrower would reclaim the article from the pawnshop and return it to its owner or would recompense the lender for the value of the item.

In the 1780s, just about 7 per cent of females who made a defence statement to explain their actions claimed that they had pawned the stolen item for another, that they had done so with permission, that they had done so to settle a debt or with the intention of returning it. For males the figure was only 0.8 per cent. Some of the women who had been involved in pawning, however, gave other reasons in the defence statements for their actions.[100] In all, the pawning of goods for the above reasons figured in about 15 per cent of the cases of female theft and 2 per cent of male.[101] While borrowing networks did not always involve pawning, and so in reality would have been considerably more extensive than the Old Bailey material indicates, the pawning cases do provide a window onto the dynamics of this informal behaviour: their characteristics and the ways in which they could go wrong. A number of borrowing network features can be teased out from the Old Bailey cases. In the first place, the networks were ongoing. In February 1780, for instance, Catherine Amer accused her roommate, Ann Friend, of stealing four pairs of silk stockings. During the trial it came out that Amer had previously borrowed and pawned two neck cloths from Friend (the latter claimed she had pawned the stockings in order to get her neck cloths out of pawn). In June of the same year, Ann Powell was accused of stealing clothes and other things from her sister's landlady. In her defence, Powell stated, 'I used to do anything she [the prosecutor] wanted; when she wanted money to pay her washerwomen she sent me to pawn things for her; she knows she gave me orders to do it to bring money to her'.[102]

Borrowing network transactions could become convoluted: in September 1782, for instance, Sarah Skettles bought a waistcoat from a cloathesman for 10s. 6d. She borrowed part of the money from a neighbour and then pawned one of her aprons in order to repay her.[103] Two years later Martha Ray claimed her prosecutor, Catherine McCue, had borrowed half a guinea from her. Ray said that when she asked the latter for it, McCue 'told me she could not pay me, and she gave me the cloak with her own hands [that she was now accused of stealing] and I went and pawned it for my own half guinea'.[104] The women in both these cases were engaged in a precarious, complex juggling act in which money was not always the basic currency regulating the exchange. Rather, at times, cash became just another commodity – being purchased and sold by the exchange of clothes or other items at hand. The exigencies of this situation clearly required a certain canniness on the part of plebeian women.

The borrowing networks were meant to meet short-term difficulties. Typically, no more than a few days passed before the giver expected the loan to be returned somehow. Thus, when Margaret Rowe claimed to have found some cotton in 1782, her landlady, a Mrs Mason, offered to buy it, but had not the money. According to Rowe, they agreed that she (Rowe) would pawn it until the end of the week, when Mason expected money with which she would pay Rowe the difference between the pawning and the real value.[105] In 1785 Elizabeth Bland told the court that her prosecutor had lent her the clothes (which she was now accused of stealing) in order to pawn them, and had given her one week to get them back.[106]

The ongoing nature of the borrowings, the precariousness and the complexity of the transactions and the need for short-term satisfaction in these networks could lead to misunderstandings resulting in theft charges. While plebeian women often behaved with generosity to one another, it is clear that lending and borrowing were transactions in the business of making ends meet just as much as waged employment. At times misunderstandings between the borrowing partners seem to have been the product of a somewhat fluid notion of private property. Both women and men seemed to feel that they had the right to use the property of others, especially when in distress. There were instances of people – usually women – pawning items from the furnished rooms they rented; on average, nine women and four men a year admitted doing so.

Those accused usually admitted they had made use of the item (by pawning it for cash), but often claimed that they had been in distress and that they had intended to redeem it. Some commented resentfully that they would have made good had they not been taken up. Ann Mitchell in 1782, for instance, pointed out that she had pawned the things repeatedly and had always returned them.[107] In 1787 Elizabeth Gosling told the court she had already returned some of the things, and in any case had not left the lodging.[108] On occasion, even the prosecutor would admit that the accused had not meant to steal the things. In 1785 Elizabeth Cooper's landlady made such an admission and Cooper was found not guilty.[109] The things were often pawned when the tenant was in distress or when an extraordinary demand for money came up. In 1788 Jane Williams's landlord demanded a week's rent in advance when she took the room. To meet this, Williams pawned the bedding, a shovel and various other things in the room. Before she could redeem the items, the landlord missed the things and had her arrested.[110] Both women and men pawned such goods, but women did so more frequently. They did seem to believe they had the right to use the items in the rooms they had rented. While the numbers cited in the Old Bailey Proceedings are small, it is very likely they would have been substantially higher had transcripts been more complete for the more minor cases, whose coverage was often minimal. Certainly, the alacrity with which landlords pressed charges suggests that the pawning of such goods was a widespread problem. These Old Bailey cases, then, offer a small window onto a different understanding of property, one which was more fluid than that being put forward by the upper classes.

The fluid notion of private property was not limited to goods from rented rooms, but is apparent in other kinds of borrowing as well. In the most extreme instance, the woman charged with theft would claim that the prosecutor had told her to use whatever she wished. Thus, Mary Robinson in 1781 told the court that Jane Stewart had said, 'I was welcome to stay with her, and was welcome to anything she had'.[111] Similarly, in 1785 Catherine Knock claimed that the prosecutor's wife had said she could take anything to pawn, and for good measure added that this woman had also allowed her to wear her clothes.[112] In all of these cases, those accused assumed, erroneously as it turned out, that they had the right to use the items to meet short-term needs.

Fluid notions of private property were not the only source of difficulties, however. As discussed earlier, lenders often needed to be repaid (in whatever fashion) within a fairly short period of time. If the borrower exceeded the length of time the lender thought proper, then, as Elizabeth Bland discovered above, theft charges could result. Other problems could also land a borrower in court: choosing to repay a debt in a manner unacceptable to the lender, for instance. Ann Wood in 1780 claimed to have left other clothes to replace those that she had pawned. In this instance, the prosecutor denied she had done so, and Wood was found guilty.[113] The complexities of the networks caused problems as well. At times third parties claimed that the lender had, in fact, stolen the item on loan, with the result that the borrower could find herself taken up on theft charges. Mary Williams claimed to be just such a victim in 1781,[114] and Susanna Kelly in the following year insisted she had no idea where Mary Walker got the items she had given her.[115]

Yet another way in which the networks could go wrong resulted from the relationship between the partners. If there were a falling out between them, the borrower might find herself charged with theft (whatever the original agreement had been). Thus, Elizabeth Green in 1781 claimed that Jane Barber had lent her a gown that she, Barber, had been altering for one Catherine Geary. Barber and Green then went out together, and when they ran out of money, Barber told Green to pawn the gown. Shortly thereafter the two 'had some words', and Green claimed that Barber had had her arrested out of spite.[116] In 1785 Jane Curtey said she had her landlady's permission to pawn the bedding, since she was in distress. Subsequently, the two had words and Curtey claimed she was taken up as a result.[117]

Finally, some women charged with theft sought to take advantage of the common knowledge that such borrowing was widespread. Thus, in 1781 Elizabeth Jones claimed that an unnamed young woman had asked her to pawn the coat she was accused of stealing on the promise of 6d. and a pot of purl. The court did not believe her.[118] While in this instance the claim did not seem very plausible, in other cases the courts were more willing to accept these justifications, especially if there were evidence of an ongoing borrowing relationship between the accused and the prosecutor. Again in 1781 Mary Hughes claimed that her mistress, Elizabeth Glover, had asked her to pawn the clothes and bedding she was accused of stealing. When the court learned from the pawnbroker that Glover had sent Hughes before to pawn things, a verdict of not guilty was returned.[119] Similarly, in 1788 Jenny Mead claimed often to have pawned things for her prosecutor. When the latter admitted to having had Mead pawn things in past, the court refused to convict.[120]

Borrowing networks, then, could go wrong in a number of ways. Medick has pointed out that social exchange made sound economic sense for plebeian women and men during this period, since 'it produced or reproduced just that solidarity to which small producers could, in times of dearth, crisis and need, most easily have recourse'.[121] In the borrowing networks, however, social exchange did not simply promote and support access to economic assistance. Rather, the two became inextricably intertwined, and the very characteristics, not to mention the informality, that made borrowing networks most useful to their female practitioners could also lead to misunderstandings and in some cases to legal action. In such an environment where trust could be so rapidly withdrawn, it was crucial to maintain a good reputation in the neighbourhood. Mutuality was a crucial resource for most, but it was extended only to those of whom lenders thought well.

If mutuality in its various forms was ubiquitous in this society, other resources were also crucially important in the struggle to make ends meet. Like mutuality, these were also dependent upon reputation. As indicated earlier, the recourse to pawning was widespread. James Treble has identified four patterns in the pawning behaviour of the poor. First, there were those who pawned belongings by the week: each Monday items would be pledged and then redeemed on Saturday, pay day for most people at this time. This cash was frequently exhausted on immediate needs, so that pawning gave the family money to buy food through the week, with the advantage of not being tied to one possibly higher-priced retail outlet willing to advance credit. Many families followed this pattern week in and week out.[122] Other families with more pressing needs would pawn belongings like blankets in the morning to be redeemed again in the evening.[123] A second pattern was to pawn goods on longer terms. Workers whose trades suffered seasonal slack periods would often pawn items to get through the difficult months, and then when the trade picked up would redeem them. Third, pawning goods could provide ready cash to meet the costs of unexpected illness or injury. Fourth, a family could gradually pawn many of its belongings in prolonged bouts of unemployment. In times of dearth all of the family's possessions could gradually find their way to the pawnshop, though this resource was limited.[124] Melanie Tebbutt quotes Eric Hobsbawm that 'the pledge shop could hardly maintain a family more than six weeks in 1842, assuming a normal income of 10s. 0d. and even £3 in pawnable property'.[125] Certainly, Francis Place and his wife had pawned 'everything but what we stood upright in'[126] long before his eight months of unemployment in 1793 were over. Finally, a fifth pawning pattern can be added to those Treble identified: pawning was also used to finance work ventures. Laundresses, for example, who were often paid by the month, or even quarter, would pawn their customers' laundry until it was due to be returned in order to raise money for immediate expenses – supplies not being the least of these.[127]

Pawning played a regular and not just emergency role in maintaining subsistence, but it was not the province of the very poorest. As Alannah Tomkins has observed, the pawnshop was rarely used by paupers. Analysing a rare pledgebook that has survived for a pawnshop in the city of York for the late 1770s, Tomkins says that the very poor were regarded as unacceptable risks: 'There was a reduced chance that they would be able to redeem their goods and pay the interest, leaving the broker with their (typically) low-value goods. The destitute were compelled to turn to dolly shops, or moneylenders requiring little or no security, where the rate of interest was even higher'.[128] The patterns Tomkins has found for York likely were not appreciably different in London. Goods were often pawned in separate lots, even though this meant people had to purchase multiple tickets. By doing this, items could be redeemed one at a time as the owner was able to pay the ticket price. Half of the pawns were short-term – less than a month – and 14 per cent of the goods remained unclaimed. By far the most popular items to pawn were pieces of adult clothing, although 'soft furnishings, household metalware ... and more valuable pieces such as watches and jewellery' were also common. Typically, clothes – especially Sunday best – would be taken to the pawnshop on Monday, the money advanced helped the family make it to pay day at the end of the week, when the clothes would be redeemed in time for Sunday. Just over 60 per cent of the customers at the York pawnshop were women, who were also more likely than men to pawn repeatedly.[129] As seen earlier, neighbours and friends lent things for pawn to those of whom they approved. Reputation and appearance also helped determine the amount of money the pawnbroker was willing to provide clients for their goods, as was apparent in the 1781 prosecution for theft of Ann Braidy at the Old Bailey. She had asked Hannah Smith to pawn some curtains and two pairs of silk stockings for her. Braidy did so because she was 'rather dirty';[130] Smith, being cleaner, either would presumably have looked less needy and hence better able to coax a higher price out of the pawnbroker, or she would have looked more respectable and hence less destitute, in order to convince him to deal at all.

Pawnshops were part of the community, and as such were trusted in a way that upper-class banking institutions rarely were. The prevalence of pawning in London can be seen from a number of sources. Aside from complaints by people like the police magistrate, Patrick Colquhoun, as to the frequency of the practice, parishes occasionally provided money to redeem belongings that paupers had pawned on the long downward trajectory to destitution. In 1796, for instance, St Martin's gave Martha White 1*s*. 6*d*. and Eleanor Evans 6*s*., and in 1814 gave Mary Draper a whopping £1 and 2*s*., all to redeem clothing.[131] There were also a number of cases in the Old Bailey records that shed light on the practice. In the first place, when people stole items and pawned them, they very often took common items of clothing. Shifts, aprons, shirts or gowns did not arouse the same suspicions among pawnbrokers, as did silver spoons or other more valuable items. This was the case, presumably, because of the existence of a huge market in second-hand clothing in London: as in York, it was a very common occurrence for people to pawn their clothing.[132] Pawning, then, was one resource among a number by which the poor sought to stave off destitution. It might merely be a small stop-gap in the downward spiral if luck was bad and conditions hard, and if pawning the belongings of others, it could be a desperate gamble indeed, possibly resulting in theft charges.

Another crucial resource, and one entwined with pawning, was the establishment of credit with local shops. It was especially important that a woman be able to buy food at those times when the family was experiencing difficulty. In some instances, families were able to establish fairly long-term credit both with shops and landlords. These tenants were generally employed in highly seasonal occupations, and it was understood that credit extended during the slack time would be made good in the busy season. As Gareth Stedman Jones pointed out,

> In order to escape starvation and in order to insure against the possibility of being thrown onto the streets at various periods of the year, it was essential to establish good credit relations with the landlord, the local shop, and the local pub. Landlords in poorer areas would be paid up in the summer. Local stores and pubs came to similar arrangements. 'Being known' in a district was thus of considerable economic importance. From the viewpoint of the labourer, it provided a further incentive against mobility.[133]

This was not just the province of labourers, however. After Francis Place, a tailor, and his wife had pawned all their belongings, their landlord (who evidently kept a shop) allowed them credit for bread, soap, coals and candles, to the extent that when Place regained employment he was in debt £6.[134]

Not all proprietors could extend long-term credit, however. Often it was only allowed to run a week or so, especially at small chandlers shops (the chief provisioners to the labouring classes), where the proprietor would face ruin if accounts remained unpaid. If credit was refused, a woman might well return 'to leave a Shift, Cap, Apron or Pocket as a pledge til the Money is paid'.[135] The Muis have shown that in some instances at least, the very small shops which catered to the labouring classes paid off their suppliers in full before the next order of stock was placed.[136] Indeed, the precarious situation of these businesses meant that plebeian Londoners often paid high prices for items purchased on credit. Tebbutt pointed out that it was often cheaper to pawn an item and to use the money advanced to pay off a credit account, rather than to let it run.[137] In part, these high prices were also due to the very small quantities of items that were habitually purchased – an ounce or even half an ounce of tea was not an uncommon request.[138] This meant that marketing was practically a daily phenomenon, and once again this duty fell largely on the wife's shoulders. In one instance the Muis uncovered evidence that the shopkeeper colluded with his women customers in preventing their husbands from finding out the extent of their credit purchases (usually tea) by falsifying bills.[139] More than this, however, the very small, frequent purchases 'enabled workers to purchase their "subsistence from day to day, or even hour to hour"',[140] and thus reinforced the short-term focus so common among these people.

Credit was ubiquitous, and it was crucial. Craig Muldrew and Steven King have pointed out that 'credit rather than weekly wages lay at the heart of the family economy'.[141] Indeed, they say that for very poor households, 'exploiting credit that might not be repaid was one essential part' of their strategies for survival. Similarly, the 'moonlight flit', leaving lodgings surreptitiously without paying outstanding rent, was a survival strategy for some poor families[142] and also ensured that what belongings they had would not be distrained. Muldrew and King conclude that 'for many poor households bad fortune such as injury, death, unemployment or an unpaid debt could make their efforts (to maintain subsistence) worthless at a stroke. As a result manipulating credit, customary entitlements, and charity must have been a more realistic option than honesty and forebearance, especially when need was pressing'.[143]

Reputation and the respectability emanating from it were vital in this society, both in terms of self-regard and the approbation of others, and for very practical reasons. Its importance could lead to quarrels that were at times violent, but also to strategies of containment and conflict resolution. This was, nevertheless, a world in which respectability needed to be re-established daily, and one in which mutuality, pawning and credit were intertwined with and often dependent upon it.

2 MAZY COURTS AND DARK ABODES

A crucial factor encouraging the retention of customary cultural practices was the spatial configuration of London's central neighbourhoods. Space matters to historians; it operates at all levels of the discipline and is woven into the very fabric of historical thought. Space is not simply an inert backdrop upon which the action of history takes place; rather, as Henri Lefebvre insisted, space is socially produced. Lefebvre argued that different societies develop spatial arrangements and configurations to meet their particular needs.[1] Building on these insights, Edward Soja has noted that while space certainly helps to shape social beings, people also make and remake space.[2] The relationship is symbiotic, and Soja has devoted himself to developing a critical social theory that achieves 'an appropriate interpretive balance between space, time and social being', that is, between 'the creation of human geographies, the making of history and the constitution of society'.[3] As Sharon Zukin succinctly put it, 'Space is now considered a dynamic medium that both exerts an influence on history and is shaped by human action'[4] – although to be sure, some groups and classes have much more influence than others. From the historian's perspective the message is clear: spatiality needs to be taken seriously.[5] It matters, moreover, not just at the theoretical or ontological levels, but at the interpretive as well. Certainly, any study of the urban poor *c.* 1780–1870 must recognize that much of plebeian life was lived in public spaces – or at least, was lived in spaces that were not private in the sense of being beyond the awareness and surveillance of others. The spatial configuration of the built environment in the plebeian neighbourhoods of central London was a crucial condition that promoted and supported customary social relations.

London, as a physical entity, was not known and understood in the same way by its various inhabitants. As John Marriott has pointed out for the eighteenth century, poor courts and alleys were *terra incognita* for the affluent – these spaces were the suspected loci of crime, and by the nineteenth century had become the focus of middle- and upper-class anxieties concerning the creation and maintenance of 'urban spaces fit for bourgeois intercourse and conviviality'.[6] In spite of the apparent unknowability of such districts to the affluent, Marriott's scepticism concerning Penelope Corfield's claim that London's streets were 'known arteries of public communication in an expanding public network' seems overstated. Rather, as Corfield also notes, London's street terrain did not generally constitute 'incomprehensible chaos' in the eighteenth century, but was instead 'a coherent and lively arena for social peregrination, perception, challenge and engagement'.[7] While the middle and upper classes had qualms about certain plebeian neighbourhoods, they had no difficulty negotiating the streets that constituted their own London world. No doubt the city must have seemed cacophonous and overwhelming to the newly arrived; yet even those who had not yet learnt the social codes of London's streets for the most part traversed them easily enough without major mishap, and at times complimented Londoners on their helpfulness to strangers. As Louis Simond, a visitor in 1810, noted, 'Whenever I have made enquiries, either in shops, or even from porters, carters, and market-women in the streets, I have uniformly received a civil answer, and every information in their power'.[8]

In no small measure, these different appreciations of London resulted from a transition that began in the nineteenth century, but which did not come to fruition in the capital's central neighbourhoods until the twentieth. According to Martin Daunton, the relationship between the house and the broader settlement around it began to shift in three important ways in English towns during the nineteenth century:

> First, the private domain of the house moved from a *promiscuous* sharing of facilities to an *encapsulated* or self-contained residential style. Secondly, the public domain of the city lost a *cellular* quality which had entailed an ambiguous semi-public and semi-private use of space, and took on a much more *open* texture. The dwelling became more enclosed and private, whilst the external space became 'waste' space or connective tissue which was to be traversed rather than used. The third change is implied in these comments on the developments in the private and public domains. The boundary or threshold between the two became less ambiguous and more definite, less penetrable and more impermeable.[9]

As Daunton explained, most labouring-class housing before the mid-nineteenth century 'had been located in self-contained little worlds of enclosed courts and alleys; but within each cell, the residents shared space and facilities in a communal way'.[10] He continued that 'Each group of houses formed its own private world within the larger city, and within that private world, space was a shared asset'.[11]

Marriott's scepticism concerning London's knowability jibes with upper- and middle-class fears emanating from these new notions of spatial configuration. Victoria Thompson's observations concerning nineteenth-century Paris are also pertinent to London. She notes that by the 1830s French observers, like their English counterparts, were focusing on the maze-like qualities of poor neighbourhoods as territories hidden from the middle class, difficult for them to navigate and whose inhabitants seemed dangerous and mysterious. Thompson says that 'More than just associating different neighbourhoods with different social groups, these authors began to imply that individuals of different classes used and understood urban space in different and conflicting ways'. She concludes that two cities emerged from such descriptions: 'a popular city that demanded surveillance and control, and a middle-class city that required freedom and mobility'.[12] Chris Otter has explored the relationship between these two concerns in a discussion focusing on the ways freedom itself was used 'as a strategy to shape conduct'.[13] Otter has built on Michel Foucault's notion of governmentality, a concept that broadens the notion of 'governing' beyond legislative acts and policies. It encompasses as well the ways in which governments, institutions and forms of knowledge attempt to shape people's behaviour: it was an 'ensemble formed by the institutions, procedures, analyses and reflections, the calculations and tactics, that allow the exercise of this very specific albeit complex form of power'.[14] Control techniques range from those meant to mould behaviour of the population as a whole to those by which an individual enacts self-control and self-discipline. The latter is especially necessary in liberal societies – such as Britain was in the nineteenth century – that sought to limit direct government activities in various spheres. Nevertheless, since it was believed that people would behave rationally and responsibly if their freedom was secure, it did become the job of government to see that this freedom was indeed protected, although frequently through 'indirect mechanisms' like infrastructure improvement and development.[15] In liberal states of the nineteenth century, cities needed to be refashioned into 'spaces within which civil conduct could be both secured and publicly displayed'.[16] The liberal subject inhabiting such spaces was to be self-governing: 'the master of the baser instincts and passions, a creature of thrift, energy, perseverance and, critically, reflexive evaluation of its own civility'.[17] Put another way, the liberal subject was the morally reformed subject. Liberal subjects constantly watched and evaluated their own and others' behaviour, and this in turn privileged a particular sense of visuality. To be respectable was to embrace this kind of visual control while distancing oneself from the 'lower' senses: smell, taste and touch. This distancing and the visual surveillance of behaviour were only possible in 'a civil, polite public arena', that is to say, they were only possible for the middle and upper classes. Plebeian women and men in overcrowded neighbourhoods remained mired in filth and squalor: 'The penumbral courts of the poor, with their communal washing and toilet facilities, overhung with a dense veil of smoke, were irregular and dark. [Bourgeois] Visuality could not predominate. The civil conduct of the respectable could not be seen and emulated. Dirt, din and stench did not instil a sense of shame'.[18] Consequently, as Otter points out, the inhabitants of such 'anti-bourgeois visual environment[s]' could not be trusted with social and political freedom.[19]

While British observers tended to focus on the moral consequences of derelict and overcrowded neighbourhoods, some did spell out the political dangers of these unknown environments. As Thomas Beames noted in 1850,

> Whilst these Rookeries [of London] remain, there must be something rotten in the state of Denmark; and we cannot forebear to recollect that some of the greatest convulsions which have shaken Europe at different times have had their origin in social discontent. We say not that the popular indignation has always triumphed, or that the stability of the governments under which these seditions occurred has always been sacrificed; we merely indicate the source whence they arose.[20]

While fear was a major component in how middle- and upper-class observers perceived plebeian neighbourhoods, the technologies meant to ensure plebeian Londoners used freedom in ways deemed responsible by their social betters were only just being developed during this period. Public inspection of the self and of others that was meant to guarantee civility necessitated a fundamental overhaul of the urban environment. To this end, urban outdoor problems – street filth, sanitation and slum areas generally – became the initial focus of reform agitation in the first three-quarters of the nineteenth century. Reform projects, however, were often sites of struggle and contest; some of the proposed changes did not work very well (gasworks had an alarming tendency to explode) or caused new problems (overcrowding escalated in neighbourhoods surrounding razed slums), while others ran afoul of vested interests of particular groups (attempts to eradicate abattoirs in central London were opposed by butchers).[21] Even if problems of these kinds were surmounted, maintenance of urban infrastructure was often a struggle for authorities. People who embraced the new codes of urban civility increasingly expected proper, regular maintenance and performance of infrastructure technologies – functioning street lamps, and regular dust collection, for instance. This required a refocusing of efforts on the part of governments, which was not accomplished in any comprehensive sense in the first three-quarters of the nineteenth century. As James Winter observed, 'no effective metropolitan government existed to promote, militate, and guide a transformative process'.[22] Nor were other levels of government any more effective. The road to the civil city was often bumpy and rarely ran straight and true.

Moreover, as Miles Ogborn noted, the contours and the features of this transition varied; they were specific to particular contexts, and it should be added, to different classes and collectivities within them.[23] To understand how plebeian Londoners experienced their spatial environments between 1780 and 1870, it is necessary to recognize the different temporalities in play, and that while sectors of the affluent may have embraced many of the values associated with modernity – individualism and a sharp delineation between the public and the private (especially as embodied in the home), for example – many sections of the plebeian population were 'doggedly persistent' in resisting 'the legal, temporal, spatial and moral imperatives of bourgeois modernisation'.[24] Marriott said this with respect to eighteenth-century London, but it was also the case throughout the first three-quarters of the nineteenth century. For plebeian Londoners, the streets – and especially the courts and alleys – were the terrain where much of their social life took place, so it is not surprising that these spaces helped to shape interpersonal relations. As vast as London was, and as unknowable as their neighbourhoods might be to the affluent, plebeian men and women were not isolated. Rather, most people had vibrant social lives composed of dense, localized networks of friends, kin, neighbours, associates and acquaintances. Most of these networks were centred on neighbourhoods, which, as seen, were at once bastions of sociability and incubators of dissention and roiling anger.

All of this meant a number of things: first, the new notions of urban spatial configuration being embraced by bourgeois Londoners – encapsulated houses, open, connective public spaces and more explicit boundaries between public and private – resulted in increasing criticism of and less tolerance for many of the plebeian neighbourhoods in the capital. Nevertheless, the inability of nineteenth-century governments to establish comprehensive infrastructure technologies guaranteeing bourgeois visuality meant that while these new ideas would fundamentally reshape the spatiality of central urban neighbourhoods, this would not happen until the twentieth century. For much of the nineteenth century, on the other hand, the physical structuration of central plebeian neighbourhoods continued to influence and help shape plebeian social relations. In order to see this, it is necessary to explore the spatiality of central London, navigating through the capital's major streets and public places to the narrow alleys, courts, yards and byways hidden away behind them, and then to look closely at the poor neighbourhoods in one particular district, the parish of St Martin in the Fields.

It is necessary to begin with caveats. Numerous historians have written about the streets of eighteenth-century London,[25] but simply to describe the smells, the dirt, the dark, the noise and the pollution is problematic, since modern sensibilities are markedly different from those of the eighteenth century: we are the inheritors of bourgeois visual culture. Fulsome descriptions of noxious smells and ubiquitous filth can make it easy for observers (and historians) today to conclude that only our own standards of urban cleanliness and notions of well-being need – and indeed, ought – to apply and that consequently, contemporary middle- and upper-class excoriations were justified. No doubt they were in many ways, but the danger is that in accepting their critique, it is all too easy to slide into accepting their assumptions and moral judgements as well. Moreover, while the contemporary critiques did share many concerns with those of urban critics today – sanitation, and the water supply, for instance – the late eighteenth- and early nineteenth-century agenda also differed from that of today. As pointed out earlier, theirs was not simply a programme to eradicate unhealthy and dangerous situations and practices; rather, demands for reforms to the city's built environment were inextricably bound up with a moral and political reform agenda that would also extirpate customary plebeian culture. As well, some of the standards commentators from this period adopted to evaluate the state of the city around them differed markedly from those of today, and so did their understanding of concepts like privacy. While modern standards obviously cannot be completely jettisoned, unproblematized judgements of London that do not recognize various differences do little to help in understanding the capital and its people during this period. At worst, the eighteenth- and early nineteenth-century city risks becoming little more than a crowded and insanitary stepping stone in a triumphal progress to the modern city.[26] Bearing these caveats in mind, what then was this urban world like?

The stench, dirt, darkness, noise, cramping and crowding found in so many parts of the capital constituted a veritable pandemonium. The sensory barrage was led by olfactory emanations: ordure, especially horse dung deposited on streets throughout the city – some 82 million pounds annually, according to Mayhew's estimate.[27] In the spring of 1842, scavengers removed some 550 cartloads of manure from city streets each week, and Mayhew claimed that in Westminster thirty-seven loads a day were removed in dry weather, fifty-six per day when it was wet.[28] Throughout the period, manure presented a health hazard all the year round, as Andrea Tanner has pointed out: 'In summer, it dried out, and the offensive dust blew into pedestrians' eyes, into the homes of the residents, and on to the goods so temptingly displayed by the capital's shopkeepers. In winter, it turned into a strong smelling mud, that clogged the street drains (where they existed), stuck to vehicle wheels and pedestrians' footwear, and caused numerous accidents'.[29]

The sharp and sour odours of urine and human waste added to this miasma, since people regularly 'eased' themselves in alleys, against buildings or in yards.[30] The vicinities of public houses, in particular, were pungent. Beer drinking producing its predictable result, the immediate neighbourhood of a pub was well marked, quite literally.[31] Houses with back gardens or yards usually had outdoor privies, which in the poorer courts were frequently in an appalling state. Houses – often those lacking sufficient space for an outdoor privy – generally had a vault or cesspit dug in the basement into which human waste was thrown. Periodically, these would be cleaned out by nightmen who brought their wagons after dark. Since their work usually entailed lugging buckets of waste through the house to the waiting wagon, this could not have been a pleasant undertaking for workers, tenants, householders or the immediate neighbours. Night soil removal was an expensive undertaking, moreover, which meant that it was rarely done at all in houses in many poor courts and alleys; instead privy and cess pit contents would overflow, in a number of instances contaminating water butts and standing pipes.[32] Indeed, John Gage quoted a surveyor of sewers in the neighbourhood of Church Lane, St Giles in 1849, 'that the privies in many of the houses had been destroyed by landlords to avoid the high periodic cost of emptying cesspits, and that the inhabitants had to walk a distance to those that were available and these were closed after a certain hour, resulting in much fouling of the streets and gutters'.[33] Communal infrastructure of this sort clearly meant that notions of familial privacy would be limited. When the nightmen did clean out cesspits and privies, they then drove their loaded wagons through the streets and dumped them either in the Thames or into covered ditches,[34] or deposited them at one of the capital's more than twenty laystalls (refuse heaps commercially sifted for recyclables).[35] Sometimes this system did not work satisfactorily, however. In the early 1780s the paving committee of St Martin in the Fields complained that 'Rubbish hath been frequently unloaded and Night Soil let out of Carts in divers parts of this Parish'.[36] Carrying nosegays may have seemed a dandified affectation, but clearly it was also a necessary one.

Street sewers and drainage systems were not the norm at this time in the poorer areas of London. Typically, a gutter – known as a kennel – ran down the middle of the roadway to collect water and refuse. Parishes periodically cleansed the kennels – paid for by a scavengers' rate – but for the most part vegetable and animal waste was left to moulder.[37] Shopkeepers habitually threw their garbage into the streets. C. P. Moritz, a tourist in 1782, complained that 'Nothing in London makes a more detestable sight than the butchers' stall ... The guts and other refuse are all thrown on the street and set up an unbearable stink'.[38] Nor were the inhabitants above using the street for garbage disposal. As James Peller Malcolm, another contemporary, sardonically noted in 1808, 'The renters of single rooms, in the first, second, and third floors, in mean streets, feel themselves above restraint. These people empty dirty water mixed with their offals into the gutters, the stench of which is appalling; but I forget, they certainly do not offend against the law – it is *dust*, not water *dirtied*, or mixed with dust and vegetables, which they are forbidden to deposit in the streets'.[39] Peller Malcolm's sarcasm was somewhat unfair, for as Hector Gavin noted in 1847, there were 'multitudes of courts and alleys that ... never had a scavenger within them'.[40] People in such places were left to bury their waste as best they could (again, often endangering the water supply) or simply to let it collect and putrefy.[41] Either way, this shared problem could lead to tensions and quarrels between neighbours, whatever option was adopted.

The streets were as dirty as they were because dust collection was haphazard at best. Parishes contracted out this service on an annual basis, but once the contract was let they seemed to have little effective control over performance. Peller Malcolm mentioned a householder who complained that the dust had not been collected 'for six long weeks',[42] and the St Martin's paving committee minutes had been punctuated by many similar charges in the early 1780s. Repeatedly, St Martin's officers noted that such complaints were 'general over the parish'.[43] Fining the scavenger 40s. made not a whit of difference.[44] According to Tanner, moreover, this was still a problem in the second half of the nineteenth century, dust contractors 'being notorious for failing to fulfil the conditions of their contracts'.[45] Added to these kinds of complaints were those such as the one in 1781 that the St Martin's scavenger was not using covered carts as he was supposed to.[46] The resulting stench would have been particularly oppressive in the narrow alleys and close courts inhabited by the poor – or at least in those where the scavenger troubled to make a collection. This was exacerbated by the proclivity of dust contractors to dump their loads illegally as close to the collection streets as possible – an especially common practice in poor districts, where people were not generally 'vociferous, literate, [and] ratepaying'.[47] Clearly, authorities during this period had a very limited ability to ensure proper performance by dust collectors and scavengers.

London's streets were generally wet and muddy. In 1765 French tourist Pierre Grosley noted of the Strand that 'I have, during my stay in London, seen the middle of the street constantly foul with a dirty puddle to the height of three or four inches; a puddle where the splashings cover those who walk on foot, fill coaches when their windows happen not to be up, and bedawb all the lower parts of such houses as are exposed to it'.[48] It was virtually impossible to remain clean when walking through the streets. John Gay's 1716 poem *Trivia* describes in relentless detail the various dangers which beset the unwary pedestrian, and continued to do so throughout the century. Clouds of ashes were blown from passing dust carts; chandlers carrying their baskets shoulder-high dripped tallow on coats; butchers' trays splashed grease and bloody liquid; sweepers' brooms sprayed mud; horses going uphill '[flung] up the mire';[49] stall keepers dashed scaly water into the streets; wheelbarrows coming up from behind marred stockings; porters rolling hogsheads bowled people over; and brewers raising and lowering goods from open cellar trapdoors created mantraps on the footpaths. Gay recommended that pedestrians try to keep close to the walls of buildings to avoid these annoyances (save the last), but admitted this could be a battle, since others also had the same ambition. Indeed, Grosley warned his countrymen that when walking in London, being pushed and shoved and often driven into the kennel was a normal experience, since

> The English walk very fast: their thoughts being entirely engrossed by business, they are very punctual to their appointments, and those, who happen to be in their way, are sure to be sufferers by it: constantly darting forward they jostle them with a force proportioned to their bulk and the velocity of their motion. I have seen foreigners, not used to this exercise, let themselves be tossed and whirled about a long time, in the midst of a crowd of passengers, who had nothing else in view, but to get forward.[50]

The phenomenon was still drawing comment in 1825, when Robert Mudie, a Scottish journalist, noted that 'in London ... the crowd sweeps along like a torrent ... it will bear you along whether you will it or not'.[51] There was, as John Badcock had explained in 1823, a system in place for those in the know: 'everyone taking the right hand of another, whereby confusion is avoided ... The contrary mode is a sure indication of a person being a stranger, or living at the outskirts of town'.[52] Although London's high levels of migration and many visitors no doubt meant it was a system ignored as much as it was observed, knowing how to walk in London became a signifier of the attainment of urban civility.

Sedan chairs, too, posed problems. Gay contended that they were not allowed within the posts which separated the footpaths from the carriageways, but according to Cesar de Saussure, yet another tourist, this distinction was not observed. Saying that sedan chairs were carried on the footpaths, he warned that if 'a Stranger does not understand the "take care" or "By your leave, sir", of the bearers, and does not make room to let them pass, he will run a great risk of being knocked down, for the bearers go very fast and cannot turn aside with their burden'.[53] By 1813 there were still some 400 sedan chairs, but by the 1820s they were becoming a fixture of the past, being superseded by the ever-increasing numbers of hackney coaches – an estimated 1,100 in 1813.[54] London's snarled and congested traffic had long been a source of friction. Already by the late seventeenth century, there had been complaints about the number of hackney coaches for hire in the capital's streets and repeated government attempts to control them through legislation.[55] While hackney coaches affected spatial practices, allowing those sufficiently affluent to use them to maintain 'patterns of sociability and shopping, work and recreation over more extensive areas', they also 'contributed appreciably to the disorder and unruly congestion of the thoroughfares'.[56] By the early 1840s traffic snarls were of monumental proportions. As James Grant explained, on major streets

> the entire open space before the pedestrian, with the exception of the pavement on either side, appears on some occasions as if it were blockaded for the purpose of impeding the advance of some hostile army. Sometimes the vehicles are so densely wedged together, that if ... one could walk on horses' backs, and on the tops of waggons, omnibuses, coaches, cabs, and so forth, without the risk of slipping his foot, he might proceed two or three hundred yards without once touching the causeway.[57]

In spite of these various street hazards, numerous observers commented on the cleanliness of the common people. Moritz said the people were cleanly and neatly dressed, and continued that 'I rarely saw, even a fellow with a wheelbarrow, who had not a shirt on; nor even a beggar without both a shirt and shoes and stockings. The English are certainly distinguished for cleanliness'.[58] That they were to any extent required constant vigilance and work. The anonymous pamphlet *Low Life or One Half of the World Knows Not How the Other Half Live* spoke of 'The wives of poor Journeymen Mechanicks, getting up [on a Sunday morning] to buy a little Soap, and wash their Husbands a Shirt, Stock, Handkerchief, and Stockings, that they may appear in the Afternoon like Christians, though they live like Brutes'.[59] Allowing for the pejorative language, the conditions of the streets would have made constant work for these women. On the other hand, the male habit of wearing dark-coloured jackets, coats and breeches would have rendered the dirt less visible – thus, the appearance of cleanness may not necessarily have been the reality. Louis Simond, in the early nineteenth century, noted that 'outside garments are of a dull, dark cast, and harmonize with smoke and mud', but also allowed that the clean linen generally perceived meant that people were 'not dirty absolutely'.[60] Certainly, the standards by which the appearance of the common people was being measured – the mere possession of a shirt and shoes, for instance – bespeak a more generous latitude in the notion of cleanliness than is common today.

While ordure, street muck and erratic dust collection undoubtedly accounted for much of the dirt of the metropolis, there was another problem as well: pollution from coal fires. As Pierre Grosley noted of the smoke enveloping London, 'This smoke is occasioned, during the winter, which lasts about eight months, by the sea-coals made use of in kitchens, apartments, and even the halls of grand houses'.[61] Coal was also used in commercial and industrial buildings. Grosley described in some detail the impact of coal smoke on London:

> This smoke, being loaded with terrestrial particles, and rolling in a thick, heavy atmosphere, forms a cloud, which envelops London like a mantle; a cloud which the sun pervades but rarely; a cloud which, recoiling back upon itself, suffers the sun to break out only now and then, which casual appearance procures the Londoners a few of what they call GLORIOUS DAYS.
>
> When the spring was completely opened, all this park [St James's], trees, alleys, benches, grass-plots, were still impregnated with a sort of black stuff, formed by the successive deposits which had been left by the smoke of winter. The vapours, fogs and rains, with which the atmosphere of London is loaded, drag with them in their fall the heaviest particles of smoke; this forms black rain and produces all the ill effects that may justly be expected from it.[62]

Grosley then went on to describe some of these effects: the staining of clothes, buildings, furniture and even books.[63] Indeed, Peter Brimblecombe has argued that the fashion for dark clothing and furnishings resulted from the ubiquitous staining by coal smoke.[64] Undoubtedly, the pollution and the dirt had various ill effects on the health of Londoners as well (although Grosley, being a short-term visitor, was perhaps less aware of these). Dr John Lettsom, a well-known London physician, was reduced in the 1770s to recommending to his convalescent typhus patients 'to loiter on the bridges across the Thames', a common stratagem of Londoners anxious for fresh air.[65] In the mid-nineteenth century, Hector

Gavin noted that a black scum from coal dust appeared on the water the poor kept in their rooms for domestic use, on the surface of water butts and even on the water surface of the reservoir in Green Park.[66]

Francis Place, looking back in 1826 on the London of his youth, wrote of the courts and lanes habituated by the poor that 'Circulation of air was out of the question, the putrid effluvia was always stagnant in these places'. Rather surprisingly, Place then claimed that London was 'in other respects a healthy place'.[67] Modern sensibilities would be hard-pressed to find evidence that this was so. While Brimblecombe says the growth of romanticism with its veneration of nature led to more and more strident criticism of London's environment during this period, he points out that even a decided critic like Charles Dickens at times 'was still able to write quite nostalgically of the pollution ... referring to smoke as "London's ivy"'.[68] After noting that coal smoke caused a grey mist throughout the city on cloudy days, Louis Simond, another visitor, went on to observe that on sunny days the coal mist shone pale orange like 'Claude Lorraine glasses – a mild golden hue, quite beautiful'.[69] As was the case with respect to the notion of cleanliness, a rather different set of criteria is being used to evaluate the state of the metropolis. By today's standards, London, even in areas like St Martin in the Fields which possessed no noxious trades, was without doubt a filthy and unhealthy city. To be sure, as Stephen Mosley has pointed out for the second half of the nineteenth century, contemporaries were certainly aware of their pollution problems. Nevertheless, as Chris Otter has noted, industry was able to evade attempts to control its pollution, and there were also factors making it difficult to control domestically produced pollution for much of the century.[70] In an era when the miasma theory of contagion was widely believed, open hearths, clearly a major source of urban pollution, were thought crucial to ensure that homes were well ventilated. According to the miasma theory, disease spread through the inhalation of air contaminated by organic putrefaction, so ventilation was thought vitally important.[71] Equally, open hearths seemed to epitomize the companionable warmth of the middle-class private family home: kith and kin gathered around the 'cheerful glow of the homely hearth'. So strong was this sentimental attachment that politicians feared the repercussions of passing legislation that might interfere with 'a citizen's freedom to enjoy the hugely popular institution of the open coal hearth'.[72] Yet again, authorities were unable to effect changes to bring about a clean and orderly city appropriate for securing and displaying the civil conduct so desired.

The capital as a whole tended often to be dark and gloomy, even in daytime, thanks to the coal smoke and the frequent fogs. The latter, exacerbated by particles in the coal smoke, became thicker, and they were more and more frequent between 1750 and 1890. The 'fuliginous cloud' so frequently enveloping the capital could plunge London into darkness, requiring lamps in shops to be lit in daylight and pedestrians to feel their way cautiously in the hopes of avoiding accidents,[73] an undertaking made more difficult by the distortions caused by the fog. As Thomas Miller noted in 1852,

> The gas-lamps appear as if placed three-story high, unless you stand close beneath them, for what light they emit is nearly all thrown upward; while a cab comes heaving up (to appearance) as large as the huge caravan which Wombwell formerly used for the conveyance of his stupendous elephant. Once take a wrong turning, and you may consider yourself very fortunate if you ever discover the right road again within three hours; for the houses wear a different appearance, and the streets appear to be all at 'sixes and sevens'.[74]

The fog even penetrated houses: 'A stranger to London, when the fog sets in at night, and he looks upon it for the first time, fancies his apartments filled with smoke, and begins by throwing open his doors and windows; thus making bad worse, by destroying all the warm air in the rooms'.[75]

There were attempts to deal with London's darkness – to establish bourgeois notions of visuality. Street lights existed throughout the capital, again provided by contractors to the various parishes. Lamps were to be found especially on the broader streets and better courts – perhaps about 14,000 in Westminster by 1809.[76] In St Martin's in 1782 there were 1,052 street lamps, according to a census conducted by the parish inspectors,[77] and 1,456 by 1813.[78] Usually there was a light every five houses or so.[79] These lamps were not bright by today's standards, whale oil being the principal illuminant by the late eighteenth century. When St Martin's was considering the introduction of gas lamps on some of the better streets in 1814, parish officers were told that one of these was equal in intensity to six or seven oil lamps.[80]

The major streets were brightened by shop lights as well. Shops frequently stayed open until nine or later,[81] and according to Peller Malcolm were 'of infinite service to the rest of the inhabitants by their liberal use of the Patent Lamp, to shew their commodities during the long evenings of winter. The parish lamps glimmer above them, and are hardly distinguishable before ten o'clock'.[82] Household window lanterns also added to the illumination. Certainly, visitors from Europe were often greatly impressed by the amount of light on London streets. C. P. Moritz confessed to being astonished, observing that the lamps were 'so near each other, that even on the most ordinary and common nights, the city has the appearance of a festive illumination'.[83] When compared to other European cities, London may indeed have been very well lit, but Grosley's observations clearly indicate the limitations of metropolitan lighting. He explained that the lamps 'yield immediate light to the foot path, but convey to the middle of the street only a glimmering, which, in the broad streets, that is to say, those which are most frequented by coaches, is hardly sufficient to enlighten and direct the way'.[84]

The general dimness of oil lamps was compounded by maintenance problems. As Otter has noted, governments during the century had to refocus their efforts to ensure the maintenance of the infrastructure, which in turn produced 'spaces divested of germs and odour, where sight, movement and civility were privileged'.[85] Intention and performance were often far apart in this period, however. There were continual complaints about the lack of functioning lamps. In December 1780, for instance, there was a complaint that five of the seventy-four lamps on Long Acre were out.[86] After the turn of the century, complaints became even more numerous. Reports of lamps going out part-way through the night or not being lit at all are repeatedly recorded in the St Martin's paving committee minutes, possibly because the price of oil had risen and the contractor felt the need to cut corners.[87] The situation was made worse by the fact that the contractor estimated that one-half of the glass lamp globes were broken each year, whether by careless lamplighters or – more likely – by vandals, he didn't say.[88] Given all of these problems, plus the weakness of oil as an illuminant, it is difficult to disagree with the judgement of one local historian that the lighting during this period merely 'rendered the darkness more visible'.[89] It is telling that links were still being regularly carried before carriages and pedestrians as late as 1807,[90] and link boys did not disappear completely until the 1840s.[91] London's lighting may have been the wonder of Europe, but the need for boys to light one's way with torches clearly indicates its limitations in the first half of the nineteenth century. If the situation was problematic on major streets, lighting in the poorer courts and alleys would have been at best haphazard, and in many cases non-existent. There were no well-lit shop windows in such places to contribute to the general illumination, and window lanterns were beyond the budgets of most poor families. Given the litany of lighting complaints from parishioners living on the better streets, it is extremely unlikely that lamps in poor courts and alleys, where they existed, would have been regularly maintained. These close and narrow byways would have been dark and dreary even on the sunniest days; at night the darkness must have been palpable.

Ill-smelling, filthy, dark and noisome places abounded throughout central London, as contemporaries were only too aware. Uproar in the streets and courts was also the norm and had various sources. Rows and fisticuffs were, according to contemporary observers, distressingly common. Grosley, like de Saussure before him, claimed that men of the lower classes fought a lot and that even women were known to do so.[92] Inevitably, a noisy crowd would gather to watch and referee. Spontaneous football matches were also noisy affairs. Gay described one such in Covent Garden in *Trivia*, and de Saussure rather bitterly commented, 'In cold weather you sometimes see a score of rascals in the street kicking a ball, and they will break panes of glass and smash the windows of coaches, and also knock you down without the slightest compunction; on the contrary they will roar with laughter'.[93]

The traffic snarls discussed earlier did not just obstruct passage; the wooden-wheeled wagons and carriages clattering and squealing along the thoroughfares were a source of unceasing noise.[94] Moritz wrote of the 'terrifying rush of carts and coaches'[95] through the streets: the congestion was serious and the din must have been constant. Theatre districts and other areas of public amusement were especially noisy with carriages at letting-out time. Mary Lamb was perhaps unusual in claiming to enjoy the cacophony in Russell Court when theatregoers were returning home. She described the noise as 'tremendous', with 'the calling up of the carriages and the squabbles of the coachmen and the link boys'.[96] In 1846 James Grant commented on the many arguments between drivers trying to make their way on the congested streets: 'They swear at each other at a furious rate, and always at the full stretch of their voices, – which as every one who has been in London will bear me witness, are of first-rate capabilities'.[97]

Pillories were yet another source of uproar, regularly attracting noisy and rowdy crowds. Grosley described a particularly turbulent encounter at Seven Dials: 'The place was crowded with people waiting to see a poor wretch stand in the pillory, whose punishment was deferred to another day. The mob, provoked at this disappointment, vented their rage on all that passed that way, whether a-foot or in coaches; and threw at them dirt, rotten eggs, dead dogs, and all sorts of trash and ordure which they had provided to pelt the unhappy wretch, according to custom'.[98] The use of pillories was restricted after 1816 (to perjury and subornation) and formally abolished in 1837. If authorities were able to eliminate some sources of rowdy street behaviour that challenged emerging bourgeois notions of public decorum, they were not always so successful.

Public execution days attracted large and often rowdy crowds. At Newgate after 1783 and Horsemonger Lane principally, Londoners gathered in large numbers to watch the hangings. While a number of upper- and middle-class observers were certainly decrying its existence, the spectator appetite for public execution did not lessen during this period, as some have supposed.[99] Noting the legislative attacks on Bartholomew, Greenwich and Peckham Fairs, Matthew White says

> Executions nevertheless remained a conspicuous ... exception to these otherwise successful measures to minimise urban disorder. The area outside Newgate prison continued to be the place of piemen, hired seating, the meeting of friends and strained glimpses of the infamous – historical continuities that display older, eighteenth-century features of inter-parochial shared experience (albeit laced with morbid fascination) that would endure for decades to come.[100]

White used a coroner's inquest from 1807 to deny that civic control and 'ameliorating' social mores caused people to lose interest in public executions. The inquest was held after thirty people were crushed to death in a crowd of 40,000 which was gathered to watch executions at Newgate. White concluded that there was still a 'powerful latent curiosity'[101] that drew people to the prison from a broad cross-section of occupations and from across the city. Aside from curiosity, 'ghoulish intrigue, vengeance, the attraction of witnessing celebrity felons, or simply the excitement of constituting a boiling crowd in its own right' all continued to draw huge numbers to Newgate for more than eighty years after 1783.[102] Carolyn Conley agrees, moreover, that this fascination was still apparent in the 1850s in London. The crowds not only watched by the thousands, but, she says, they watched with relish.[103] V. A. C. Gatrell has discussed attitudes to execution crowds at length in *The Hanging Tree*. He refuses to see the increasing criticisms of these crowds in the first half of the nineteenth century as a product of the growth of humanitarian sentiment. Rather, he excoriates the squeamishness of the affluent and notes the limits of their sympathy for the person about to die – basically to individuals most like themselves. It is telling that upper- and middle-class critics focused so frequently on the supposed animality of the execution crowd. Thomas Miller, for instance, described these spectators as emerging from 'blind alleys and secluded nooks – haunts of vice and infamy – the uneducated heirs to crime and wretchedness'.[104] Ranging themselves along the barriers at Newgate, Miller compared them to 'hounds that are ever foremost at the death'.[105] He ended his description by recounting a fight – one of more than a score – this time involving two women: 'blinded with their long hair, they tore at each other like two furies; their bonnets and caps were trodden underfoot in the kennel, and lay disregarded beside the body of the poor dog, which, while searching for its master in the crowd, was an hour before kicked to death by the savage and brutal mob'.[106] Such middle-class attitudes, while certainly sensational, make sense if viewed through the lens of the bourgeois visual environment and the type of person it was meant to promote. Clearly, in the first half of the nineteenth century the execution crowd remained a large and noisy site of contestation.

Street sellers also added to the general noise, calling out continually, flogging their wares. St Martin's parish officers received complaints in 1806 and 1813, for instance, concerning street sellers in Bedfordbury and Chandos Streets, 'persons standing in that neighbourhood with barrows and baskets for the sale of fish and fruit'.[107] The smell of the wares – especially the fish – as well as the noise of the sellers and their customers likely lay behind the complaints. Street performers also contributed to the hubbub throughout the period – Hogarth's *Enraged Musician* (1741) has only to be recalled, for instance.[108] The conflict between often affluent residents and usually plebeian street performers continued to rage throughout the period – in 1864 Charles Babbage was moved to begin a campaign against street performers, and especially organ grinders, whom he called organ pests.[109] Again, notions of proper street decorum and usage remained a site of struggle and contest.

There were many other causes of noisy street quarrels. Parking problems have a longer history than one might suppose, and were certainly an ongoing issue during this period. Repeatedly, the St Martin in the Fields paving committee minutes registered complaints: in 1780 that a sedan chair was obstructing passage into Buckingham Court; in 1802 and 1803 that barrows were obstructing St Martin's Court, St Martin's Lane and the corner of Drury Lane; in 1805 that coach makers in Long Acre were leaving their just finished products on the footpath; and in 1813 that hay wagons were being left in James Street Haymarket.[110] For every formal complaint lodged with the parish, there must have been scores more which were resolved by direct action on the part of the complainant.

Moreover, this was still the age of the hue and cry – it was the legal responsibility of bystanders to assist in arrests which were usually effected by the victim of the crime. While its use may have been less common than in earlier centuries, Old Bailey court proceedings contain numerous references to baying crowds in hot pursuit of accused law breakers. In 1783 John Hyde was accused of stealing a coat. He maintained that he had bought it not knowing it to be stolen property. The crowd took his part, calling for him to break the prosecutor's windows in revenge. He threw some mud, but denied actually breaking any glass.[111] A year later Edward Robinson was accused of picking pockets at a football game. The crowd took him and ducked him, keeping him in the water for half an hour.[112] Crowds regularly intervened, noisily taking sides in these legal dramas. These noisy altercations also demonstrated some of the customary cultural practices discussed in the last chapter. A preliminary examination of two of the sessions of the Old Bailey in 1800 (February and September) also provides evidence that people still looked out for one another and watched carefully the goings-on in the streets at the turn of the century. There were 232 cases in these two sessions, and in 162 of them it is possible to determine the circumstances of the apprehension of the accused. In ninety-six of the latter cases, those accused were arrested immediately; either they were employees of the prosecutor; the prosecutor otherwise knew their identity; or they were reported by suspicious pawnbrokers. In sixty-six other cases – 41 per cent of the 162 – neighbours and strangers chose to intervene in various ways, almost always to help the victim of the crime effect an arrest. Neighbours and passing strangers were still giving information to victims; they noted suspicious behaviour, often intervening to question the person. They helped give chase and responded to the hue and cry. In 9 per cent of these cases, it was stated that the cry was made. It must have occurred much more often, however, given that in more than fifty cases – 31 per cent – witnesses said they pursued or helped take the accused.[113] With the establishment of the metropolitan police in 1829, this began to change, however. In the February 1845 session at the Old Bailey, for instance, there were 170 cases heard. In seventy-three of these, the circumstances of the arrest were unclear. In the ninety-seven cases for which the circumstances were apparent, there were ten – just over 10 per cent – in which the cry was made, and another twenty-one in which neighbours or strangers offered assistance in various ways – in all, in 32 per cent of the ninety-seven cases people offered assistance to the victim. While at first glance, it did seem that people were less willing to intervene in 1845, a more careful examination indicates otherwise. In twenty-three of the ninety-seven cases, policemen effected arrests as the crime was in progress, usually as a result of their having noticed suspicious behaviour beforehand. If these cases are set aside, then in the seventy-four cases remaining, in 41 per cent of them people were willing to assist the victim in the various ways described above – the same percentage as in 1800. In spite of the presence of a professional police force designed to intervene in instances of malfeasance and to prevent crime where possible, it would seem that people continued to look out for one another in much the same ways as they had before the coming of the force. When constables were at hand, people readily made use of them, especially to protect property, whatever they may have thought of some of the other activities of the force. Nevertheless, in those instances where the police were not to be found, Londoners did not stop assisting one another. In finding and apprehending those accused of wrongdoing, the police seem to have been folded into customary cultural behaviour rather than radically altering it. This is of a piece with Jennifer Davis's observation that 'Criminal prosecutions did not replace informal sanctions against perceived wrongdoing, but were used in addition to them'.[114]

London's crowded streets may have been overwhelming, both in terms of noise and sheer numbers of people and vehicles, but it was not a city of anonymous multitudes. Rather, it teemed with small neighbourhoods consisting of a street, a court or an alley or two. In Westminster, the former mansions of the wealthy had been divided and re-divided to accommodate poor families. Courts and alleys were built over their back gardens consisting of jerry-built edifices with paper-thin walls. Peller Malcolm estimated that there were some 3,000 houses in London and Westminster which were in 'a dangerous state of ruin'.[115] Under-built or derelict houses collapsed throughout the period – two such in Little Russell Court in 1812 alone, for instance.[116] To contemporaries, the close courts and alleys occupied by the poor seemed particularly malodorous and dirty; most had narrow entrances, often obscure and unnoticed, and seemed dark and often fearsome places to outsiders. Indeed, their very self-containment made these courts and alleys unknowable and threatening to many upper- and middle-class observers. Already by the mid-eighteenth century, Henry Fielding had complained, 'Whoever indeed considers the cities of *London* and *Westminster* ... the great irregularity of their Buildings, the immense Number of Lanes, Alleys, Courts and Bye-places; must think, that, had they been intended for the very Purpose of Concealment, they could scarce have been better contrived. Upon such a View, the whole appears as a vast Wood or Forest, in which a Thief may harbour with as great Security, as wild Beasts do in the Desarts of Africa or Arabia.'[117] Such criticisms only intensified in the nineteenth century. The enclosed nature of such spaces can be seen in some of the poorest neighbourhoods in St Martin in the Fields, a parish of some 26,000 people in the early nineteenth century. Several patterns are apparent in these spaces: entrances were often very narrow indeed. In some areas like the Bermudas – an infamous slum just behind St Martin's church – they led into a labyrinthine world of courts and alleys all but invisible from major streets. In other neighbourhoods like Bedfordbury, to the north of the Bermudas, alleys were narrow at points of egress but ballooned out in the centre to create spaces for sociability.

The neighbourhoods of the poor afforded little privacy to those living within them. Indeed, expectations concerning privacy and even the way in which it was understood differed in this period from later notions. The boundaries between public and private in such spaces were often porous, and the two spheres did not necessarily align themselves with home and not-home.[118] Rather, as Linda Pollock, Lawrence Klein and Joanne Bailey have all shown, the notion of 'private' seemed to be aligned with secrecy (which could occur outside the home), while 'public' denoted matters 'exposed to the perceptions of some others or of people in general',[119] which could certainly occur within the plebeian home. Amanda Vickery has recently taken issue with the notion that privacy was aligned with secrecy, claiming instead that

> Though the public/private conceptual dichotomy was invoked in many discursive contexts in the long eighteenth century, it was rarely deployed to characterise an inside/outside, female/male division of space. In fact, what writers designated as belonging to the private sphere tended to vary according to the particular public they were counterposing. Consequently, privacy for eighteenth-century historians is a moveable feast, rather different from ... Pollock's secrecy.[120]

It is difficult to see how this undermines the claims of Pollock, Klein and Bailey, given that none of them equated privacy with the home. Pollock, for example, notes that privacy 'did not involve a perception that an arena existed that was totally beyond the range of and totally separate from the state'.[121] There are, moreover, seemingly unwarranted elisions in Vickery's understanding of the concept. It is not at all clear that privacy and the private sphere are directly equivalent, as she seems to assume. Nor is it the case that security – especially of property – is the equivalent of privacy, as Vickery also seems to suppose in the first chapter of *Behind Closed Doors*.[122] At the very least, these elisions require clear justification, and her definition of privacy needs to be clarified.

The understanding of privacy put forward by Pollock, Klein and Bailey accords well with Lena Cowen Orlin's observations for early modern London, that privacy was 'less a material condition than a consensual act'.[123] Similarly, what she says of the tensions engendered by this situation applied equally in the late eighteenth century, another period of rapid urban growth: 'Housemates expected certain conventions to be honoured: when two people retired to a corner, they signalled their desire for a private conversation … But the built consequences of population growth and an expanding economy brought many into closer contiguities than had been the case in the recent past'.[124] She notes that plebeian Londoners could no longer assume their neighbours 'would respect their social boundaries, especially given the provocation that the structural boundaries between households were often as insubstantial as those between housemates'.[125] The tensions engendered by these kinds of living arrangements only got worse over time. By the late eighteenth century, as Vickery recognizes, 'Living cheek by jowl with comparative strangers robbed the London house of any automatic association with privacy as we understand it. Indeed, more solitude and anonymity was probably found outside the house than in'.[126] These notions of public and private call into question Shoemaker's claims that in moving into the home, sociability by definition became more private and less subject to neighbourhood pressures. Ironically, by the nineteenth century, improvement schemes made the situation even more difficult for many plebeian Londoners. As such schemes were introduced, overcrowding in plebeian homes became more severe. Slum clearance quickly came to be seen by the affluent as one of the major benefits resulting from the construction of major thoroughfares. As H. J. Dyos noted, 'the line taken by new streets was generally determined by its effectiveness in clearing as many slum dwellings as possible'.[127] According to Tristram Hunt, this reflected a shift in reform ambitions from the early nineteenth century: 'whereas Nash and earlier developers had used roads as shorelines to hem in the poor, to hide them behind a stage set of Regency wonder, the ambition now was to drive straight through, opening up the dreaded rookeries'.[128] The number of displacements caused by street improvements and rail line construction was huge. After Trafalgar Square was begun in 1829, for instance, nearby streets were also levelled, resulting in a drop in St Martin in the Field's population by 4,282 in 1831. The construction of Victoria Street left some 2,500 people homeless, while another 5,000 people were evicted from the rookery in St Giles in the Fields by the mid-century development of New Oxford Street. The average number of people per house in Church Lane, which ran parallel to this street on the south side, rose from twenty-four in 1841 to fifty-two in 1851.[129] Moreover, between 1859 and 1867 alone, railway schemes displaced 37,000 in central London.[130] Not until the 1870s were any of the improvers required to re-house the displaced – a requirement that in practice was easily evaded and yet again demonstrates the limits of government efficacy.

Even in areas that were not subject to grand redevelopment schemes, there were noticeable changes. For example, by 1868 the courts and alleys running off Bedfordbury – one of the very poor areas in St Martin in the Fields – were reduced in number: Stable Yard and Charles Court disappeared, and the same was true of the courts running north off the Strand between Bedford Street and Bull Inn Court. By the 1860s entrances to the courts and alleys were being widened – Goodwin's Court's eastern entrance, and Taylor's Court's western, for example. Even back streets were becoming thoroughfares to be traversed rather than enclosed spaces for sociability. As Lis and Soly have observed, 'The clearance of slums and the demolition of those urban areas with numerous yards and alleys after the middle of the nineteenth century enabled policy makers to "open up" local communities; new housing projects were designed in such a way that public spaces offered little scope for social interaction'.[131] It is with the advent of such shifts in the built environment that privacy, centred on the enclosed family home, could even begin to become physically viable. In the period of this study, however, there were not enough of such changes in street configuration or in housing conditions to ensure a major shift in plebeian behaviour in central London.

As A. S. Wohl noted, when neighbourhoods were razed, 'The sudden and dramatic elimination of eye-sores, not the eviction of the inhabitants' caught the imagination of the public.[132] Before the 1850s overcrowding was not a major concern, in part because it was hidden away inside houses – it was largely invisible – and in part because the stench and filth of the streets were so glaringly apparent. The latter were regarded as particularly problematic, since 'The main concern of the day was the epidemics that ravaged society, and the current pythogenic theories of disease, which attributed fever to noxious gases and effluvia from decomposing faecal matter ... [drew] ... attention from overcrowding within the home to drains and sewers outside it'.[133] It was also generally assumed that evicted people would move to better housing in the suburbs. In point of fact, as pointed out earlier, they did not. Displaced people tried to find alternate lodging in their immediate neighbourhood for several reasons. First, men in a number of trades needed to be close to their work: 'porters, market workers, building labourers, dock hands, tailors, jewellers (who often shared their tools), street vendors, and ... all the casually employed' fell into this category.[134] Indeed, in 1866 it was estimated that at least 680,000 workers were still tied to central London. Other reasons also kept families in the old central neighbourhoods: if credit had been established with a local shop, this would have been too crucial a resource to be cast aside lightly. Equally, if women belonged to informal borrowing networks, this too was a resource worth preserving. Finally, a number of people were enormously fond of their neighbourhoods. In *Ragged London in 1861*, John Hollingshead asked a shoemaker who lived in a poor, badly overcrowded neighbourhood near Regent Street why he continued to do so. The man 'spoke about his long residence in the parish, his familiarity with its people and its ways, and his dread of going into another neighbourhood, which he said would be like a "foreign country"'.[135] When New Oxford Street was constructed between 1844 and 1847, the Irish clung to their neighbourhood, some refusing to leave their homes even after the building roofs had been removed.[136]

Beginning in the 1840s, a number of philanthropic and speculative builders did start to erect model apartment buildings throughout central London, but there were never anywhere near enough of them, and very rapidly these landlords began to discriminate in favour of regularly employed, and often skilled, workers as tenants. The very poor who had been displaced often could not afford the rents, and in any case they found the many restrictions hedging about occupancy and the utilitarian, barrack-like appearance of many of these buildings unpleasant and irksome.[137] What this meant in practice was severe overcrowding in the housing stock that remained in central London. The Strand district medical officer noted in 1858 that inmates at Pentonville Penitentiary received 800–900 cubic feet of air in their cells. Rooms in old houses in the Strand district, now the homes of the poor, allowed from 164 to 310 cubic feet of air per occupant.[138] As Donald Olsen point out, moreover, 'Down to the twentieth century most working-class Londoners lived in homes that had not been built with them in mind; down to the nineteenth century all of them did'.[139] This kind of housing was particularly problematic, for as Dyos noted,

> By special irony the large houses vacated by the middle classes in their trek to the suburbs were capable of declining fastest after they had been given up ... No slum was worse than property transferred in this way. The quite normal process of bringing land once settled at a low density into heavier occupation sometimes got badly out of control; and back gardens, often quite small ones, were divided and sub-divided into alleys and courts which could scarcely avoid going badly wrong once rot had set in.[140]

Typically, a family rented a room or two in a subdivided house. Householders, the status to which people in the labouring classes aspired, rented a whole house, but then normally let out several rooms to lodgers. The pattern of subletting was often Byzantine. As John Hollingshead observed, 'four, if not more, landlords are interested in the rent. The leases are invariably sub-let, three deep'.[141] Gage gives an example in the St Giles rookery of a ground landlord receiving £20 a year in rent for a house, 'and after passing through one or two middlemen the final landlord netted £70 a year for a property worth not more than £10 a year, a profitable activity at the expense of the destitute'.[142] The householding family usually lived on the main floor, renting rooms – often furnished – on the first and second floors (if the house had both) to better-off trades families. According to Joanne McEwan, first-floor front rooms were the most desirable – and the most costly – since the ceilings on this floor tended to be higher.[143] The poorest people often rented space in the cellar or the garret, neither of which made comfortable homes. Cellars were dark, often damp and if located near a cess pit, noxious. George Godwin's 1859 description of cellar dwellings undoubtedly fit the situation throughout the period:

> In addition to the want of light and air, these places are in most instances intoler-
> ably damp. The back kitchen is generally used by the numerous tenants in the house
> for washing: in many the cess-pool closet and dust-heap are placed there; and in
> eight cases out of ten the contents of the closet are passed under these places in
> badly-formed drains, that allow the gases to spread around, and quietly poison the
> inmates.[144]

Garrets were 'mere shelters under the tiles',[145] many with only small skylights for illumination, and most without hearths for cooking and warmth. The occu-pants of a house passed each other constantly on the staircases, often having to walk through the private rooms of others in order to gain access to their own – situations that frequently led to arguments and tension. Paper-thin walls in houses meant that conversations and quarrels in other rooms were often clearly audible to neighbours. Family disputes were neighbourhood property, as were the comings and goings of all. The rooms themselves were often subdivisions of larger chambers in the formerly grander houses, and Orlin's observation for Elizabethan London still obtained in the late eighteenth and nineteenth centu-ries: paper-thin walls were meant 'to demarcate territory, often temporarily and flexibly, rather than to effect privacy'.[146] Moreover, the rooms the poor called home were not salubrious. Godwin described the dwelling of a light porter who had been thrown out of work: 'The room is little more than 7 feet long by 6 feet wide; the greatest height 6 feet 9 inches. The narrow bedstead, which is doubled up in the daytime, reaches, when let down, close to the fire-place. The roof and part of the walls are green and mildewed with damp: through parts of the roof the sky is distinctly visible'.[147] This room was home to the man, his wife and their young daughter, but was not, according to Godwin, an 'example of the direst stage of London poverty'.[148] Unskilled labourers, who formed approximately two-thirds of the labouring classes, regularly faced the threat of unemployment. When it materialized, these families could rapidly find themselves removing to rooms such as just described.

Those who were poorest of all sought refuge in the common lodging houses that abounded in London. According to an anonymous upper-class observer in 1835, there were 'hundreds and thousands' of such places in the capital, ranging from that of

> The poor tenant of a room or cellar, with its two or three shake-down beds upon the
> floor, to the more substantial landlord with his ten and twenty houses, and two or
> three hundred beds. Among these the houseless wanderer may find shelter, from a

penny to three half-pence, two pence, three pence, four pence and six pence a night, on beds of iron, wood, and straw or on that more lofty couch a hammock; and some (that is, the penny-a-night lodger) have often no softer resting place than the hard floor. This common lodging-house business is a thriving trade; only small capital is required; for an old house will do, no matter how the rain beats in, or the wind whistles through, in a back street or filthy lane, for the more wretched the neighbourhood, the better; old bed-steads and beds, clothes of the coarsest description, with a few forms, and a table or so, for the kitchen, are all that is necessary for the concern. The front room, or what is usually termed the parlour, is generally fitted up into a shop.[149]

This observer visited one such common lodging house in St Giles in the Fields in central London. His description was graphic:

The door, which led into the street … was fast nailed up, and bore evident marks that many a sick man had leaned against it. The door-light – the window above the door – had been taken out, or, what is more likely, knocked out, and its place supplied with a wood shutter, which was raised up during the day, to let in the light, and air; and, as for the window itself, with the exception of a few panes of glass in the centre, here and there patched with brown paper, it was almost wholly made up with squares of wood – giving ocular proof that glass was of a very brittle nature in St. Giles …

We next proceeded to the kitchen – and a den-like retreat it was – dark and gloomy; by the partial light let in by the few remnants of glass, it seems well calculated to harbour felon thoughts. The room itself was moderate enough in size – a good fire, and an excellent grate, containing a copper of boiling water … The floors and walls did not differ much in colour – the former being a dusky hue that knew of no other purifier save the birchen broom; and the latter, a dirty red – a daub long since and clumsily made. A cuckoo-clock ticked on one side of an old cupboard, and before the window was spread a large deal table … A small table (whose old-fashioned, crooked, mahogany legs, showed that it had once been in a more honoured place; but the rough deal covering with which it had been repaired, denoted that it was now only fit for a *cadger's plate*) – stood at the other end of the room, behind the door.[150]

While this description fairly rings with upper-class disapproval, it is clear that for those who had regularly to seek refuge in such lodging houses, the environment was not salubrious. At best, such dwellings offered fusty cosiness; too often, they were unclean, dark, overcrowded and violent.

London by today's standards was, then, fairly apocalyptic. It was noisy, filthy, reeking and riddled with courts and alleys that were mazy, dark and close. Having said this, it is apparent that modern sensibilities are considerably more exacting in some ways than were those of the eighteenth and nineteenth centuries. While the abundance of evidence clearly shows that contemporaries saw great problems, some of them also thought the people were cleanly, the city in some respects healthy, the street lighting a wonder and coal pollution not without positive merits. It was a city in which the poor tended to be hidden from view, living in courts and alleys behind more fashionable streets and seldom sharing the spaces frequented by the upper classes. It is apparent that the spatiality of London's streets and neighbourhoods made privacy of the kind increasingly championed by the middle class enormously difficult in plebeian neighbourhoods. Moreover, it is also apparent that such streets were still sites of spectacle and sociability, and finally, that governments did not yet possess the capacity effectively to reorder urban infrastructure. To be sure, various efforts to establish and maintain the infrastructure necessary for a bourgeois visual environment had begun to be made in the first three-quarters of the nineteenth century, but they were often fragmentary or ineffectual.

Thus far the conditions of late eighteenth- and nineteenth-century London as experienced by the poor have been described in fairly general terms: the smells, the dirt, the darkness, the noise and the crowding. In much of what follows, the focus will be on the poor people of St Martin in the Fields, a large Westminster parish. Most of the contemporary commentators whose work has figured prominently in this chapter were committed to the establishment of bourgeois visuality and the values and behaviour concomitant to it. They tended to write about the conditions and the neighbourhoods they found most offensive, and this presents problems in trying to identify the localities where poor men and women lived, since less sensational but equally poor courts and alleys may have been overlooked. To identify the neighbourhoods where the poor lived in St Martin's, it will be necessary to have recourse to other kinds of sources, as well as contemporary descriptions.

St Martin in the Fields was a city unto itself, consisting of not quite 26,000 souls, according to the first census in 1801. Geographically, the parish sprawled over 305 acres in Westminster, although much of this land was not inhabited. Green Park and more than half of the Queen's Gardens and St James's Park fell within St Martin's boundaries, and so, technically, did Buckingham Palace. The Haymarket, Cockspur Street, Charing Cross and Whitehall formed the western perimeter of the parish's inhabited areas. St Martin's stretched eastward to Drury Lane, and northward from the Thames to Castle Street, which ran east–west between Long Acre and Seven Dials (see Figure 2.1). The parish consisted of ten wards, and was a doughnut, moreover, with St Paul Covent Garden the hole at its centre (see Figure 2.2). Like most other parts of west and central London during this period, St Martin's was not experiencing the very rapid growth that characterized suburban areas of the capital.[151] By 1821 the parish population had grown by 2,500 – a not quite 10 per cent increase, when London's as a whole grew from 959,310 to 1,379,543 in the same twenty-year period.[152] In spite of St Martin's relatively small population increase – small at least for the era – the parish's household density remained relatively stable.

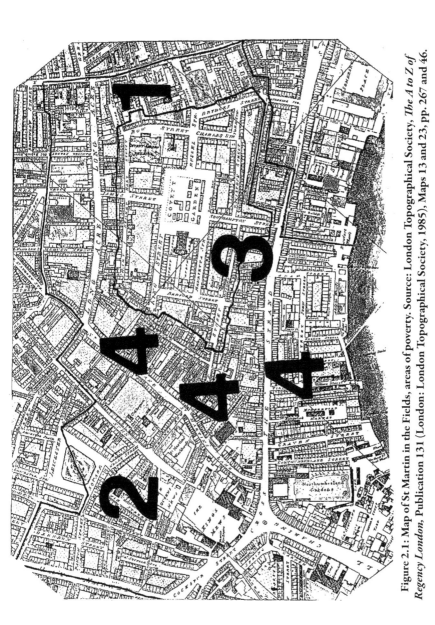

Figure 2.1: Map of St Martin in the Fields, areas of poverty. Source: London Topographical Society, *The A to Z of Regency London*, Publication 131 (London: London Topographical Society, 1985), Maps 13 and 23, pp. 267 and 46.

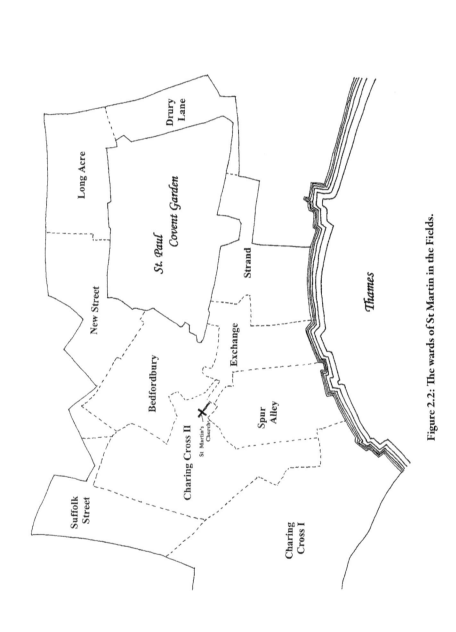

Figure 2.2: The wards of St Martin in the Fields.

Earlier in the eighteenth century, St Martin's had been a very fashionable residential area – if also somewhat risqué given the presence of prostitution in the environs of Covent Garden. By the 1780s, however, the social elite had moved westward, and the titled residents who remained were found in the south-western part of the parish. Charing Cross was considered the beginning of the West End by the late eighteenth century,[153] and Spring Gardens and the vicinities of the royal palaces retained their social cachet. In the eastern reaches of St Martin's there were grand houses, now subdivided. Roughly two-thirds of the houses in Westminster contained lodgers.[154] While the socially prominent tended to live in the south-western parts of the parish, the comfortably off middling classes – merchants and professionals especially – were found south of the Strand around the Adelphi. Even the most fashionable and prosperous areas contained pockets of immiseration, however. Charing Cross, while a busy starting point for the coaching services fanning out from London,[155] also had 'as many dark holes and corners within a few yards' of it, 'which shelter almost as much sickness, crime, and poverty, as any back hiding-places in Whitechapel or Bethnal Green'.[156] That this comment was made after the slum clearances occasioned by the building of Trafalgar Square throws the situation at the end of the eighteenth century into even starker relief. The King's Mews, on which much of Trafalgar Square now stands, had had an unsavoury reputation. Since the king's servants had used the mews to buy and sell horses privately, this attracted 'large numbers of the rougher element in the population'.[157] The mews was also a favourite haunt of thieves, since, as one contemporary observer noted disapprovingly, errand boys and porters 'set down their loads – the former to play, the latter to drink; and while they are in the midst of their fun, away go the goods committed to their care'.[158]

Residential segregation in the eighteenth century generally occurred by street, and consequently, neighbourhoods tended to be small. The middling and upper classes lived in the more salubrious squares and avenues. Moritz, for instance, described George Street in the York buildings district south of the Strand thus: 'I went down the little street in which I live to the Thames, nearly at the end of it, towards the left, a few steps led me to a singularly pretty terrace, planted with trees, on the very bank of the river'. He continued, 'There reigns in those smaller streets towards the Thames so pleasing a calm, compared to the tumult and hustle of people, and carriages, and horses, that are constantly going up and down the Strand, that in going into one of them you can hardly help fancying yourself removed at a distance from the noise of the City, even whilst the noisiest part of it is still so near at hand'.[159]

The poor, on the other hand, sheltered in the courts and alleys found behind such streets. As John Hollingshead observed in the mid-nineteenth century: 'We may all have hurried for years along the bright open highways, scarcely glancing at the little doorways scattered here and there between the busy shops, and yet these doorways – holes – call them by what name we will – are the entrances to many thousands of closely packed homes ... The air in them is close and heavy, and they are dark on the clearest day'.[160] While the rich and poor may practically have rubbed shoulders, the latter, in their dark holes and corners, were all but invisible to their wealthier neighbours. A couple of small blocks from George Street, still on the south side of the Strand, was Hungerford Street with its disreputable market – 'a mass of fishy hovels'[161] – where the young Charles Dickens eked out his miserable existence in the blacking factory.[162]

One final point needs to be made concerning neighbourhood segregation: it wasn't just the abodes of the poor that were invisible to upper-class eyes, the poor themselves rarely intruded into much upper-class space. Godwin noted that even when poor children crept from their close courts and alleys to the fashionable squares, 'eagerly peeping through the enclosures at the shrubs and flowers', they would be 'driven back by stalwart street-keepers and policemen'.[163] Segregation did not just determine who lived where; it also ordained who used various spaces and places. So where were the poor to be found? Contemporary commentators identified a number of such neighbourhoods in St Martin's.

Before construction commenced in 1829 on Trafalgar Square, the area behind St Martin's church had been one of the most nefarious slums in all of London: the Bermudas. According to J. Holden MacMichael, 'The accounts which adventurers gave of these islands … no doubt suggested this curious name for a congeries of courts and alleys remarkable for their labyrinthine nature'.[164] Enclosed by St Martin's Lane, the Strand, Bedford Street and Chandos Street,[165] this rookery contained an abundance of cook shops, known as Porridge (or sometimes Pottage) Island, 'where the poorer classes could procure cooked meat'.[166] The area had long been known for its turbulent nature; Ben Jonson had called it the place 'where the quarrelling lesson is read'.[167] The presence of this slum, moreover, affected the character of both the Strand and St Martin's Lane. Although one of the principal shopping thoroughfares in London, the Strand's north side, especially between St Martin's Lane and Church Lane, was the unfashionable part of the street.[168] There were no fewer than thirty 'dark little courts and alleys'[169] running north off this side of the street, which, according to Dorothy George, bore an infamous character.[170] Similarly, the west side of St Martin's Lane was more fashionable than was its east.[171]

The poor also lived in the area where the Strand met Drury Lane. There had been many upper-class complaints throughout the eighteenth century about the condition of the courts and alleys in the neighbourhood. John Gray, in *Trivia*, warned his readers,

> O! may thy Virtue guard thee through the Roads
> Of Drury's Mazy Courts, and dark Abodes
> The Harlot's Guileful Paths, who nightly stand,
> Where Katherine-street descends into the Strand.[172]

In 1764 the anonymous author of *Low Life or One Half of the World Knows Not How the Other Half Live* spoke of bawdy houses around Drury Lane and in Russell and Bridges Streets, claiming that entrance into a number of the local courts and alleys was impossible, 'they being so crowded with young fellows and ragged Whores'.[173] Two years later Sir John Fielding inveighed against the ruinous houses that were let as brothels, saying that they made 'Exeter Street, Change Court, Eagle Court and Little Catherine Street so infamous that it was dangerous for persons to pass and repass'.[174] Indeed, by 1770 this area had become the main locus of prostitution in the Covent Garden neighbourhood. Martlett Court and Cumberland Court especially have been described as 'whores' nests'.[175] The presence of two large theatres in the neighbourhood – Covent Garden and Drury Lane – undoubtedly served to attract prostitutes. Indeed, in 1786 *The Times* condemned the boxes at Drury Lane as 'licenced stews for the abandoned and profligate to meet and pair off from'.[176]

The neighbourhood also suffered the presence of two burial grounds, one in Russell Court belonging to St Mary-le-Strand, and one in Drury Lane (just north of Little Russell Street) to St Martin's. That the Russell Court burial ground most probably served as Dickens's model for the cemetery in *Bleak House*, and the St Martin's was described as a plague-spot 'in the midst of thousands of people',[177] leave little doubt as to their impact on the neighbourhood. In the Russell Court graveyard, consisting of an area of some 400 square yards, more than 20,000 bodies were interred in a fifty-year span.[178] The grim conditions in the St Martin's ground were described by a parishioner in a letter of complaint to the vestry in 1787:

> The Burial ground belonging to the parish which is in Drury Lane has long been and still remains so shocking a nuisance that to describe it is beyond my power – My back Windows – commanding a View of it, I have Occular Demonstration – the poor are Tumbled into one Common Hole and there lay exposed Day and Night uncovered, a Sight which is not only shocking to human nature but renders every house round it perfectly disagreeable, and the Smells horridly Offensive – I should not, Sir, be in the least Surprized if in the hot Weather, a Plague arising from the Putrifaction of human Bodys should communicate itself to the Surrounding Neighbourhood and then Spread Generally through the Metropolis ...
>
> I have seen Dogs and Rats and Ducks gnawing at the half putrified flesh of the deceased poor who are buryed, I am very sorry to observe without the last Funeral Ceremony ...
>
> There is, Sir, a kind of wooden Covering which the man lays on when he pleases, but if it is on for 24 hours it is off for a week, and when on is not of the least efficacy in confining the Stench, so that I am obliged to keep my windows down ...[179]

The situation did not improve in the nineteenth century. In 1839 George Walker noted that this burying ground had become so saturated with the dead that it had been shut up. The ground was subsequently raised '*level with the first floor windows surrounding the place*, and in this superstratum vast numbers of bodies have, up to this period, been deposited ... a pit was then dug ... in one corner of the ground' whose top was 'covered only with boards', with the consequence that 'inhabitants of the houses are frequently annoyed by the most disgusting and repulsive sights'.[180]

If Drury Lane was scarcely a desirable address according to contemporaries, the situation north of Covent Garden was often little better. While Long Acre was noted for its fashionable shops and workshops,[181] there were a number of byways running off it that were decidedly insalubrious. Rose Street, in particular, was described by Godwin as being 'thickly inhabited by the poor and in some instances a bad class of people'.[182] He continued that there was a water shortage, since the communal water casks were not filled often enough to supply the street on a steady basis. Godwin singled out No. 18, which had eight rooms each let to separate families. When he visited, the house had had no water for several days (the 120-gallon cask belonging to the house was filled once a week on Saturdays). Indeed, he found no one in the neighbourhood regularly had any water left by Sunday.[183] Another street, Angel Alley, had six houses with 150 people living in them and one water closet. Water was more plentiful on this street, since there was an underground tank; but there was only surface drainage, and the refuse from the water closet collected in a cess pool 'most probably in the neighbourhood of the subterranean water tank'.[184]

Finally, according to contemporaries, the poor also lived along the west side of Covent Garden in the neighbourhood known as Bedfordbury, which was north of the Bermudas. It took its name from the eponymous street, a narrow byway filled with shops. It was not at all fashionable, as one contemporary made clear in his grudging estimation: 'in spite of much dilapidation here, and the presence of a horde of undesirable people, the thoroughfare occupied a place, even if a small one, in the commercial life of London'.[185] Indeed, according to one historian, the neighbourhood could be dismissed as 'a nest of low alleys and streets'.[186]

This survey of contemporary comments has identified a number of enclaves where the poor lived. The area around Drury Lane, in particular, attracted attention. In part, the notoriety of the people thought to be dominant in the courts and alleys of the neighbourhood – the prostitutes and the thieves – accounts for this. As well, the Irish rookeries of St Giles in the Fields were found just on the other side of Drury Lane, and these achieved an infamous reputation as the locale of the most extreme poverty. Indeed, by the 1840s a visit to the Drury Lane neighbourhood had become *de rigueur* for socially conscious tourists and commentators.[187]

Comments from contemporaries often highlighted the very worst streets and the most sensational conditions, which raises the problem of the reliability of these descriptions and evaluations of the poor: can these claims be trusted – just how sensationalized were they? Did these observers focus unduly on the notorious poor – the prostitutes, the idle and the dissolute? To answer these questions, it is necessary to turn to other kinds of sources that allow a more systematic analysis, especially with respect to where the poor lived in St Martin's. One such source is the settlement examinations. After October 1816, the parish of St Martin in the Fields began to examine much more systematically those applying for poor relief. In the process of determining whether or not an individual qualified for assistance from St Martin's, parish officials began to note down the person's current address in most instances – a departure from previous practices. The greatest number of examinations by far are found in the records of the year from 23 October 1816 to 22 October 1817. Thereafter the number of examinations falls sharply – from 1,984 in the first year to 783 in the next.[188] The reasons for this are not given, although possibly parish officials tired of what must have been an exacting and time-consuming exercise, or the economy began to pick up after the calamitous depression of 1817. Whatever the explanation, there is one extraordinarily full year of records that can be used to identify more systematically where the poor lived. To cope with the fact that some individuals were examined more than once during the course of the year, they have been counted only once if they repeatedly gave the same street as their address. In all, 111 such examinations were eliminated. Another 379 examinees gave extra-parish addresses, and 172 people either gave no address, gave a false address, had no lodging, or were in the workhouse. Finally, in five cases the address was unclear. Once all of these have been subtracted, 1,317 examinees remain. Since streets within St Martin's varied wildly in length, the number of those examined has been divided by the number of houses on the street.

The thirty streets with the most examinees reveal four areas in St Martin's where poverty was prevalent (see Figure 2.1). The examinations also reveal a different emphasis in the parish map of poverty from that conveyed by contemporary commentators. While certainly constituting one of the four areas in which there was much poverty, the courts and yards between the eastern perimeter of Covent Garden and Drury Lane that figured so prominently in the contemporary literature are much less so in the settlement records. In all, fifty-eight men and sixty-two women from the Drury Lane neighbourhood were examined. Only Middlesex Court, Little Catherine Street and Charles Street had high ratios of people examined to numbers of houses – some twenty-three women and twenty-three men in thirty-two houses. Since poor relief, as will be seen, was not a popular option, it may well be that people in this neighbourhood preferred to resort to prostitution and theft, as the contemporary sources indicated.

The area near Leicester Square and Whitcomb Street was a second part of the parish in which the poor were numerous, according to the settlement examinations: eighty-nine men and 104 women from this neighbourhood were questioned by parish officers. Princes Court, Blue Cross Street, Long's Court and Edwards Court and Whitcomb Street itself were the addresses provided by fifty-two women and forty-nine men in ninety-eight houses. This area had not been extensively discussed in the contemporary commentaries (although the nearby Haymarket was frequently described as being rife with prostitutes plying their trade). A third area in which many poor people lived was made up of the small courts running north off the Strand between Bedford Street and Drury Lane. Here, sixty-six men and fifty-four women were examined. Bull Inn Court, New Exchange Court and Southampton Place (also called Marygold Court) all had high ratios: thirty-one men and twenty-nine women from forty-five houses gave these addresses.

The last area in which the poor were prominent provided the lion's share of the examinees. Four streets which ran south from the west end of Long Acre were very well represented among the settlement examination addresses – Rose Street, Angel Court, Conduit (or Bird in Hand) Court and Lazonby Court. The thirty-nine houses on these four streets not only were the home to forty-seven women and thirty-three men examined, but also formed the northern terminus of the most distinctive pattern revealed by the settlement examinations: there was an arc of poverty that swept down from the western extremity of Long Acre along the west side of Covent Garden and onwards south of the Strand to the Thames. Below the four Long Acre streets, Bedfordbury Street and a number of the courts behind it – Shelton, Turners, Pipe Makers, Charles and Brew House Courts, Taylor's Buildings and Lemon Tree Yard, plus nearby Whitehart Court – were home to sixty-four women and fifty-eight men (in 104 houses) whom the parish examined. Immediately below Bedfordbury, the Bermudas provided the greatest concentration in the entire parish of addresses of those examined. Vine Street, Thackham's Court, Church Lane, Moor's and Little Moor's Yard, Chandos Street, Hewitt's Court, Church Court, New Round Court, Old Round Court and Seymour Court contained 204 houses, the homes of 148 women and 135 men examined by the parish officers of St Martin's. South of the Strand, several courts and alleys concluded the progress. Off Alley, Charles Court[189] and One Tun Court consisted of seventy-six houses, providing sixty-three of the women and forty-one of the men examined. In all, 363 men and 422 women from streets found within the arc were examined.

While neighbourhoods forming this arc were certainly discussed in the contemporary literature, with the possible exception of the Bermudas, they did not generally receive the attention accorded to the apparently prostitute- and Irish-infested courts of Drury Lane. Yet it is clear from the settlement examinations that the western arc constituted the most serious belt of poverty in the parish. To be sure, the major streets still were the domiciles of the better off, but the many small courts and alleys behind them were the locus of real immiseration, especially around the area of the greatest concentration of poverty: Bedfordbury and the Bermudas. If the more sensational and illicit forms of poverty caught the eye of contemporary observers, it cannot be assumed that the settlement examination information simply contradicts these writings. The poor tended to avoid the recourse to poor relief if at all possible, so it may be that the men and women living around Drury Lane were not conspicuous in the settlement examinations precisely because they were relying on activities like prostitution and theft in order to make ends meet. In short, their preferred makeshifts in the struggle for subsistence may have differed from those pursued by the people of Bedfordbury and environs.

Unlike contemporary opinion, moreover, the patterns revealed in the settlement examinations can be corroborated by other sources, which are discussed in the Appendix, revealing that the area of greatest poverty was indeed the western arc of which Bedfordbury neighbourhood was the heart. This difference indicates, on the one hand, that contemporary comment needs to be handled carefully, and on the other, that the London poor were not a homogenous group sharing the same priorities and preferences in making ends meet. It is necessary to be sensitive to the priorities, preferences and behaviour of different collectivities within plebeian London in order to understand the nature of social relations. In pointing out the importance of the built environment in helping to shape these, a form of spatial determinism is not being posited. The spatial configurations of neighbourhoods and the infrastructures supporting them cannot predict human behaviour: which collectivities would accept, adapt, resist or manipulate part or all of the bourgeois discourse; whether it would be embraced and internalized or adopted strategically and provisionally when it was in the best interests of individuals to do so, or whether elements of it would be combined with some of those from customary plebeian culture. Rather than being deterministic, as Chris Otter has pointed out, material systems 'produce certain spectra of possibility. We might say that the discourse and practice of polite conduct and civility make more sense in a park, museum or boulevard than in a communal privy; a certain set of possibilities is etched into their stones'.[190] The built environment and its systems afforded possibilities, helped shape plausibilities and presented constraints on the ways plebeian Londoners dealt with one another and with the socially and politically powerful. Spatiality matters.

3 THE DAILY GRIND

London was at once the financial, commercial and political centre of the country as well as being a major international *entrepôt*. The capital also set the *ton* socially, especially during the Season, and its huge size and dramatic growth during this period generated domestic demand for goods and services. The benefits arising from this vibrant, expanding economy, however, were not shared by all, or even most, Londoners. To understand the impact economic factors had upon plebeian social relations, it is necessary to examine the kinds of employment on offer to men and women, and the state of the most populous trades. Economic fluctuations, seasonality and, in the manufacturing sector, market pressures from provincial competition were all critical factors affecting employment, and, as such, had direct consequences influencing plebeian Londoners' aspirations and behaviour. The role of work in the retention of customary culture needs to be examined.

While the metropolitan economy, unlike those of northern industrial towns, was broadly based, this did not guarantee stability, particularly for workers in a number of trades in central London. Historical interpretation of the standard of living for these people has been fraught, and frequently contradictory. Michael Ball and David Sunderland, in their sweeping but polemical study of the structures, processes and changes in London's economy between 1800 and 1914, are dismissive of most previous interpretations – especially pessimistic accounts. In making their argument, however, they attribute extreme positions that seem to caricature the claims of a number of historians,[1] and they have an abiding faith in the explanatory power of economic theory that does not always seem justified or proven. While relatively optimistic interpretations of the standard of living based on trends in real wage indices may hold for the country at large, the situation in the capital during this period was more problematic. Life remained precarious for many plebeian Londoners throughout the first three-quarters of the nineteenth century, as Leonard Schwarz and David Green have shown.[2] Schwarz has examined the London economy between 1700 and 1850, arguing that overall it did not change fundamentally during this period. He does show that London manufacturers reorganized production in order to compete during the industrial period, which had a direct impact on labour in this sector. After

1820 this resulted in a period of crisis in some, but not all, manufacturing trades. Moreover, because manufacturing was not the major employer – in 1851 33 per cent of men and 34 per cent of women were employed in this sector – the difficulties in a number of trades do not obviate Schwarz's overall claims for gradual change in the manufacturing sector as a whole and for continuities in the social, employment and income structures.[3]

Green's book, *From Artisans to Paupers*, is more narrowly focused with respect to both chronology and subject matter. His period is 1790 to 1870, and London's artisans and their struggles to deal with economic change are of particular concern. Market-driven changes in production in the manufacturing sector meant that as the first half of the nineteenth century wore on, artisans and labourers in a number of trades were paid less and their employment became increasingly insecure – this in spite of broad improvement in living standards generally. Some historians have found contradictions between the interpretations of Schwarz and Green – the former being seen as a gradualist with respect to economic change in the capital, and the latter as considerably more pessimistic.[4] Indeed, Green has taken Schwarz to task, saying that in trades like watch making and silk weaving changes were certainly not gradual; if anything, they were 'little short of catastrophic'.[5] Nevertheless, the differences between them seem to result, at least in part, from their different foci and chronologies. For his part, Schwarz does not see fundamental ruptures between his interpretation and Green's. In a positive review of the latter's book, Schwarz admits, in rather a mixed metaphor, to coming 'from a predominantly eighteenth-century stable with a tendency, therefore, to see the nineteenth-century bottle as half full rather than half empty', and continues that Green is 'quite justified in stressing the instability of the London economy'.[6]

Economic fluctuations seem to have had a greater impact in the capital than elsewhere, especially in the manufacturing sector,[7] which, while not the mainstay of the economy, was particularly important in the old central districts.[8] As Schwarz has noted, real wages fell in the second half of the eighteenth century and in London did not exceed the 1740s level until the 1840s.[9] During the era of the French Revolutionary and Napoleonic Wars, there were three crisis points: 1794–6, 1799–1800 and 1812–13. Poor harvests in all three periods led to dramatically higher food costs. While real wages rose in this period, as Green has pointed out, price increases rose even more quickly. After the wars, demobilization combining with trade recession and high taxes led to another period of difficulty, more than outweighing the increase in real wages. The recovery in the 1820s was curtailed by the financial crisis of 1825, which ushered in several years of difficulty – even in 1831 there were still 12,000 unemployed carpenters in London, for example.[10] Then, in the 1830s and 1840s, growth of the railway network 'eroded London's viability as a manufacturing centre', since the capital lost its insulation of high transport costs.[11] More and more, sweating and the forcing down of wages generally were seen as necessary in a number of trades to deal with the increasing competition. Economic conditions were difficult in the early and late 1840s, and Green has pointed out that in the second quarter of the nineteenth century 'years of recession outnumbered those of boom'.[12] Even nature seemed to turn against working people during this period, with one winter in four between 1814 and 1855 having unusually low temperature averages of 1 to 2 degrees Celsius. Particularly cold winters occurred in 1814, 1830, 1838, 1841 and 1847.[13] In such years, outdoor workers were adversely affected and all plebeian Londoners had to spend more to warm themselves. All in all, the second quarter of the nineteenth century was a particularly difficult period for working people in the capital. The mid-1860s also brought hardship, however. The collapse in 1866 of the discount banking firm Overend & Gurney had a deleterious impact throughout the economy of London, and indeed of the country as a whole. As Stedman Jones observed, the winter of 1866–7 saw 'trade depression, the collapse of the Thames shipbuilding industry (with widespread ripple effects), the cholera epidemic, the bad harvest and the exceptionally severe weather conditions', all of which contributed to high levels of unemployment and pauperism in the capital, neither of which began to recede before 1872.[14]

Generally speaking, life in Britain during this period was insecure for many. Roderick Floud has estimated that during the period between 1830 and 1914, while some 30 per cent of the population 'lived below the margin, perhaps a further 40 per cent or even more lived so close to the margin that they could be, and often were forced below it by a variety of life events'.[15] These claims accord well, as Floud himself notes, with the findings of Charles Booth in the late 1880s that 31 per cent of Londoners lived in poverty.[16]

To understand the impact economic factors had upon plebeian social relations, it is necessary to examine the structure of employment for men and for women. To make this manageable, employment patterns in the parish of St Martin in the Fields in particular, and of Westminster where appropriate, will be the focus of study. The 1841 census was the first to identify occupations systematically, although it did so somewhat problematically, especially with respect to the occupations of married women, as will be discussed later in the chapter.[17] While problems certainly exist within the census data, determining occupational structure before 1841 is even more fraught – especially for women. Moreover, given the various claims for the gradual or the catastrophic nature of economic change in London, the most populous trades in the parish need to be identified and the conditions in each set out throughout the period.

Paid work was crucially important, although as Muldrew and King have noted, it was part of a household economy of resources, 'a component of a complex matrix of earnings and access to credit'.[18] Its role in this friable economy was vital, but not always central to it, since most plebeian families lived on credit. Wages could become weekly deposits maintaining access to credit at shops or with landlords, or to maintain a tenuous hold on goods in pawn. Wages prevented this complex mesh from unravelling, and as such merit close consideration. In exploring waged work, it is also necessary to consider the effects of seasonality and the impact of the life cycle. By examining the effects of these various constraints, the cultural priorities of plebeian Londoners with respect to making ends meet can be better understood and situated.

In determining people's occupations, it is necessary to resort to a variety of sources, particularly for the period before 1841. Conditions within the major occupations can then be examined, which can be accomplished first by referring to the parish's settlement examinations and to a number of trade histories and manuals, and second by looking for geographic clustering in particular trades and occupations within the parish. Occupation and home address can be related in order to determine whether poor trades were in fact found in poor areas of St Martin's, as identified in the last chapter. Turning first to the identification of male trades, a number of early nineteenth-century sources can be compared to the later, more comprehensive census material in order to determine how stable the occupational structure actually was in St Martin's during this period. In an age when plebeian Londoners walked to work, the location of family dwellings were usually determined by proximity to the husband's employment, so it makes sense to concentrate on this in an exercise seeking in part to relate occupation and address. Once the sources have been evaluated, however, women's work will be considered systematically at a later point in the chapter.

Poll books from the period provide occupational information for the more respectable of St Martin's male residents, although clearly these sources can only tell part of the story. While the first universal occupational compilation for St Martin's is contained in the 1841 census, a list for males twenty years and older who were employed in retail trade or in handicrafts as masters or workmen exists for Westminster in the 1831 census. The range and variety of occupations in this complex and dynamic society are overwhelming, so to keep the project within manageable bounds, a grouping scheme is necessary: the occupational classifications which W. A. Armstrong developed, based on the work of Charles Booth.[19] Of the poll books – complete lists of all those who voted – two are particularly useful, since they give both addresses and occupation: those for the 1802 and 1818 Westminster elections.[20] The representativeness of these lists depends on voter participation, and there were marked differences in voter levels between them: 1,035 men voted in 1802, while 1,854 did so in 1818. In spite of this difference in voter participation and the sixteen-year gap between them, there was striking similarity in the dispersion among Armstrong's groups (see Table 3.1), evidence that life in St Martin's did not change drastically during the period.[21] Thus, for parish residents who had the vote at least, manufacturing was the most important sector, while dealing ran a healthy second. In 1802 these two sub-groups accounted for 81 per cent of total occupations, and in 1818 for 80 per cent. In terms of manufacturing trades, the parish reflected the general pattern of the time, in that tailoring and boot- and shoemaking were the most numerous occupations. Indeed, the list of ten most numerous trades – manufacturing and otherwise – for each of the years is very similar, although there is considerable fluctuation with regard to position within the lists. Table 3.1 also gives the number of gentlemen, since this group was substantial.

Table 3.1: Occupational groupings for Westminster and St Martin's.

	1802 Westminster Poll Book	1818 Westminster Poll Book	1841 St Martin's Census*	1851 St Martin's Census*	1861 St Martin's Census*
Agriculture and Breeding	1 (0.1%)†	4 (0.2%)	39 (0.3%)‡	88 (0.7%)	80 (0.8%)
Property Owning	53 (5.1)	113 (6.1)	1508 (11.9)	312 (2.6)§	252 (2.4)
Dealing	368 (35.6)	717 (38.7)	1522 (12)	1707 (14.3)	1587 (15)
Domestic Service	22 (2.1)	27 (1.5)	3890 (30.8)	3297 (27.5)	2756 (26)
Transportation	11 (1.1)	24 (1.3)	464 (3.7)	618 (5.2)	619 (5.8)
Industrial Service	10 (1)	10 (0.5)	524 (4.2)	402 (3.4)	329 (3.1)
Professional and Public Service	50 (4.8)	85 (4.6)	1247 (9.9)	1653 (13.8)	1228 (11.6)
Building	54 (5.2)	110 (5.9)	498 (3.9)	481 (4)	458 (4.3)
Manufacturing	466 (45)	764 (41.2)	3228 (25.6)	3408 (28.5)	3286 (31)
Mining	0	0	0	11 (0.09)	18 (0.2)
N =	1035	1854	12,920	11,977	10,613

*   These figures include men and women in the parish.

†   The first figure is the number in each group, while that in parentheses is its expression as a percentage of the whole.

‡   Some occupations appear in more than one of the nine groups. Thus, for 1841 the total figure of 12,920 contains 284 double listings between the groups. In figuring the percentages, this last figure has been subtracted from 12,920, and 12,636 used as the total figure.

§   The surprising difference in the property owning category is explained partly by the very different instructions enumerators received in 1841 and 1851 (described on p. 84). Another possible reason to account for the very different levels of the property owning in the parish is the falling population of St Martin's throughout this period. Most people in the working class could not move far, since they needed to be close to work and credit resources. It may be that it was the affluent who disproportionately left the parish.

With respect to the major occupational groupings, there were marked differences between the censuses[22] and the poll books, which was to be expected. A number of trades that had been invisible, because their practitioners were unlikely to be voters, greatly influenced the overall picture in the censuses; in particular, the domestic service group, accounting for slightly less than a third of the total number of those employed, was a major factor in these changes. Previously invisible trades in a number of groups also helped shift the balance away from manufacturing, building and dealing. Thus, in the transportation group, the porters, the watermen, and a dramatic increase in the number of carmen themselves account for the higher percentage of this sector in the census data. The same is true for the industrial service group, where clerks and labourers account for the difference. The somewhat surprising increase in the public service and professional group can be accounted for by the presence of barracks soldiers, the policemen of the metropolitan force, and greater numbers of soldiers and sailors living in the community. Finally, the last – and even more surprising – group to show a substantial percentage increase in 1841 was property owners. Comparison here is impossible, however, since in 1802 and 1818 property owners were clearly gentlemen, while in 1841 those described as 'independent' were people with no calling, but living on their own means – a much broader category than that in the poll books. Thereafter, in 1851 census enumerators received more stringent directions that limited the numbers of 'independents': the instructions with respect to the occupations of the affluent were much lengthier (two pages versus the one paragraph of 1841) and much more explicit, with the result that a far greater number of people were described as having an occupation. In spite of these incompatibilities, the marked differences between the poll books and the censuses generally reflect the much broader base of the latter, rather than a fundamental shift in occupational patterns.

A direct comparison of particular trades across these sources is also revealing. In the comparable sectors of the poll books and the census materials, seven of the top ten trades are common across the period (see Table 3.2), although there was a fair degree of jockeying within the lists. Thus, the poll book data do appear useful in understanding the occupational structure of the parish, and Schwarz's claim for structural continuity holds for St Martin's. The situation overall for the parish was a gradual decline in population throughout the period, largely due to the various improvement projects, but stability in terms of occupational structure, if not always in the conditions within particular trades.

Table 3.2: Dealing and manufacturing male trades common to all years.

Trade	1802	1818	1831	1841	1851	1861
Tailor	3	1	1	1	1	1
Shoemaker	1	3	2	2	2	2
Grocer	5	4	4	7	6	8
Publican	2*	2	5	4	7	7
Baker	8	7	6	5	4	6
Coachmaker	9	9	10	3	3	4
Jeweller	5	5	9	6	10	9

*   Publicans and victuallers have been combined to make the 1802 list consistent with the others.

Independent evidence concerning conditions obtaining in the trades appearing across the six lists can be found in the settlement examinations, in trade manuals, in contemporary comments and in historians' descriptions of them. St Martin's settlement examinations survive for a number of years during this period: 1780–95, 1816–27 and 1834–40. Some of these are rough examination books and the amount of information varies strikingly among examinees. Nevertheless, much useful data can be gleaned, particularly from the late 1816 to 1819 rough examination books, with respect to occupation and conditions thereof.[23] Beginning in October 1816, the parish examined 2,405 people in this three-year period. Home addresses within the parish were provided for 1,294 of the examinees, much higher than in earlier or later period records. Occupations were listed for 209 of those examined, again higher than was the norm. The settlement exams do have to be treated cautiously, since it is unclear why particular people were chosen for examination,[24] and parish officials rarely gave the occupations of the women being examined. Of the 1,381 women examined, occupations were listed for only seventeen – just over 1 per cent. Nevertheless, bearing these caveats in mind, a number of the over-represented male trades discussed above do appear frequently in the settlement examinations. More than half of the 192 men examined for whom trades were given were employed as shoemakers (51), tailors (37), porters (7) or labourers (7).[25]

That labourers and porters should figure prominently in settlement examinations is not surprising, since both occupations were often the refuge of the unskilled. Neither required an apprenticeship, and, indeed, both were often regarded as unrespectable by those further up the social ladder. Dorothy George quoted one observer that 'we should properly distinguish the porters, sailors, chairmen, and the day labourers who work in the streets not only from persons of condition, most of whom walk a-foot, but even from the lowest class of shopkeepers. The former are as insolent a rabble as can be met with in countries without laws or police'.[26] In part, this disapproval probably resulted from the fact that both occupations belonged to the casual labour market – where very short-term hiring and irregular work were the norm. In Covent Garden, unlike Smithfield, porters were not licensed, ensuring that work would be 'very irregular outside the peak summer months'.[27]

While the shoemaking trade, on the other hand, did require an apprenticeship, entry into it was not difficult. Apprenticeship premiums were low, beginning at £5.[28] It was also a popular trade with St Martin's parish officials, who bound out pauper children with a £2 premium. The trade didn't require a large capital investment in order to set up, nor did it require great physical strength, or skill outside the bespoke sector. Indeed, George says, shoemaking and tailoring were taken up 'by some of the many deformed people of the age'.[29] Adding to the woes of the shoemakers was the state of the trade during this period. A divisive strike in 1812 had seen the beginning of the importation of cheap shoes from Northampton,[30] a move that continued to force down wages throughout the first half of the nineteenth century. Hard on the heels of this strike came the major recession of 1813. By this time, according to Schwarz, women and children had entered the trade in large numbers,[31] and as usual, their presence added to the pressures on wage levels. Indeed, one of Henry Mayhew's inform-ants claimed that wages, even in the first-rate shops, 'remained stationary from 1812 to 1830',[32] when they were reduced. All of these problems, then, made it increasingly difficult for the majority of shoemakers to make a good living by their trade. The ease of entry into the trade meant that the occupation was over-populated,[33] and not surprisingly, it figured prominently in tallies of the poor.

Tailoring, the largest handicraft trade, was another occupation which was easy to enter. Apprentice fees were low (£5 was common), capital expenditure was light, and physical requirements were less onerous than in many other trades. Nevertheless, it had its own difficulties, the chief of which was the sea-sonality of work. Like all trades dependent upon upper-class patronage, tailoring faced a slack summer period when the gentry and aristocracy returned to their estates. Estimates as to the length of time involved increased during the period, in part due to the shortening of the Season: in 1747 Campbell maintained that a tailor could expect to be out of work for three or four months.[34] Rule quoted tailors that the slack period lasted six months,[35] while the Statistical Society of London was even bleaker, claiming that a tailor might well only work three or four months of the year in total in the 1840s.[36] As Green has pointed out, tailors who were limited to sewing, rather than measuring and cutting cloth, and doing finishing work, were particularly hard hit.[37]

If seasonality was a major problem for tailors, they were, nevertheless, able to maintain a strong union, which protected the better sectors of the trade until the 1830s. In part it did this by limiting women to particular kinds of work, and by insisting that work not be done at home (thus ensuring that women would be marginalized). During the war period demand was high, principally because of military needs. It was met, however, by the introduction of the non-unionized slop system: 'large wholesale "warehouses" from which fabric was given out to small masters or unemployed journeymen who in turn employed other workers, often women, in their own homes, or in sweatshops'.[38] As such, this spelled trouble for the trade, since the competition among these warehouses meant the lowering of piece-rates and the lengthening of hours. It also meant that as conditions in the less honourable sectors worsened (that is, sectors in which workers did not adhere to the prices set by the trade society, but undercut them), more pressure to lower wages and lengthen hours was felt in all sectors of the trade. With the end of the war, this meant very difficult times indeed for many small honourable masters. By the late 1820s the tailors' union was beginning to lose strikes meant to keep low-paid workers – especially women – out of the trade. The strike in 1834, inspired by Owenism, was ruinous for the tailors. Indeed, where in 1824 there had been one worker in the dishonourable sector to four in the honourable, by 1849 there were twenty dishonourable workers for every three honourable in the tailoring trade.[39] By the 1830s cheap ready-made warehouses had begun to invade the West End, formerly the preserve of the bespoke sector.[40]

If the long-term picture for tailors was increasingly grim, conditions in the poorer sectors of the trade had always been difficult. In 1747 Campbell said tailors were 'as numerous as Locusts ... and generally as poor as Rats'.[41] In the nineteenth century the overpopulated condition of the trade was made worse by seasonal migration. According to the Statistical Society, 'large numbers of journeymen arriv[ed] in London from the country at the commencement of the season, and remain[ed] in town as long as there ... [was] ... any work to be obtained'.[42] For all of these reasons, then, the well-being of tailors – especially those outside the bespoke sector – was always fragile. That they would turn up disproportionately in descriptions of the poor was practically a foregone conclusion. The picture that emerges for workers in male trades is therefore one of uncertainty. These men very often faced irregularity in work, and low pay in following their trades. This was the case, moreover, in a number of the most populous occupations in the parish: tailors, shoemakers, labourers and porters all faced uncertainty in attempting to earn a living.

Unfortunately, the situation was even more difficult with respect to women's work. Numerous historians have used census data to explore the dimensions of women's employment, and just about as many have pointed out the short-comings of this source.[43] Census enumerators consistently underestimated the number of women who were employed, especially with respect to those who were married. While Michael Anderson has questioned whether the problem was quite as serious as some have insisted, more recently several historians have argued that almost all plebeian women worked, at least at some points of their lives. Amy Erickson has pointed out that in eighteenth-century London virtually all married plebeian women worked, thus debunking conventional notions that wives limited their activities to homemaking save in times of economic crisis. Andrew August has concluded that late nineteenth-century plebeian women in London did remain in the home while their children were young, but at other points in the life course, almost all of these women engaged in waged work,[44] and moreover, that 'wage earning formed a regular and accepted part of the experience of poor women in London throughout their lives'.[45] These views have been criticized,[46] but the fact remains that as a snapshot, the census would necessarily underestimate the waged work of women if the latter was linked to some points in the life cycle but not others. Whatever the problems with the census data – and women's employment is without doubt underestimated, even if historians cannot agree by how much – as Anderson has observed, 'Unless we can find alternative and representative sources allowing firm estimates of the proportionate contribution to family incomes of casual and part-time work, the census enumerators' books must remain, for many parts of the country at least, the best indicator that we have of the variations in married women's gainful work activity in the mid-nineteenth century'.[47]

In the 1841 census, there was an occupational summary for Westminster but not for the city's parishes.[48] This changed in 1851, and thereafter parish summaries were provided, giving information for both male and female employment. As ever, these sources indicate that far fewer women than men worked for wages. The 1841 census data for Westminster shows that 95 per cent of men twenty and over were employed. For women in this age group, on the other hand, the employed figure was much lower at 39 per cent. The St Martin's summaries indicate a higher percentage of employed women: 50 per cent in both 1851 and 1861. This may well result from the fact that the affluent, as indicated earlier, had moved westward, so more westerly Westminster parishes may have had lower numbers of women working, which in turn would lower the overall figure. Given that the censuses generally underestimated women's work, these figures should be taken as the minimum – the lower bound of female employment.

While they were regularly expected to make financial contributions, women's paramount responsibilities remained their family duties, especially when the children were young. This was a point in the life cycle when the family was most susceptible to poverty, but as August has noted, it was also the time when married women were less likely to work: a wife was expected to make her financial contribution in the interstices of family responsibilities. Francis Place summed up the common situation when he said that his wife assisted him in making breeches and waistcoats in their home whenever she had 'time she could spare from her child and her other domestic concerns'.[49] Moreover, the vagaries of the employment market meant that this juggling act was probably a regular part of the experience of most plebeian women. In engaging in paid employment, the wages they earned were small: Horrell and Humphries have estimated that by the mid-nineteenth century approximately 80 per cent of the family income was provided by husband/fathers, while women and older children contributed the rest. Horrell and Humphries also believe that older children would have contributed more than their mothers, and that for both wives and older children, paid work became scarcer in the second half of the nineteenth century. As meagre as the financial contribution of wives was, it was also crucially necessary when so many families lived at or near the margin.[50]

The women's pattern with respect to the range of occupations in which they were found also differed from that of men. Table 3.3 gives the number of females in the various occupational groups. Girls and women formed significant proportions of only four groups: domestic service, manufacturing, public service and the professions, and dealing. In the parish summaries for both 1851 and 1861, these four groups accounted for 96 per cent of employed women. The 1841 figure for Westminster women was only 81 per cent, but appears to have been skewed by the very high number of 'independents' in the professional and public service category (19 per cent as opposed to 4 and 3 per cent for the two later censuses), and the correspondingly lower numbers in the manufacturing and dealing categories. It is clear that women's occupations were much more narrowly concentrated than were those for men.

Table 3.3: Female occupations by group and trade.

Group	1841 Westminster Number of Women	1851 St Martin's Number of Women	1861 St Martin's Number of Women
Manufacturing	5,535	1,049	1,105
Dealing	1,300	397	297
Public Service and Professional	1,181	182	176
Industrial Service	63	4	1
Agriculture	8	5	9
Building	39	2	1
Transport	27	8	5
Property Owning	6,806	155	133
Domestic Service	21,744	2,570	2,151
N =	36,703	4,372	3,878
Trades			
Domestic Servants*	19,390	2,127	1,703
Needlework†	4,052	639	718
Laundry Work	1,762	223	238
Charwoman	567	220	191
Teacher/Governess	478	78	68
Nurse	447	51	54
Lodging House Keeper	293	86	63
Food Retailer‡	338	142	106
Shoemaker§	281	128	106
N =	27,799	3,725	3,302

*   Nurses have not been included in this figure.
†   This includes bonnet and cap makers, dressmakers, milliners, shirt makers, seamstresses and tailors.
‡   Butchers, cheesemongers, fishmongers, milk sellers, fruit sellers, green grocers, grocers, poulterers and publicans.
§   This includes the category 'shoemaker's wife'.

The top nine trades within the four occupational groups in which women were found in numbers accounted for slightly more than 85 per cent of the women in St Martin's who were employed in 1851 and 1861 (see Table 3.3). For men in the same years, the top ten trades accounted for 41 per cent and 43 per cent respectively. If these figures are related to the data for occupational groups, then clear patterns begin to emerge. The majority of working women – always at least two-thirds – were to be found in the low-paid domestic service sector, employed as house servants, laundresses, charwomen and nurses. While women only formed just over three-quarters of the total number of domestic servants in 1851 and 1861, duties within the household were sexually segregated so that male and female servants were not competing for the same jobs (thus making the occupation in effect segregated).[51]

Being a house servant was an occupation that for most people was a stage in life rather than a final career destination. For example, ninety of the 313 people examined in 1790 based their settlement on a year's service. Since this was only one of a number of ways by which one could achieve a settlement, the actual number of people who had been yearly hired servants was undoubtedly higher. This was especially so for men, who were more likely to have been apprentices or to have rented accommodation for 4s. or more a week (sufficient to give a settlement). In the event, seventy-one women and nineteen men claimed a settlement on the basis of service.

The average age of the women at the end of the period of service they described was twenty-four years, while that for men was twenty-two years. Admittedly, these may not have been the last service positions held, since others of shorter duration may have followed, or the examinants may have omitted stints which would have given an unwanted settlement. Nevertheless, service does seem to have been largely the province of the young, and this is apparent in the age distribution of those employed in it. Of the sixty-five women for whom age at the end of the service described was given, forty-nine were less than thirty, and sixteen of these less than twenty. Another eleven were thirty to thirty-nine years, two were forty to forty-nine, and three were fifty to fifty-nine. All were unmarried save four childless widows who returned to service after their husbands' deaths. Among the fifteen men for whom ages are available, five were less than twenty, another eight were less than thirty and two more were less than forty. Thus, for both sexes, service was for the most part an experience of youth.

If yearly hired servants were then primarily young and unmarried, their experience in this field does not seem to have been as uniform or secure as might be supposed. The term 'servant' could cover a wide array of duties and experiences. In some instances these were strictly those of the domestic servant, while in others duties may have included work in a particular trade. Among the lowest paid of the servants described in the St Martin's records were those who had been employed outside London, and those employed in public houses. Eleven of the women who had been servants made less than £5 plus diet and lodging a year, three of them had worked out of town, three in pubs, and one in a coffeehouse.

The most common wage among the women was £5 per annum plus diet and lodging. Twenty of the forty-six women for whom wage information was available earned this amount. Those who described their employers by trade, rather than by address, often earned more, perhaps indicating that their duties involved more than domestic work. The chief exception to this, as noted above, was the public house. None of the six women who worked at a pub earned more than £5, and as seen above, three earned less. Those few who worked at socially prestigious addresses, on the other hand, also tended to earn more, and were often paid in guineas. The five women who earned 8 guineas or more, for whom addresses are provided, all worked on streets whose median rent level was above £25, and which were located in the western reaches of the parish or in the residential district south of the Strand.

The men tended to earn more than their female counterparts. Only three (one of whom had been a boy) earned less than £5 – one employed outside London, one in a pub and one by a weaver. While 67 per cent of women earned £5 or less, only 39 per cent of men did so. As for women, however, work in public houses was a prominent occupation among low paid men. Two-thirds of the men (twelve of them) earned 8 guineas or less, thus repeating the pattern of wage differentials according to gender that was seen earlier. Five of the men examined claimed to have earned between 14 and 20 guineas as yearly hired servants. In two instances these men worked for aristocrats, and in the third as a skilled worker, a pastry cook. The other two men were employed in other Westminster parishes, and their employers were not identified.

Perhaps not surprisingly, the better paid often worked for the socially prestigious, or were more skilled. While experiences certainly varied, service was probably an uncertain affair at best for the majority. Many were employed by people whose economic status was not significantly higher or more secure than their own. Thus, there are occasional references in the examinations to masters failing, and even when economic failure wasn't a spectre haunting employers, paternalistic concern couldn't be assumed. Three women were forced to turn to the parish after they became pregnant, and even more tellingly, the Duke of Norfolk felt no compunction to care for his coachman's insane wife (in spite of the husband's eleven years of service).

Indeed, the uncertainties of service are readily apparent in the autobiography of Mary Ann Ashford. Her book is extraordinary in the fullness of its account of service life. She entered the occupation at thirteen, an age she regarded as unusually young. She did so after the death of both her parents, and remained in service until her marriage. What comes through in Ashford's account is the uncertainty of service, and the canniness required of a yearly hired servant to manage. In her first place Ashford only lasted two months, and very nearly lost her earnings when her mistress refused to pay her. She was fortunate that she had been befriended by a churchwarden during her father's final illness. He had her employers summoned to the Court of Requests and obtained Ashford's wages – more than a pound.[52] For most servants, however, this kind of assistance simply wouldn't have been available. Ashford seems to have been in a better position because her father had been a respectable householder. She remained in her next place for nearly three years, in spite of having to do the most laborious drudge work, and her mistress's refusal to teach her any kind of skill (so she could not leave). In the winter she had to spend long hours pumping water from the basement until she was 'nearly exhausted with pumping, and almost poisoned with the smell'. In spite of all this, Ashford did not see the situation as all bad, saying, 'I was well fed – living just the same as they did, and partaking of whatever they had'.[53] In this instance, it seems clear that her employers were scarcely better off than she, and that expectations on the part of servants were not high.

Over the next three years Ashford worked for a number of people and had various problems, ranging from insufficient food to below-subsistence wages. Her solution to her problems was to move on, and when in between positions to rely on the help of friends. At nineteen she took a position and remained for three years, eventually leaving because of loneliness (she was the only servant). After this she again took a number of positions, one of which again demonstrated the caginess necessary for a servant. She had taken a position with a Jewish family, and in a paragraph which revealed both the anti-Semitism common in London at the time, and the importance of a reference, Ashford says, 'I went as house-maid, in a Jew's family, in Leman St., Goodman's Fields; but, in a short time, I heard that there was great difficulty in getting a place, after living with Jews; and as Miss W— (her former employer) had given me an excellent character, I could not think of losing it, and told the lady I would only stop till she could get a servant, and must have my three years and a-half character returned'.[54]

Thus, it was necessary to be aware of societal predilections quite as much as it was to be a good worker. Ashford remained in service until her marriage, when she was able to contribute the savings she had accumulated from her work to setting up a household. In all, Ashford's experience demonstrated the uncertainties of servant life, the canniness necessary on the part of employees, and the fact that service was a stage through which many people passed in the earlier part of their lives.[55]

In the rest of the occupations in the service sector, the workforce was almost exclusively female. Humphries has found that the sexual division of labour increased during this period, and she believes it was due in large measure to the need to control female sexuality in order to prevent illegitimate children overwhelming families' fragile resources.[56] Laundresses, almost always female, worked either full- or part-time, and often at home. Similarly, charring, another wholly female trade, had peak periods which demanded a flexible workforce. Fridays were especially busy, in preparation for the weekend.[57] Thus, these occupations were often more easily accommodated within the cycle of family responsibilities than would have been the case for full-time employment.

In the manufacturing sector, most women were employed in making various kinds of clothing. Dressmaker/milliners, seamstresses, tailors, stay makers, embroiderers, shirt makers and glovers accounted for 4,397 women, while another 364 were shoemakers, bonnet and straw hat makers. In all, these trades accounted for 86 per cent of the women employed in manufacturing in Westminster. Within most of these trades,[58] women made up more than 90 per cent of the workforce. According to Sally Alexander, 'The needle was the staple employment for women in London – apart from domestic service', and she continues that 'Distressed needlewomen were a notorious problem of London life'.[59] Even in the most respectable needle trades, dressmaking and millinery, the lot of most workers was difficult. Alexander says of the women who worked for fashionable West End firms, 'Long hours, ill-health and early retirement were the rewards of many of the ... young women employed in the "better-class" house'.[60] For the most part, they were 'between twenty and thirty and lived in St. Martins [*sic*] in the Fields, the Strand, or St. Giles'.[61] Most of them worked at home, and were no better paid than women in poorer sections of the trade. As Alexander baldly concluded, 'All women's needle-work was very low paid'.[62] Once again, however, some flexibility in meeting family obligations was possible, because much of the work was done at home.[63]

In only two trades dominated by men – tailoring and shoemaking – did significant numbers of women work. As has been seen, in both these trades work was irregular and pay low. In dealing, women were most often lodging house keepers, an employment that allowed them to remain at home and thus, once again, did not interfere with family responsibilities. They were also found among booksellers – Pinchbeck said they ran 'numerous little "pamphlet shops" in important thoroughfares'.[64] They worked as bookbinders, often serving 'as job hands at rush periods when extra labour was needed ... for instance, when Christmas annuals were being produced, or for a few days each month in the production of innumerable monthly publications'.[65]

Women were also active in trades purveying food to the public – as grocers, publicans, and victuallers among the shopkeepers, and as street sellers. Again, they were often employed as assistants to husbands and fathers, or the work was part-time. Pinchbeck says of the shopkeeping sector, 'These were businesses which women could manage perhaps more easily than any other, and in which they almost invariably assisted'.[66] According to Dorothy Davis, possession of this kind of small shop catering to the labouring classes was the ambition of many couples, and was usually run by the wife.[67] The Muis point out, moreover, that it could make a substantial contribution to the family income, since tax records have indicated incomes averaging £40 to £50 per annum for the very smallest shops.[68] The street sellers worked on a smaller scale. In London they commonly sold fruit, vegetables, fish or milk.[69] Pinchbeck says of these women,

> As a class, street sellers belonged to the lowest rank of traders. Some of their occupations were considered disreputable; a good deal of their work was casual and the majority appear to have lived from hand to mouth, frequently depending on the pawnbroker for means to purchase a stock in trade. For wives of labourers, however, who had almost always to do something to supplement the family income, street trading was an easy way of earning a livelihood, especially for those who had neither trade nor capital.[70]

In the last employment sector in which women figured prominently (according to the census), public service and the professions, they were concentrated in teaching. The profession of governess was one of the few open to women who had been raised in the middle and upper classes, but there were also women from more humble backgrounds who operated 'dame schools'. While the quality of education provided may often have been suspect – there was apparently little distinction between child-minders and those who claimed to be operating these schools[71] – this type of employment once again allowed a woman to remain in the home, and as seen before, provided greater flexibility in dealing with family responsibilities.

A number of patterns concerning the employment of women begin to emerge from this data. In the first place, as seen above, the majority of women were employed in a fairly narrow range of trades within the narrow range of occupational groups already identified. This narrowness accords with the findings of a number of historians. Sally Alexander, for instance, identified four principal categories of work for women in London: that concerning all aspects of household labour (washing, cooking, charring, serving, laundry work, etc.); childcare and training; the distribution of retail food and other articles of regular consumption; and finally the manufacture of goods (in trades that were usually subject to the sexual division of labour).[72] Certainly this scheme would take into account almost all of the trades just discussed. L. D. Schwarz is even more succinct in discussing women's work in London. He says that 'As late as 1851, almost 60 per cent of the employed female labour force in the capital was employed within the three occupations of service, needlework, and laundry'.[73]

There were also a number of other features common to women's work experience. In the first place, the situation of women workers was made difficult by a general characteristic of their work: the low pay which most of them earned. Gilboy estimated that in the late eighteenth century women might earn on average five to six shillings a week, while Alexander said that in 1848 the average wage of single women and widows was only 6s. 10d.[74] According to Horrell and Humphries, women typically earned one-third to one-half a man's daily wage, an amount on which it would have been difficult to keep body and soul together.[75]

The reasons for these low wages were twofold. In part, as Alexander pointed out, patriarchal notions which permeated the family also ensured that women would be subordinate in the workforce. A woman's family responsibilities were assumed to take precedence over productive work, and wages reflected this.[76] Joyce Burnette's recent claims that women were paid less because they were not as strong as men, and hence were less productive, do not seem compelling. Her argument that market forces rather than ideology determined women's wages itself seems an ideological intervention on behalf of the power of the free market. As a number of historians have pointed out, moreover, Burnette has used cultural and social explanations very selectively in her work, and there is substantial evidence contradicting her claim that competition eliminates wage discrimination.[77] Since the range of occupations open to women was fairly limited (again, in part a result of prevalent notions concerning the kinds of work proper for women), there was a labour surplus in most trades open to women. The high competition for work in these trades in turn ensured that wages would remain low.

This was exacerbated by yet another pattern in women's work: much of it was part-time. This meant that many women pursued more than one occupation in trying to make ends meet, which was apparent in the pauper reports collected by J. S. Taylor for the London parish of St Martin's Vintry. Margaret Phillips, a seventy-four-year-old widow, tried to make ends meet by selling fruit in the street and by sweeping street-crossings. Mary Swinney, a thirty-six-year-old widow, sold meat and butter, and went out charring and washing.[78] As such, this situation was a two-edged sword. For married women, this meant that they could continue to fulfil family responsibilities, while also contributing to the family income. This was particularly the case when the work could be performed at home, as was often the practice in the needle trades. Being able to fit in productive work around family duties undoubtedly gave them much-needed flexibility. Nevertheless, the ability to work part-time also meant that (as seen above) there was a very large pool of available workers for these trades, which undoubtedly helped keep wages low. For single women, or for those who were the only bread winners, the irregularity of work and the low pay offered could spell disaster. Even in relatively well-paid trades like glove making, the irregularity of work would have made it difficult for these women to sustain a living income.

Finally, a number of historians have noted one more pattern: participation in particular trades was age specific. According to Peter Earle, 'young women were mainly domestics, those in the next higher age-group clustered in the needle trades, while charring, washing, nursing, and hawking tended to be the preserve of older women whose declining eyesight and arthritic fingers prevented them from maintaining themselves "by their needle".[79] Alexander found that this pattern was still apparent in the mid-nineteenth century. Most servants, she says, were between the ages of fifteen to twenty-five,[80] 'whereas the majority of charwomen, washerwomen, manglers and laundry keepers were middle-aged and older'.[81]

To sum up, the fairly narrow range of occupations, and the ability to carry on work part-time (often at home), meant that the trades in which women worked almost always had a labour surplus. The employment situation, moreover, was exacerbated by the very high percentage of Westminster's population – 48 per cent – that was between the ages of fifteen and forty. This concentration served to increase further the competitive pressures of the labour market. This excess of workers, combined with patriarchal notions concerning women's work, made certain their wages would be very low. While this situation allowed married women to juggle their responsibilities, it also ensured that, like men's work, women's employment would be irregular and highly uncertain at best.

Children's labour was another resource that family could deploy in their attempts to make ends meet. The extent to which they did so during the period of the industrial revolution has been the subject of historical controversy, however.[82] While admitting that the censuses almost certainly under-report child labour, Peter Kirby has argued that the data can be used to reveal relative levels of child employment in various regions. Using the 1851 census occupational summaries, he has argued that compared to the rest of the country, the level of child employment in London was low. Kirby found that 23 per cent of London boys aged ten to fourteen were employed, compared to 42 per cent for the rest of the country, and 12 per cent of London girls aged ten to fourteen worked, compared to 24 per cent for the rest of the country.[83] In part, the lack of agrarian and large manufacturing and industrial employment opportunities in the capital accounted for this, as well as the fact that adult wages tended to be higher in London than elsewhere.[84] In spite of Kirby's criticisms of Hugh Cunningham's work, these findings do seem to accord, at least for London, with the latter's claim that child employment was less common in the eighteenth century than hitherto supposed, largely because there was insufficient work for them to do.[85] The St Martin's evidence would tend to back this position. To take the extreme case, it was certainly in the parish's financial interest to apprentice its pauper children as soon as possible, and this was so for two reasons. First, it was cheaper to pay the £2 premium and to provide clothing than it was to maintain the child in the workhouse. And second, if the master was located in another parish, as generally was the case, then St Martin's would have been freed from future responsibility for the child (since it could now claim a settlement in the parish of employment). In spite of these apparent incentives, the average age of pauper apprentices in St Martin's never fell below nine years, and was often higher. In St James, Westminster, a parish adjacent to St Martin's, there was a rule that pauper children could not be apprenticed before the age of 12½ if they were 'strong, healthy and well-grown'. If not, they were not put out until 13, 13½ or 14 years of age.[86] As well, the overall number of apprenticeships fell throughout the period in St Martin's, perhaps indicating that work was increasingly hard to find.

Thus, the average number of apprenticeships a year from 1790–4 was thirty-seven, from 1795–9 it was thirty-nine, from 1800–4 it was thirty-one, from 1805–9 it was twenty-four, and from 1810–14 it was thirteen. The fact that the parish increasingly relied on northern textile manufacturers could also indicate the scarcity of local work. Before 1800, only once, in 1796, did the parish send as many as half its apprentices to these firms. From 1800 to 1815 inclusive, there were only four years when at least half the children did not find themselves in northern textile industries.[87] Three of these years, moreover, fell during the depression of 1811–13, and with the textile industries closed to them, parish officials managed to place only nine, four and five children in apprenticeships in each respective year. Thus, the evidence seems to indicate that it was difficult to find work for children, a situation that could create hardship for the family. When the children were young, moreover, the need to care for them also limited the wife's ability to earn. Further evidence that children were indeed a financial burden is also contained in Francis Place's autobiography. Place says at several points that large numbers of children often brought wretchedness to their families. Even of his own family, which at the time was of average size, Place said, 'we had then two living, both girls, this tyed up my wife's hands and made my loss of time (through underemployment) of serious consequence to me'.[88] In pointing out the relative paucity of work for children in the capital, it is nevertheless difficult to believe that in the troubled trades of central London, children were not frequently working alongside other family members in their parents' trades. In the absence of reliable sources, however, the extent to which this was the case cannot be known. The situation with respect to women and children's employment was made even more difficult by the fact that most historians believe work opportunities for both groups declined in the second half of the nineteenth century. While there is less agreement as to the reasons for this decline, it could only have added to the burdens of instability under which these people laboured.[89]

If uncertainty was a hallmark of work in London for both sexes, there were obviously times when people were more likely to feel the pinch of destitution. Depression years were problematic, especially when they were accompanied by harvest failures, high food prices and harsh winters. Equally, the life cycle was important in determining how well people would roll with the economic punches. Similar economic constraints did not necessarily affect people in the same ways. Indeed, even the same people had a varying ability to cope with economic hardship, depending on where they were in the life cycle. This can be seen in part by referring to the St Martin's settlement examinations. As stated earlier, those examined were chosen by relief officials in hopes of passing them (and the expense of their maintenance) to another parish, and so tended to be those most likely to require long-term support – precisely the people who were most vulnerable.

The settlement records for 1790, a year in which there is a good run of examinations, reveal a number of patterns. The records of the 313 people examined in
this year afford the opportunity for comparison with those for the workhouse.[90]
The first group that can be identified in the settlement records is the elderly. People aged sixty years or more formed 12 per cent of all those examined. Women
only slightly outnumbered men in this age group, but gender differences are
apparent. Ten of the sixteen men had a dependant (usually a wife, sometimes
children), which undoubtedly made subsistence more difficult to achieve. Not
one of the nineteen women in this age group, on the other hand, had a male
breadwinner. Thirteen were widows, four had never married and one had been
deserted by her husband. Thus, the records seem to indicate that elderly women
on their own had trouble making ends meet, while responsibility for dependants
could tip elderly men into destitution.

The different experiences of men and women at various stages in the life cycle
are also apparent from these records. Among the unmarried, the vast majority
of both sexes were in their twenties and thirties. Women far outnumbered men
– eighty-three to fifteen, in fact – and single parenthood was a major reason
for this disparity. Twenty-seven single women had children and another fifteen
were pregnant, thus accounting for just over half of the unmarried women.
Six of these forty-two women had been taken as rogues and vagabonds, as had
another woman without children. Two women had lost their father and master
respectively, and apparently had no access to other kinds of assistance. This left
thirty-seven unmarried women who were not burdened by children, yet who
had come to the attention of parish authorities. A number of these women may
have been prostitutes – some of them who entered the workhouse were assigned
to wards for the disreputable. Others were likely ill, or unable to find work, but
the extent to which this was so cannot be known for certain on the basis of the
records which have survived.

If a certain amount of information can nevertheless be teased out of the
documents with respect to unmarried women, the same is not the case for men
so described. The fifteen entries which describe unmarried men are stubbornly
opaque, since parish authorities were much less careful in describing the marital
status of men than they were of women. Marriage did not determine settlement
for men, and this status was unspecified for thirty-two men overall – as opposed
to only eight women, of whom five were labelled as vagrants. It seems likely
that these men were either unmarried or had deserted their families, since none
had dependants. Fourteen of them had been taken as rogues and vagabonds,
and were examined as such rather than as paupers. Of the men in the overall
non-specified group who entered the workhouse, four died shortly thereafter.
Although the men in the non-specified group were most commonly in their
fifties, their median age was thirty-six, and those who died were all in their twen-

ties and thirties. Thus, it seems likely that a number of men in their prime were falling into destitution through illness or injury – especially given that not all illness or injury would have resulted in death (meaning that illness was likely more prevalent than the records indicate).

In another stage in the life cycle, the survivors of fragmented families also demonstrated differences according to gender. Few widowers turn up in St Martin's settlement examinations, but the five who did all had children. Widows, on the other hand, were conspicuous by their presence. It is apparent from some entries that the lack of a male breadwinner was the major factor causing problems. The situation was often exacerbated, however, by the presence of children. Twenty-three of the forty-three widows had children with them, and not all of these children were small. Of those for whom ages were given, thirty-two were under ten, fourteen were between ten and twenty, and three were more than twenty. It would seem that the presence of older children – potential wage-earners – did not necessarily ease the financial burdens of these women.

The other group of women from fragmented families who figured prominently in the settlement examinations were wives who had been deserted, for whatever reason. Absconding husbands, spouses serving abroad, who had been impressed or who were in jail or an insane asylum are all described in the examinations. In all, thirty-four women claimed that their spouses had gone from them. Once again, the difficulties of making ends meet without a male breadwinner were made worse by the presence of children. Three-quarters of these women had children with them, although among this group offspring were much younger. Thirty-six of the children were under ten, while only four were ten or more. The younger age of children can be accounted for, at least in part, because their mothers were almost four years younger than the widows.

It is apparent that women in fragmented families, whether widowed or deserted, had greater difficulty in achieving subsistence than their male counterparts – at least if numbers are any indication. In part, the presence of children added to their difficulties. Indeed, this pattern can once again be seen in so-called 'complete' families. Parish officials almost invariably interviewed the husband when he was present. Thirty-six men were examined who described themselves as married. Only fifteen of these couples did not have children, and of these, two were taken as rogues and vagabonds. Two more wives were described as insane, undoubtedly placing an added burden on their spouses, and in another the husband was ill and died shortly thereafter. Of the twenty-one couples who did have children, ten had three or more to provide for. Thus, while children weren't always the determining factor tipping a family into destitution, they did seem to add to the woes in the majority of complete households. In a significant minority of families, a larger number of children seems to have created even more onerous economic burdens.

Overall, then, at certain stages in the life cycle, the achievement of subsistence could prove especially problematic. The increasing fragility that accompanied age certainly made life more precarious, and women who were unmarried, widowed or who had been deserted by their husbands all had greater difficulty in achieving subsistence. Men who lacked spouses able to contribute to the family income and to care for children also faced difficulties, if seemingly less severe than those facing their female counterparts. Finally, the presence of children in and of itself often seems to have worsened the situation of families in trouble.

If the evidence hitherto offered points to the relative importance of the life cycle and of employment difficulties in producing immiseration, one final source will also corroborate this: the annual reports of the Mendicity Society. This was a charity meant to assist London beggars, which will be discussed more fully in the next chapter. The annual reports for the years 1818, 1819, 1821, 1823, 1828 and 1829 all contain alleged causes of distress experienced by the beggars with whom the society dealt.[91] The four main causes of destitution were age and infirmity, sickness or accident, loss of a husband and alleged unemployment. 'Alleged' unemployment (and the society was suspicious) was clearly the single greatest cause of distress in every year, falling below 50 per cent only twice in 1818 and 1821. At 16–22 per cent, sickness or accident, which could strike at any point in life, together constituted the second most common cause in every year but one, 1829, when they accounted for 9 per cent of those seeking assistance. The two causes that could be related to the life cycle – age, and the loss of a husband – accounted for 12 to 24 per cent of the cases. Thus, while stresses occurring at various stages in the life cycle were important factors, the single greatest danger facing the plebeian Londoners who turned to the Mendicity Society seems to have been the precariousness of work. Admittedly, the extent to which fraudulent reasons for begging were given cannot be known. Nevertheless, the figures for unemployment were so very much higher than those for other causes that it seems likely that the former would retain their primacy in any case.[92]

Clearly, the employment picture for the whole family was precarious at best. Aside from the difficulty of finding work for children, a labour surplus, irregularity of work and seasonal underemployment plagued adult male and female trades in London, making subsistence uncertain for plebeian families. As David Vincent noted of the autobiographies he analysed, 'what comes across ... is that constant financial insecurity was the lot even of those working men who had the good fortune to avoid recruitment into the ranks of the casual labourers or the factory proletariat, and spent their lives in seemingly prosperous and well protected skilled trades'.[93] If families earning less than 20s. a week likely faced great difficulty in making ends meet, and if unskilled male workers were making approximately 10s. a week while their wives could expect to earn no more than 6s., then it is apparent that achieving subsistence must have been a continual struggle for the majority of plebeian Londoners. According to the family budget that Thompson and Yeo provided in *The Unknown Mayhew*, a labouring class family was likely spending 13s. 4½d. on rent, food, beer, candles, soap and coal in 1841. When clothing costs were added, it is apparent that even quite minor dislocations could have tipped the scales to destitution.[94] Certainly Francis Place and his wife managed to meet immediate demands in 1791, when their income was seventeen shillings a week, but as he also observed, 'Nothing could be saved from this small sum'.[95] For those who lived outside the family – especially women – the achievement of subsistence would have been even more difficult.

Clustering, the predilection of people in particular trades to locate in different areas of the parish, is also revealing, since these choices can be mapped on to the neighbourhoods defined as poor and affluent in the last chapter. In examining the seven trades common to the six trade lists discussed earlier, it is apparent that clustering did exist, although more so in some occupations than others. Both shoemakers and tailors, for example, were particularly numerous in the west end of the inhabited part of the parish, especially in the streets, courts and alleys around Bedfordbury. According to the censuses of 1841 and 1861, the vast majority of the parish's shoemakers and tailors were found within the perimeter marked out by Leicester Square, the King's Mews (later Trafalgar Square), the foot of Northumberland Street along the Thames to George Street, and then up along Bedford Street through to Long Acre. Indeed, 81 per cent and 77 per cent of St Martin's shoemakers, and 79 per cent and 80 per cent of the parish's tailors in 1841 and 1861 respectively, lived within this area. The pattern also seemed to obtain earlier in the century: of the forty-two tailors who gave parish addresses listed in the settlement records of 1816–19, thirty-one of them lived here, while thirty-nine of the forty-eight shoemakers did so.

Bakers tended to locate on major streets – nearly half in 1841 (62 of 129), were to be found on the Strand, Long Acre, Drury Lane, Bedfordbury and St Martin's Lane. Few were located on the streets earlier defined as poor, and none were found in the comfortable residential district south of the Strand. As well, very few bakers were found in the area immediately south of Leicester Square. Before the construction of Trafalgar Square and the reconstruction of the streets south of St Martin's church, there was a particularly heavy concentration of bakers in the Bermudas – almost 25 per cent of all bakers in 1802. By 1841, after the destruction of the Bermudas, this concentration had disappeared.

The three other manufacturing trades among the top seven exhibited somewhat different patterns. Jewellers were found in the Strand and the streets running into it, and in a broad band which ran over to the Haymarket south of Leicester Square. Most lived on larger streets, and few were found in Bedfordbury. Coachmakers, as is generally known, were heavily concentrated on Long Acre and the streets running into it. They also lived in Castle Street, Long

Acre, and a sprinkling was found on the streets and courts of the west end of the parish. Trades people in the dealing sector – publicans and grocers, principally – were found throughout the parish. Publicans[96] tended to locate on the bigger streets, and as with other trades, few were located in the residential district south of the Strand. Grocers,[97] on the other hand, tended to be most numerous in the west end of the inhabited part of the parish. There were none in the residential district south of the Strand. A lesser number were found in the streets around Long Acre and in the north-east corner of the parish.

A number of trades that became visible in the censuses also need to be considered: domestic servants, labourers, soldiers, clerks, porters and laundresses. Domestic servants can be set aside, since they rarely formed independent households, but generally lived with their masters. Similarly, the vast majority of soldiers, more than 82 per cent, lived in barracks, and also will not be considered. Of the other groups, the labourers exhibited the most clustering. The vast majority of them lived in the courts and alleys of Bedfordbury. A much smaller number of them were found in the streets and courts behind Drury Lane and off Long Acre, and a few more were to be found in the streets and alleys south of the Strand near Charing Cross. As will be recalled, all of these areas were defined as poor in the last chapter. The clerks also showed preference for particular areas of St Martin's, and were especially numerous in the residential district south of the Strand. They preferred to live on the larger, generally more affluent streets of the parish, with many of them settling on the Haymarket, St Martin's Lane, Long Acre and Charing Cross. There was an enclave south of Leicester Square, another in the north-east corner of the parish, and in 1841 there were no fewer than thirteen clerks on Mercer Street.

The porters, on the other hand, exhibited little clustering, tending to be spread homogeneously throughout the parish. This tendency was not surprising, given that St Martin's completely surrounded Covent Garden. Finally, laundresses (including manglers and washerwomen) also showed some clustering. The laundresses were found in the courts and alleys of Bedfordbury and up to Long Acre. There was a broad band south and east of Leicester Square. Some were found in the residential district south of the Strand, especially west of George Street over towards Hungerford Market. There were some as well on the east side of the parish, on the streets and courts behind Drury Lane. Since most of these women were probably married, the neighbourhood in which they lived was likely determined by their husbands' trades. Indeed, a comparison of laundress addresses with those of the other trades discussed in this chapter reveals very similar dispersion patterns for the labourers (an unskilled trade), and for tailors and shoemakers (two of the easiest trades to enter, and hence two of the most populous). Whatever the wives of artisans in the more exclusive trades[98] might have been doing to contribute to the economy of the family, it wasn't laundry – at least according to these sources.

It is apparent, then, that there was clustering, although the degree of it varied with trade. Tailors, shoemakers, laundresses and labourers were found in large numbers in Bedfordbury, and the last group in Drury Lane and Long Acre wards as well. More prestigious trades like jewellers and coachmakers did not locate in Bedfordbury, or in back courts. The clerks, with greater pretensions to respectability, tended to be the only group found in any numbers in the residential district south of the Strand. Thus, the conditions in a number of trades, whether unskilled like labouring and portering, or easily entered like shoemaking and tailoring, made them practical career options for the poor. Once enrolled in their ranks, these same conditions ensured that the majority of practitioners would remain within the ranks of the marginal. It is also apparent that those following these trades tended to live in particular areas of the parish previously defined as poor, and this in turn is further evidence for the precariousness of these trades. Indeed, while clustering was a tendency rather than a hard-and-fast rule, the practitioners of various trades were drawn to particular parts of the parish: the better-off trades to the more salubrious areas, and the poorer to the neighbourhoods identified above. This meant that for people in a number of precarious trades, neighbourhood solidarities were densely textured, constructed not just on the propinquity of others, but on shared work experiences as well.

In conclusion, then, it is apparent that work for both men and women was uncertain. Many of the biggest trades for men in central London suffered from irregularity of employment and low pay. Women's trades experienced these problems to an even more severe degree, given there were so few kinds of work available. The many, many women who needed to work were lower paid as well, because of patriarchal beliefs and their need to find work that could be accommodated to family responsibilities. Neighbourhood clustering by trade, while a tendency rather than a hard-and-fast rule, still meant that solidarities would be densely textured for many, imbricating propinquity and shared work experiences. Susceptibility to hardship at various points in the life cycle – especially when there were dependent children – increased the need for neighbours to rely upon one another, and this was especially so for fragmented families. In the face of so much uncertainty, prescriptions for individual initiative and sturdy self-reliance made little sense, since they were inadequate protection against privation, while injunctions to work hard were in most cases simply insulting – far better to continue to trust customary cultural practices.

4 USING CHARITY AND POOR RELIEF

In the absence of an adequate welfare safety net, customary cultural practices centring on mutual reliance remained necessary and widespread. These practices continued to be relevant, moreover, because the social assistance that did exist at this time – chiefly poor relief and philanthropy – was becoming progressively more difficult to accommodate within the precarious configuration of makeshift resources through which the poor maintained subsistence.

A third kind of formal assistance was provided by friendly societies, organizations meant to provide security against problems brought on by accident, illness and age, and often to provide for funeral expenses.[1] In St Martin's in 1803 there were forty-two such societies, according to parliamentary returns, with a total membership of 3,259 people.[2] Friendly societies became particularly important in the second half of the nineteenth century, and by 1914 there were slightly fewer than 29,000 in the country, with a membership of 7.6 million.[3] If most of these people had families, then it is obvious that by the late century a sizable percentage of the labouring classes was able to benefit from this kind of assistance. For London as a whole in the early nineteenth century, Martin Gorsky has estimated, 8 per cent of the population and 34 per cent of families belonged to such societies, although he cautions that problems with the sources likely means that the true figures were lower.[4] There were, moreover, problems inherent to the organization of these societies. Funeral expenses were often a drain on finances, as was the fact that meetings were held at public houses, where members were expected to drink. As well, the ratio of contributions to payments was often ill-calculated, with the result that these societies very often collapsed under their own financial burdens and obligations. Finally, since regular contributions were demanded – and all benefits were lost if payments lapsed – it is unlikely that this kind of assistance would have been available to those most buffeted by the winds of economic vicissitude.[5] It is difficult to disagree with Prothero's comment that while the function and the appeal of these organizations should not be underestimated, their assistance was limited: 'they did provide some protection, though in the main only for those above subsistence level, against some of the hazards of life'.[6] It was, in short, the better off who were most likely to benefit from belonging to a friendly society during the period of this study. Most of the people discussed in this chapter were likely beyond the reach of friendly society assistance: either their needs exceeded the limits of the assistance available, or as they spiralled downward economically, friendly society dues were allowed to lapse.

Poor relief and philanthropic assistance were becoming more difficult to accommodate because of the ways in which, from the late eighteenth century, London parishes and many charitable bodies began to change their practices. By this time, reformers and authorities were beginning to make concerted efforts to reshape poor relief and philanthropy in order to effect the moral reformation of recipients. Bernard Harris has discussed the contemporary reservations concerning the Old Poor Law: that it bred a sense of entitlement, discouraging the willingness to labour, weakened social bonds between classes, and crowded out voluntary charity to the detriment of both giver and recipient alike.[7] It was necessary, according to contemporary upper- and middle-class commentators, to recast poor relief as a privilege rather than a right, and to allot a greater role to voluntary charity. Mitchell Dean has noted these ideological preoccupations, which he associates with the emergence of liberal governance. He says that the poor were expected to become more 'responsible', and that this was especially so for men. It was crucial that the individual liberty central to the liberal state be used rationally and conscientiously – in ways that promoted social stability and economic growth. Poor men at all times were to be held accountable for the well-being of their families: subsistence was to be achieved through their good efforts rather than through reliance upon public assistance. As Dean has pointed out, 'in regards to matters of poverty, the private sphere is not so much one of personal freedoms and rights but of the economic responsibilities of a certain category of social agent, the male breadwinner'.[8] With respect to poor relief, rules and regulations reflecting these aims were enacted throughout the period from the 1790s onward. This meant that 1834 was less a juncture in the poor law system than the culmination of a decades-long shift in thinking and in practices. As Alan Kidd has noted, the agenda for charity also shifted: 'As early as the 1790s, proponents of "scientific charity" co-ordinated giving, collated information about the poor, aimed to "re-educate" the giving class and organized district visiting of working-class homes. Even in the hands of evangelical charities the gift had to be discriminating … a prime motive of charitable giving to adults was the reinforcement of norms of self-help'.[9] All of this meant that while still critically important in a crisis, charity and poor relief became less reliable resources for those who lived at the margin.

The predispositions of contemporary commentators and officials described above were a poor fit with the realities of the time, recognizing neither the inability of men, nor even of waged work generally, to guarantee subsistence. As has been seen, uncertainty was a hallmark of employment in St Martin's during this period for both men and women, and families could not expect to make ends meet by relying on it alone, not even when women and children were able to contribute. Instead, waged labour was embedded in a dense matrix of resources that Olwen Hufton memorably termed the economy of makeshifts. Waged work was crucially necessary, but was not alone sufficient in the struggle to maintain subsistence. Rather, it and other formal resources like poor relief and charity meshed with informal mutuality, credit and pawning networks. These resources would be accessed in turn or combined in flexible permutations in the ongoing battle to maintain subsistence. Immediate flexibility in the face of unpredictable vicissitudes was crucially necessary for these people: they had to be able to respond to changing circumstances at once. It is the argument of this chapter that from a relatively early period, philanthropic relief and workhouse assistance became increasingly less useful in this struggle as they were reshaped in order to effect the moral reformation of recipients, and in the case of poor relief, to keep down costs for rate payers. There is ample evidence that genuine need rather than fecklessness frequently underlay the recourse to these kinds of assistance.

The situation with respect to charity was complicated, and it is unfortunately not possible in a study of London to adopt the methodology that Alannah Tomkins put to such good use in *The Experience of Being Poor*, linking charitable and poor relief records to create partial biographies for the urban poor. Nor can individual recipients of charity be tracked systematically over time in the way that is possible for workhouse inmates. Given the huge population of St Martin's, its mobility, plus the great number of charities available to the poor in the capital, the linkages possible in London are necessarily more modest and limited largely to the poor law system. For these reasons, the greater part by far of this chapter will be devoted to the poor law, and especially to workhouse inmates. It is possible that charitable assistance may have helped lower poor relief numbers, but this is difficult to prove in London. In the first place, while the range of charities was extensive in the capital, it was difficult, as Harris has pointed out, to know how much money they spent, and how much of it was actually allocated to the metropolitan poor rather than to overseas missions, the erection of buildings, or social events. Certainly, claims that charitable spending outstripped poor relief expenditures need to be treated with caution.[10] It may be as well, as Andrea Tanner has claimed, that the existence of an extensive charitable nexus gave London paupers more flexibility in choosing either poor relief or charitable assistance, and more negotiating room, but given the inability noted above to link charitable client lists (where they have survived) to poor relief recipients in any systematic way, it is again difficult to know how significant an impact such apparent choice might have had.[11] There are figures perhaps comparable from the city of Oxford: Richard Dyson says that 30 to 40 per cent of householders in the small Oxford parish of St Giles received either charity or poor relief between 1760 and 1830.[12]

The increasing demands of scientific charity that assistance be offered only to the deserving, with the consequent (often visible) investigation of potential recipients, made it less easy to accommodate for plebeian Londoners who needed to maintain a facade of solvency if they were to retain access to credit with shopkeepers and landlords. Of the charities assisting the poorest of the poor, the Mendicity Society was likely the most infamous for investigations of its clientele. This large, highly respectable charity, enjoying royal patronage, grew out of several private investigations of London beggars begun by Matthew Martin in 1796. By 1818 a permanent charity had been established whose approach to the problem of beggars was two-pronged: punishment for those whom it deemed fraudulent, and assistance and encouragement for those thought deserving. It hired its own constables to patrol the streets looking for beggars who, when apprehended, were brought to the society headquarters in Red Lion Square or handed over to magistrates. During its first fourteen years, society constables apprehended more than 9,500 people whom they deemed to be vagrants, of whom 4,800 were convicted.[13] In order to ensure that it offered help only to the deserving, the society distributed tickets to members of the upper and middle classes, who were encouraged to give these, rather than money, to beggars. The latter then turned the tickets in at the society office, where the circumstances of their cases were carefully examined. The society also operated a begging-letter department where subscribers could send letters they had received soliciting assistance. These would be investigated, and the subscribers notified as to their worthiness. In ten years the society examined some 28,000 letters,[14] some of which have survived in the papers of the second Earl Spencer.[15]

What Martin, and subsequently the Mendicity Society, sought to accomplish was to bring beggars back within established systems of relief which were increasingly discriminating among their clientele on the basis of moral status,[16] and to extend those systems to deal with the poor who did not fall into one of the various classifications for relief. To accomplish this, the society investigated the character of applicants carefully, first in an interview in which they were asked questions eliciting information about family life, employment history, settlement and the rent paid. Applicants were also asked whether poor relief had been received, whether belongings were in pawn and if there was debt of any kind. Finally, they had to explain how they came to be begging. Equally crucial, a reference – 'a credible person who will vouch for your veracity and general character' – had to be provided, and was checked.[17] The interview was followed up by at least one home visit, and often 'repeated and unexpected visits' were thought necessary.[18] To guard against misinformed or careless references, society visitors also spoke to the applicant's neighbours, to the landlord and to local shopkeepers. Its visitors, moreover, were highly visible in the plebeian neighbourhoods where they conducted their investigations. As a mid-century admirer of the society explained, the visitor 'must be dressed as a gentleman, to give authority to his questions among applicants and his interviews with referees'.[19] In the determination of worthiness, society applicants could expect little discretion or privacy.

While the Mendicity Society was widely admired, there were those who were uneasy about its intrusiveness. In 1825 one critic complained that the society pried 'into all the secrets of a man's life and family', laying open 'his entire history'.[20] The society's constables also came under attack for high-handed and brutal behaviour. In an 1825 case, well publicized in the press, several constables tried to arrest a couple for begging. According to witnesses, the constables began beating the man, who was holding a young child, hitting him repeatedly about the head with sticks. A gentleman riding by tried to intervene to stop the beating. The constables threatened to have the gentleman arrested for vagrancy, and subjected him to 'much gross abuse' and 'opprobrious epithets'.[21] After the arrest, the magistrate hearing the case dismissed the vagrancy charge against the man, and instituted assault charges against the constables, one of whom was subsequently found guilty. Employee problems were exacerbated by the fact that the society felt no particular loyalty to its staff. In 1829, for example, one of its porters, Phillip Bragg, faced a family crisis: after a prolonged bout of cancer his wife died; his children then caught small pox, and he fell deeply into debt trying to cope. The society itself made no attempt to help Bragg, noting rather primly that 'The Managers would feel much pleasure in rendering aid to his Family, but they are prevented by inability, also their pledge to the Public, that their funds are applicable only to the purposes, and objects of the Institution'. After noting with disapproval that none of the wealthy in Bragg's neighbourhood had helped the family, presumably 'because the matter was not sufficiently made known', the assistant manager appealed to Lord Spencer to give them alms.[22] In the eyes of the society, employees in difficulty differed not at all from the beggars with whom it dealt. Its members seemingly did not consider their own responsibilities as affluent London employers to whom the matter surely had been made sufficiently known. It is apparent that a decidedly unpleasant combination frequently governed the behaviour of this charity: staff whose behaviour could undercut the society's intentions and a rigid adherence to bureaucratic rules with few attempts to find creative ways to be humane.

In spite of the society's deep suspicions, data appended to Matthew Martin's *Letter to Lord Pelham* of 1803 indicate that its clientele, for the most part, came from the ranks of the most vulnerable: the vast majority were women with children, at least two-thirds of whom lacked male breadwinners.[23] Nor did they seem to take the decision to beg lightly. Given the nature of neighbourhood life at this time, people who fell into destitution often tried to hide it from their neighbours, especially if forced to pursue options of which the neighbourhood might disapprove. Henry Mayhew found that people who were forced by need to beg often tried to disguise this. He said, 'the sale of small articles in the streets may, perhaps, be an excuse for begging; but in most cases I am convinced it is adopted from a horror of the workhouse, and a disposition to do, at least, *something* for the food they eat. Often it is the last struggle of independence – the desire to give something like an equivalent for what they receive'. Mayhew said people did this from 'the aversion to be thought a common beggar'.[24] Indeed, people clearly did not wish to be recognized by friends and acquaintances. One woman whom Mayhew interviewed, for instance, said she sold matches in the street. She lived in Whitechapel, but said she went to Shoreditch to sell them, 'thinking I would not be known'. The next week she returned to the same spot, 'holding my head down like a bulrush, for fear that somebody would pass that knew me'.[25] Possibly she was shaping her response to what she thought Mayhew wished to hear, but begging did not seem to be a popular option among the destitute. Of sixty-two poor needlewomen who attended a meeting Mayhew had called, ten said they had been forced to enter a workhouse, nineteen said they had pawned their work, thirty-one claimed to have gone without food for a day, but only three women admitted to begging in the streets.[26]

In an environment where reputation in the neighbourhood was very important, and begging an activity to be concealed if possible, the Mendicity Society practice of home visits involving a stranger, clearly from a higher class, coming to the neighbourhood to interview a potential client would most certainly have excited comment by the neighbours. Similarly, appeals to 'creditable persons' in the neighbourhood – including landlords and shopkeepers – also helped to broadcast the individual's plight, as did society officers redeeming pawned goods. These society practices made the individual's indigence public knowledge, and consequently made it difficult to retain access to neighbourhood resources needed to regain and maintain financial independence. Since the vast majority of Mendicity Society applicants came from the most vulnerable sectors of the community, such public investigation of character must have seemed spurious, demeaning, economically harmful, and in the end decidedly unhelpful.

Charities intended to assist a more reputable clientele faced a different set of problems. People who were more receptive to the constellation of values being promoted by scientific charity – generally the most skilled or the most secure financially – may have seen the receipt of assistance from a charity meant to help those thought most reputable as a confirmation of status. Alan Kidd has observed that the meaning of charity could be redefined. He noted the conditional nature of charity at this time – that it should be given only to the deserving and not simply to the needy – and concluded that it 'could be viewed as an attempt to overcome the one-way nature of the charity relationship', since 'giving was made dependent upon the return gift expected from the recipient, i.e. the status of being deserving'. Thus, charity was thought to function 'as a means of enhancing solidarity and strengthening mutual ties' between classes.[27] Given this conditionality, however, charity could also be redefined from below, and it could be turned towards ends that donors never anticipated.

This can be seen in the case of Mary Ann Ashford, a plebeian woman proud of her respectability, who applied to the British Lying-In Hospital on Brownlow Street. Ashford was married to a sergeant tradesman who taught shoemaking to the boys of the Royal Military Asylum. This institution was an orphanage for the children of soldiers killed in service. Ashford's husband was steadily employed the year round and was provided accommodation for his dependants within the asylum, thus giving this family much more security than was the norm for shoemakers. When her first confinement approached, Ashford accepted a letter of admission to the British Lying-In Hospital, a highly respectable charitable institution that would admit only married women. Her lady sponsor, who was out of town, had the Royal Military Asylum doctor pay her annual subscription to the hospital (which was accepted by the charity) and sign Ashford's letter. Thinking the hospital quieter and not wishing to disturb her not very healthy husband, Ashford accepted the offer. She presented herself to the charity's committee, but not as a humble supplicant. Rather, she seemed to regard the interview simply as a standard bureaucratic procedure. Things went awry, however, when one of the committee members refused to accept Ashford's letter because it was not signed by the original sponsor. After affronting her by asking (rudely and coarsely she thought) when her baby was due, he decided there was time to write to the sponsor and refused to accept the letter until such confirmation had arrived. Ashford wrote,

> I left Brownlow Street very much vexed; and, what was very annoying, the other persons, whose letters had passed, went, as is customary, to Bow Street to swear to their marriage certificates; and as they could not tell what had passed in the committee room, or why I did not go with the rest, stared me quite out of countenance. I did not get home till near tea-time; and whether the long walk and agitation I had undergone made any difference, I do not know, but I am taken ill the next day; and on Monday, the 17th of August, my first child, a female, was born.[28]

Ashford did not simply content herself in her autobiography with blaming the committee for her premature labour. She went on to name and shame the curmudgeonly committee member – Sir William Knatchbull as she thought – and she recounted a prescient dream she had shortly before the committee meeting. In it, she was annoyed and frightened by a porcupine that refused to let her pass. The creature 'burst suddenly open, and the face of a very cross, ugly, old man came forth'. She was, she wrote, shocked the next day upon walking into the committee room to find 'the very cross, ugly face I saw in my dream': the churlish committee member.[29] Ashford rounded out her public revenge for the slur to her respectability by noting with satisfaction that her lady sponsor 'was so much offended that she placed her subscription to some of the other hospitals'.[30] An application process that Ashford clearly expected would affirm her status as respectable instead called it into question, first through the committee doubting the veracity of her letter, and then in letting other plebeian women believe that she was not legally married. Her revenge was sharp, and it was public. The pen, it would seem, was mightier than the curmudgeon. It is apparent that Ashford felt no shame or hesitation in applying to this charity. Rather, she seemed to think this assistance was her right: admission to this hospital ought to have been a confirmation of her respectability. In a curious way, then, charities meant to help the upright and worthy did not reinforce independence in the way in which scientific charity was meant to do. The meaning of the gift had shifted. Moreover, the contrast between charities intended to help those thought disreputable and those targeting the most worthy reflects a point made in earlier chapters: plebeian Londoners, while sharing much in important ways, nevertheless were not homogenous, and nor were their responses to new cultural demands and expectations being placed upon them.

If charity was complicated, the story with respect to poor relief was perhaps more straightforward in as much as its clientele was drawn almost wholly from the ranks of the most needy. In order to understand who turned to the workhouse and why, and how it was used, it is necessary to focus closely on the sources. In the case of St Martin in the Fields, it is fruitful to concentrate on the old poor law period – in this case from the early 1790s to 1830 – for several reasons. First, on a practical level, a particularly rich range of poor relief records has survived for these years. Moreover, the *London Lives* database allows workhouse admission and discharge records for individuals to be linked through time up until 1819 (the point at which the St Martin's records in the database end) in order to create institutional biographies, a task that is far too onerous to attempt manually. Ideologically the period was formative: in the years between 1790 and the early 1830s, debates about the poor law system reached a crescendo. While there is debate among historians as to just when these shifts began, the 1790s saw an intense and wide-ranging discussion concerning the causes of and solutions for the ever-mounting levels of poverty. A second period of intense debate occurred after the war, with calls for the abolition of the system peaking in 1817. Finally, after considerable investigation and discussion, in 1834 the system was subjected to a fundamental overhaul with the passage of the Poor Law Amendment Act into law.[31] An examination of actual practices during an era in which the whole approach to poor relief was being rethought is certainly worth undertaking, especially as less work has been done on this period than on either the eighteenth century or the New Poor Law. Finally, there is evidence that the poor were turning away from repeated reliance upon the workhouse during these decades, and the reasons for this need to be explored. In particular, it will be argued that the falling numbers in some of the inmate groups regarded with most suspicion – high repeat entrants and in those who absconded from the house illegally – were less the result of a moral transformation in which inmates embraced new canons of respectability associated with individual responsibility, than they were of the growing inability to use workhouse assistance as part of the economy of makeshifts.

It should be noted at the outset that poor relief recipients, and in particular workhouse inmates, did not exist in isolation from the rest of the plebeian community. As will be seen, inmates, for the most part, were people who lacked family or friends to whom to turn when crisis struck, or whose needs had exceeded the ability of such to assist them. This was certainly apparent in the case of William Hart, for example, who contracted smallpox in 1794, at age eighteen. He had just moved to the town of St Albans the month before, and no one would take him in. His master, for whom he had worked for several weeks, did try to assist him, but the old woman with whom he lodged refused to let him stay, since she 'kept a shop (in her home) and was afraid of losing her customers'.[32] Hart was able to return to the town where he served his apprenticeship and to receive assistance there from friends and from the parish: he entered the parish pest house and got free medical care. Had he been forced to remain in St Albans, the consequences could have been disastrous. As Hart observed, 'it was a favourable circumstance (though it appeared a calamitous one at the time) that no person could be found to take me in at St Albans, for if they had the expense would have been very great to me, and I had not much money, being out of my time only a few weeks'.[33] Hart was a respectable cooper, but rather than feeling shame for receiving this public assistance, he felt only relief, and rapidly regained his position within the plebeian community thereafter.

Poor relief in St Martin's became a vehicle for attempts to impose new notions of individual responsibility upon paupers, and this was occurring well before the passage of the Poor Law Amendment Act. Many workhouse inmates, however, did not accept these changes passively, but tried to bend an increasingly unhelpful relief system to meet their needs. To explore this, it is necessary to examine first the changes that parish officials introduced, which were recorded in the overseers' minutes and reports and in pamphlets published by the parish. Workhouse admission records exist for the entire period from 1783 to 1833, and discharge records for most years. Settlement examinations, unfortunately, have survived for only some of the years under consideration: 1790–4 and 1816–20. In order to explore continuity of behaviour over several sequential years and to have some sense of the period as a whole, institutional biographies have been constructed for paupers between the periods 1790–4 and 1815–19. The poor relief records will also be examined at five-year intervals, and references will at times be made to other years, and to census data concerning the workhouse.

As was pointed out earlier, some 30 per cent of London's population was either destitute or at risk of becoming so during the nineteenth century, and it is obvious that the poor relief system did not assist all those in economic peril;

nor was it intended to do so. In the census years of 1801 and 1811, for example, poor relief was offered to 5 per cent of the population of St Martin's. This level very likely underestimates assistance given to the casual poor – those who could not claim a legitimate settlement in the parish that would entitle them to relief – especially with respect to out relief. The parish not only offered admission to its workhouse but, according to the overseers' minutes, offered relief in kind to the poor – coats, gowns, shirts, shoes and so on, as well as one-time monetary pay-outs to the casual and weekly pensions for the settled. The latter usually ranged between 1 and 4s. in the 1790s and rose to as much as 5 to 7s. on occasion in the early nineteenth century. From the 1790s through to the end of the wars in 1815, the average number of instances of out relief offered by the parish was 217 annually. The out relief lists contained in the overseers' minutes are, however, problematic in several ways: they frequently indicated that pensions or relief in kind were to be given to an individual and their family, without specifying how many people the family contained. As well, the lists provide only names and no other identifying features. Thus, it cannot be known for certain, for example, whether the Mary Forsyth who was given a shift and shoes in December 1794 was the same Mary Forsyth who had left the workhouse in March of the same year. Nevertheless, there are many names identical to those of inmates in the workhouse, undoubtedly indicating short-term parish support for friable household economies at least some of the time after discharge from the workhouse. According to the overseers' minutes, such pensions when awarded typically lasted one month after discharge.[34] The parish daybooks contain bi-weekly summaries of workhouse admissions and discharges, and for reasons not explained, the amounts paid in discharge pensions to inmates leaving the house were recorded in twelve of the summaries between 1 April 1819 and 29 April 1820. In all, the parish paid £17 1s. 6d., making it likely that the annual figure for workhouse leavers was in the neighbourhood of £35 to £40.[35]

Although the minutes note that overseers were 'to attend in rotation to relieve the casual poor', it is unclear how much casual out relief is recorded in these entries.[36] A report from 1839 on the casual poor assisted in St Martin's claimed that in the parish, it had 'for a very long period, been the custom to admit into the Workhouse all Persons that were destitute, without ... enquiring to what Parish they belonged',[37] and there are relatively few such notations in the daybook records, especially after the 1790s. While the amount of assistance given to the casual poor may have been significant, the overseers' minutes simply do not permit an estimation of who these people were, and the numbers of such who were assisted. All of these problems make it very difficult, using these sources, to estimate the overall number of people assisted in St Martin's each year, and the rough 5 per cent figure given above should be taken as a minimum, with the actual figure perhaps several points higher.[38] Nor do these estimates look at poor relief over the long term: doing so would very likely result in significantly higher percentages. Dyson, for example, has estimated that in the city of Oxford in 1803 and in 1813–15, paupers made up 6 per cent of the population, a figure similar to that for St Martin's.[39] Elsewhere, he has examined the proportion of households from one poor small Oxford parish, St Giles, who received poor relief over twenty-five years: at the beginning of the period 33 per cent were in receipt of assistance; by the end of the cycle 47 per cent had received assistance at one point or another. Clearly, over time the percentage of the population needing help was significantly higher than the figures for a single year would indicate.[40]

As David Green has pointed out, parishes in London were, in any case, more reliant on workhouse assistance than was the norm in most other parts of the country. In 1803 more than 29 per cent of Middlesex paupers – 17,000 – were in workhouses. By 1815 there were 19,000.[41] Not all parishes possessed workhouses; some combined to share a house, while others farmed out their paupers to entrepreneurs running private institutions.[42] St Martin's, however, like a number of other parishes in the West End, had its own workhouse, which was one of the largest in the capital. It was built to accommodate 700 people, and was located on Castle Street, Leicester Square, to the south of Hemmings Row. It had been enlarged in 1783, and by the next decade was frequently accommodating more than 800 people. The St Martin's house was particularly well thought of in the early nineteenth century; one guide book praised 'the general arrangement of the house', which it thought reflected 'great credit on the churchwardens'.[43] By the 1860s, however, the workhouse's reputation had gone into serious decline, as the *Lancet*'s withering condemnation of its infirmary attests: the ventilation of the house, the number of 'proper water closets' and the nursing arrangements were all excoriated, and the managers found 'neglectful'. Tramp wards were 'abominable', and the house itself was described as 'a gloomy, prison-like structure', although the extent to which these criticisms resulted from an actual decline in conditions, or from changing attitudes and standards, is unclear. In 1868, three years after the *Lancet* article, the parish of St Martin in the Fields was incorporated into the Strand Poor Law Union, and its workhouse was pulled down in 1871 to make way for an extension of the National Gallery.

The number of admission entries recorded each year in the daybooks could vary significantly, ranging from a low in 1805 of 572 to a high in 1819 of 1,325. The overall pattern during the nineteenth century was a gradual diminution in the number of admissions, although with much oscillation. The same pattern held with respect to individuals in the house: overall diminution but with several spikes in numbers. Table 4.1 shows the overall number of inmates for these years, plus the number of adults in the house. In the discussions that follow, the 1785–1825 figures are drawn from the by-weekly daybook summaries, while the figures for 1841, 1851 and 1861 come from census enumeration books.[44] The number of children in the house fell sharply after the establishment of the Infant Poor House at Highwood Hill in 1821.

Table 4.1: Workhouse admissions of St Martin in the Fields.*

	1790	1791	1792	1793	1794	1795	1800	1805	1810	1815	1816	1817	1818	1819
Total Admissions	1206	1104	1024	1002	932	947	1116	649	843	992	1135	1291	1151	1325
Total Women	686	593	556	552	521	550	585	344	394	457	526	548	463	519
Total Men	244	219	243	201	173	152	203	129	178	225	304	365	303	330
Total Children	260	277	208	234	220	237	323	173	267	291	297	366	368	460
No Sex or Age	16	15	17	15	18	8	5	3	4	19	8	12	17	16
Women as % of Total	56.9	53.7	54.3	55.1	55.9	58.1	52.4	53.0	46.7	46.1	46.3	42.4	40.0	39.2
Women as % of Adults	72.5	73.0	69.6	73.3	75.1	78.3	74.2	72.7	68.9	67.0	63.4	60.0	60.4	61.1
Men as % of Total	20.2	19.8	23.7	20.1	18.6	16.1	18.2	19.9	21.1	22.7	26.8	28.3	26.3	24.9
Men as % of Adults	25.8	27.0	30.4	26.7	24.9	21.7	25.8	27.3	31.1	33.0	36.6	40.0	40.0	38.9
Children as % of Total	21.6	25.1	20.3	23.4	23.6	25.0	28.9	26.7	31.7	29.3	26.2	28.4	32.0	34.7

*   These are crude admission figures, uncorrected for repeat entrants.

Green has pointed out that workhouses in London anticipated many of the reforms associated with the Poor Law Amendment Act of 1834,[45] and, as noted earlier, the St Martin's workhouse was certainly part of this general trend. Parish authorities had long attempted to differentiate among the inmates by allocating them to wards according to their sex, age, character and ability to work. This was made clear in the *Rules and Regulations for the Government of the Workhouse of the Parish of St Martin in the Fields and of the Infant Poor at Highwood Hill*, published in 1828, and closely based on the Workhouse Standing Orders of 1817.[46] The 1828 pamphlet explained the various rules that governed the workhouse. While particular regulations changed, the general organization of the workhouse had been the same in previous decades. Men and women 'of good disposition, regular behaviour, decent dress, or who have been in better circumstances'[47] were each to be warded together. Indeed, in 1817 two wards had been set aside specifically for former householders, or the wives of such.[48] Men and women who were judged to be 'of irregular behaviour', and who were 'unclean, and of a vagrant disposition',[49] were also assigned wards of their own. Mothers and their infants had a special ward, as did lying-in women. Boys and girls deemed capable of work were each assigned to separate wards, as were sick men and women.

From the ward assignments contained in the workhouse daybooks for the period from 1790 to 1815, it is apparent that these general divisions were already in existence in this earlier period, although perhaps not as rigorously enforced. In 1799, for example, a single ward had been appropriated for aged men and their wives. This kindness did not seem to survive the increasing concern for sexual segregation that characterized the 1820s, however.[50] In this latter decade, parish authorities tried to effect a complete separation of the sexes through construction of a wall in the yard and various 'internal alterations' within the house. The overseers hoped that these changes would have moral benefits, and they stated overtly that the changes were meant to classify and divide paupers. As well, the alterations were meant to achieve pecuniary benefits – the latter to be achieved by reducing the overall number of inmates.[51] Those whom officials regarded as feckless presumably would have been less inclined to enter this stricter workhouse, or so parish authorities apparently hoped. Previous to this change, however, it is clear that segregation, although the desideratum for administrators, was not completely successful, and that paupers were at times intermingling.[52]

Life in the workhouse was highly regimented, and became more so throughout the period. Generally speaking, there seems to have been a tightening up in workhouse practices from 1793 onward. Rising and retiring times were set, as were the hours of work and meal times. Menus, while more varied than those from some other workhouses, still featured a high degree of repetition. Liquor was strictly forbidden except for medicinal purposes, although by 1817 inmates could smoke in passages and on the grounds.[53] In 1795, after complaining that people under order of removal were escaping from the house, the overseers decided boys would no longer attend the doors. Instead, a new door porter was hired. Inmates stealing provisions were to be compelled to live off the same until the goods were used up. It was in this year that the parish began to send the most obstreperous of those deemed insane to a private madhouse. In 1796 cleanliness became an issue: a reception place for cleaning new inmates and their clothing was set up, although the fact that this order was repeated in 1805 raises doubts concerning its effective enforcement. The distribution of gin to the sick was also more closely monitored. In 1798 the lower shed was converted to the penitentiary. Two years later, a twenty-four-hour advance application for liberty of the gate was introduced, and it was decided inmates would not be supplied with food during the day of their leave. In 1801 there was a move to control the supply of sheets, seemingly to cut theft rates. In 1805 inmates were made to wear special clothing marked with the parish name, which almost certainly would have been recognizable should the pauper have ventured into the community at large. Their own clothing was cleaned and set aside to be returned upon release, unless they remained longer than twelve months, in which case the clothing was used for others.[54] Blue and yellow dresses were introduced for women who were pregnant with or the mothers of illegitimate children,[55] and refractory individuals wore special badges and dresses.[56] In 1805 the baths were to be better maintained, and a reallocation of wards was carried out.[57] Stricter rules governing the whereabouts of inmates during the day – they were not allowed to remain in their wards – were brought into effect, and once more new door porters were hired, again seemingly to cut down on absenteeism.[58] By 1812 all articles belonging to the parish were being stamped, although the repetition of this order in 1817 would again seem to call into question the efficacy of the first order.

Visits by outsiders were also strictly regulated, and in the case of women pregnant out of wedlock, forbidden. Visitors had to have a churchwarden's prior approval, and by 1811 were limited to Tuesdays and Thursdays. By 1817 visitors were searched upon entering and leaving the workhouse.[59] Inmates were allowed out into the community at specified times, but this freedom was again hedged about by many restrictions. In the early 1790s paupers were allowed out every other Thursday.[60] By 1828 men and women were no longer allowed the 'liberty of the gate', as it was termed, at the same time.[61] Moreover, inmates had to have been in the house for three months before they could even apply to go out.[62] No woman bringing an illegitimate child into the house could go out without her offspring, until she had been in the house at least a year.[63] Heads of families with children in the house, whether male or female, had to have special permission before they were permitted to go out. All those who were allowed out required a signed pass, and those who returned after the hour specified, or who had been drinking, were subject to discipline.

Other punishments were imposed on malefactors against house rules or the standards of morality, and these normally took the form of a stoppage of pay for work performed, the stoppage of rations, the refusal of liberty of the gate, or commitment to the penitentiary. Unlike some parishes, however, St Martin's did not seem to allow corporal punishment.[64] In more serious cases, inmates were committed by a magistrate to Bridewell. Since magistrates could not always be depended upon to side with parish officials, however, the parish, like a number of others, began in 1816 to send inmates it deemed refractory or difficult to John Sutton's City Farm in Islington.[65] By 1821 children were being sent to the infant poor house that the parish established at Highwood Hill, and inmates judged insane and obstreperous were sent to Mr Warburton's Private Madhouse in Bethnal Green. These external, special-purpose institutions served to intensify the segregation process even further, and no doubt had an impact on the numbers of paupers to be found in the workhouse.

These strict and unvarying routines must surely have been tedious to the inmates subjected to them. As well as stultifying boredom, however, these regulations made it difficult to escape the poor relief system. Household goods as well as clothing had to be delivered up to parish authorities when paupers were admitted to the workhouse.[66] Aside from reinforcing the dependence on pawning – if the goods were going to be forfeited anyway, one might as well have the pledge money as nothing – this practice, if strictly implemented, also meant that those leaving the workhouse would be trying to set up a household virtually from scratch. It is unclear from these records whether goods were regularly returned. Workhouse assistance had never fit easily into the economy of make-shifts, but from the 1790s onward became even more difficult to accommodate.

In theory, however, there was an opportunity to gather a nest egg against leaving the institution. St Martin's officials demanded that inmates work, and refusal to do so could result in a trip to Bridewell. The pay scale was very low – most kinds of work paid 1*s*. or less a week, much lower than wage levels for comparable work in the community at large. In 1797 Eden described the principal pauper employments in the St Martin's workhouse as 'spinning flax, picking hair, carding wool, etc.',[67] which was still the case in 1817.[68] Inmates were also paid to perform virtually all manner of domestic work – laundry, sewing, portering, plastering, for example – in order to keep the house functioning. Given the very meagre pay levels, it would have taken a long time for inmates to accumulate enough money truly to be helpful in the readjustment to life in the community. It is apparent that the notion of less eligibility underlay practices in the St Martin's workhouse in a period when women and unskilled men could typically expect to earn 6*s*. and 10*s*. respectively. Moreover, the very idea that inmates would have been inclined to save for future needs in the first place may have been unrealistic, for, as has been seen, the focus of plebeian Londoners tended to be very short-term, concentrating on immediate needs. As noted earlier, the parish also sought to ease the transition back into the community by paying the inmate a small pension – usually a shilling or two a week for a month after discharge. Clearly, while a help, pensions were of little use if not supplemented by wages almost immediately. In recognition of this fact, the parish authorities (especially towards the end of the period) sometimes allowed inmates liberty of the gate during their last week in the house in order that they could look for work. While undoubtedly helpful when it was allowed (the reasons particular individuals were granted this privilege are unclear), it was certainly no guarantee that solvency could be regained.

Finally, if the confiscation of goods, minuscule levels of pay and inadequate pensions weren't sufficiently large obstacles to the recovery of financial independence, workhouse readmission policies made the decision to leave – and an inmate was free to do so at any time – even more risky. The threat noted above was part of a deliberate policy to discourage readmission. In 1817 the Standing Orders stated 'That any Pauper returning to the House after having been Discharged unless from Sickness, shall not be allowed any Pay for their work for Two Months after their Readmission'.[69] While intended to discourage readmissions, this provision, coupled with the three-month detention period upon admission, meant that the workhouse was becoming more rigid when, as has been seen, flexibility and the ability to juggle a number of short-term resources were the most successful coping strategies for many people at this time.

At times the overseers' minutes do seem to indicate a willingness on the part of parish authorities to allow the poor some flexibility in their use of the house.

In forty-five cases, officials allowed people to admit sick or vulnerable family members to the house while staying out themselves, to continue to work to support themselves or the rest of the family. The price the parish charged for doing so, however, was steep: in thirty-two instances the parish imposed a weekly charge of 3 to 5s. The weekly charge was cheaper than this in only four cases, but more expensive in nine others. These fees would have been beyond most families turning to workhouse assistance – and indeed in two cases the parish was forced to waive them for periods of time. It is difficult not to conclude either that these fees were meant to dissuade the poor from this strategy, or that more affluent families were using the house in this flexible manner. If the latter, then clearly workhouse assistance was not always seen as being irredeemably shameful. Poorer families undoubtedly also used the house in this way, but either officials did not impose fees, or such families hid what they were about. Throughout this period, then, the parish tightened discipline within the workhouse and segmented and segregated the pauper population, although it seems clear that officials were not always able to implement the new regulations to their complete satisfaction, as the repetition of orders and the hiring of new staff would seem to indicate. Green states that stricter relief practices in London dated from the 1820s, but in the case of St Martin's the process began considerably earlier in the 1790s.[70]

The overall purpose parish officials hoped to achieve with the institutional regime of the workhouse was never explicitly stated, but seems to have been twofold. First, there was an increasing concern with the moral state of the inmates, and rules were continually introduced or tightened up in order to isolate those considered depraved and to inculcate 'proper behaviour'. Warding policies, limits on visitors, sexual segregation and the insistence on work all served these functions – though to be sure the line between reforming and controlling behaviour was not always clearly drawn. In the second instance, there was also an abiding concern to keep relief costs down. Sporadic protests by parishioners against high costs undoubtedly helped keep this concern prominent on St Martin's agenda. The various rules meant to protect parish property and to make the house unattractive to those regarded as feckless helped serve this purpose, as did the discouragement of repeat entrants. While some regulations like the insistence on productive work clearly served both purposes, these two aims did not always run in tandem. Indeed, the balance the parish tried to strike between the two often seemed to result in a kind of holding action: rules were passed, but not always strictly enforced – likely because of the expense – and this was especially so in the early years of the period. A second factor mitigating against efficient enforcement of the new regulations was the recurring problems the workhouse had with its staff. A new taskmaster was appointed on 27 August 1794, another on 4 November 1795, and a third on 19 October 1796, who was subsequently dismissed less than a year later on 14 June 1797. No reasons were given for this high turnover. On 22 October 1794 the nurse of two wards for disreputable women was let go for selling liquor. On 23 August 1797 the matron was dismissed for 'improper conduct' which was not further explained. The baker was dismissed on 15 November of the same year for selling bread. On 2 September 1801 the overseers threatened the ward nurses (who were inmates) with fourteen days in the penitentiary if they took money or gratuities from inmates or their visitors. The beer provisioner was suspended on 26 October 1803 on suspicion of buying soap from an inmate. On 10 September 1812 the baker was dismissed over unspecified allegations, while on 13 September 1816 the surgeon-apothecary was let go for 'acting in a very unfeeling manner' towards a female inmate.[71] Employee recalcitrance would certainly have made the enforcement of the stricter rules more difficult, to say the least.

The workhouse population, upon whom these strictures were imposed, was a large one. The identity of the inmate population can be gleaned from the admission and discharge records that are contained in the workhouse daybooks,[72] where officials recorded the name and age of the person to be admitted. The number of times applicants had been in the house, the wards to which they were assigned, and by whose order admission was granted were also listed. Finally, family members were shown as a group. On the discharge pages, names and the reasons for leaving were given, as were the wards from which people came. Ages were recorded somewhat haphazardly until 1800, when this information was routinely provided. Throughout the period, admission and discharge entries were grouped into two-week segments – that is, from board meeting to board meeting, at which time a summary of admission and discharge activity was recorded.

Crude admission figures, uncorrected for repeat entrants within the year, reveal a number of patterns concerning the composition of the workhouse population (see Table 4.1). Some were to be expected: during the war years the number of adult males in the house was depressed. Enlistment, plus the high demand for war work in a number of trades like tailoring, made the need for poor relief less pressing for many men. Nor was the St Martin's workhouse chiefly the abode of children, the elderly and the sick, as was the case by the 1860s.[73] In this decade, the *Lancet* indicated that the workhouse population 'really consists almost entirely of diseased or infirm persons who require more or less of medical attendance'.[74] In the earlier period children constituted less than a third of the house population, 23 per cent between 1790 and 1794, and 30 per cent between 1815 and 1819. The elderly (anyone sixty or older) made up an even smaller group in the workhouse: 12 per cent in both runs of years. Among adults, women far outnumbered men in the workhouse admissions records. Indeed, they always formed at least 60 per cent, and frequently two-thirds, of the adult admissions, and this was so even in 1815, when demobilized soldiers began to swell the male ranks. Women aged sixteen to forty-four were especially prominent. In the early nineties they constituted 44 per cent of adults in the house, while men in their age group made up only 14 per cent. In the period from 1815 onward, women in this age group still accounted for 38 per cent of house adults, while men sixteen to forty-four formed 20 per cent. Clearly, women were more likely to fall into destitution at a younger age than their male counterparts. Given what has been said about the impact of downturns in the economy and life cycle constraints, the predominance of younger women in the house is not surprising. While there have been debates concerning the nature of poverty – whether life cycle pressures or endemic employment problems were at its heart – these factors often acted in concert in the lives of the poor, and the combination regularly tumbled people into destitution, and from there into the workhouse.[75]

Illness and injury were other factors that led many people to seek poor relief, which is apparent from the workhouse admission records. Throughout the period, the sick or injured constituted between 20 and 30 per cent of adult admissions, and in six of the nine years examined, made up at least a quarter of the adult admissions. A far greater percentage of adult male admissions was due to illness or injury than was the case for women. The average for the nine years was 39 per cent for adult male admissions and 21 per cent for adult female. While male admissions were almost twice as likely to be for illness or injury than were female, women were more likely to become ill or injured at a younger age than were men. Fifty-three per cent of the male admissions for illness or injury were for men aged sixteen to forty-four; the comparable figure for women was 64 per cent, possibly due to complications from childbirth. This was also a very difficult stage in the life cycle, when the presence of young children meant that families frequently had great difficulty in making ends meet. Within these families, moreover, food was more likely to be disproportionately allocated to the highest wage earner, the husband, and to the children, which would undoubtedly have helped make younger women more vulnerable to illness.

Years of dearth, difficult stages in the life cycle, and illness and injury all led many men and women to turn to the workhouse, and would seem to indicate that vulnerability rather than degeneration lay behind the decision to enter the house for many, if not most, inmates. The question remains, however, whether this was the case for high-repeat entrants to the house. People who had entered the workhouse numerous times throughout their lives were often regarded with great suspicion by poor relief officials. The workhouse, for these inmates, was an ongoing resource in their battle to make ends meet, so they were, seemingly, the individuals most in need of moral reform. The first thing to note about them, however, is the fact that they weren't very numerous. In all, between 1790 and 1794, 119 women and seventeen men had been in the workhouse ten times or more. To put this in context, during these five years the St Martin's workhouse daybooks record 3,988 adult admissions. About 15 per cent of the adult admissions would have been people who entered more than once during the period, so the high-repeat entrants typically constituted roughly 4 per cent of adult inmates admitted to the house during these years. Clearly, the fears of pro-abolitionist commentators that poor relief led to the widespread demoralization of recipients do not seem to be borne out by the low numbers of high-repeat entrants.

One of the most obvious characteristics of the high-repeat entrants was the gender imbalance: they were overwhelmingly female (see Table 4.2). The number of men may have been artificially low due to the outbreak of war in early 1793, although the number of such men in the period from 1815 to 1819 was only a little higher at twenty-two. Women constituted 88 per cent of the high repeaters between 1790 and 1794. The gendered disparity parallels in a more extreme form that for all inmates of the workhouse: as noted earlier, on average women formed 60 to 66 per cent of the adult population of the house. The disparity in numbers between the sexes of high repeaters bespeaks the greater difficulties women faced in making ends meet, which is apparent in a number of ways. In the first place, the high-repeat women found it difficult to maintain subsistence from an early period in their lives. Exactly two-thirds of these women first entered the workhouse between the ages of sixteen and forty-four; they were women in their prime. Only 10 per cent of the high-repeat women first entered the workhouse in old age (defined as sixty years or older). For the men, on the other hand, difficulties tended to come later in life. Only slightly more than one-third of these men entered the house for the first time between the ages of sixteen and forty-four – half the rate for the women. Just under two-thirds of the men entered the workhouse for the first time when in their fifties or older, a point by which time prime employment years were behind most of them. Moreover, on average, the high-repeat women entered the house seventeen times, while for men the average was thirteen admissions. If dying in the workhouse is taken as a measure of failure to escape from the poor law system, then the differences between the sexes for these high-repeat entrants all but disappear: 66 per cent of high-repeat women died in the house, while 65 per cent of the high-repeat men did so. These women and men may have begun their workhouse careers at different points in the life cycle, but both sexes seemed to have great difficulty, for whatever reason, in escaping the need for poor relief.

Table 4.2: St Martin in the Fields workhouse high-repeat entrants.

	16–44	Young/ Middle*	45–59	Young/ Old†	Middle/ Old‡	60+	TOTAL
MEN 1790–4	4 (24%)	2 (12%)	4 (24%)	0	3 (18%)	4 (24%)	17
MEN 1815–19	9 (41%)	6 (27%)	0	2 (9%)	3 (14%)	2 (9%)	22
WOMEN 1790–4	35 (29%)	28 (24%)	6 (5%)	16 (13%)	22 (18%)	12 (10%)	119
WOMEN 1815–19	11 (24%)	11 (24%)	3 (7%)	4 (9%)	11 (24%)	5 (11%)	45

*   Young/Middle = men and women who first entered the workhouse when they were 16
     to 44 and continued to enter when they were 45–59.
†   Young/Old = men and women who first entered the workhouse when they were 16 to 44
     and continued to enter when they were 60+.
‡   Middle/Old = men and women who first entered the workhouse when they were 45–59
     and continued to enter when they were 60+.

In examining the admission and discharge records for these people, a number
of reasons for their persistent recourse to the workhouse and the different age
patterns of the men and women become apparent. First of all there was illness,
which, unlike death in the workhouse, did exhibit gender-specific patterns.
Seven, or 40 per cent, of the seventeen men had been placed in a sick ward at least
five times, which may well have been indicative of long-term health problems or
injury at work. For the women, the percentage was much lower, 5 per cent, or
six of the 119 female high repeaters. Since no one who entered the house repeatedly was sick all of the time, the overall number of admissions was also tallied
up from all of these individuals. In all, the 119 women entered the house 1,987
times. On 191 occasions, admission was to a sick ward, constituting 10 per cent
of the female entries. For the men, there were 228 admissions in all, of which
fifty-seven, or 25 per cent, were to sick wards. Clearly, illness or injury were much
greater factors causing men to enter the house repeatedly. Given that so many of
the male trades common in London during this period required heavy labour,
men were likely more prone to work-related injury and illness.

A major factor causing women to enter the workhouse repeatedly, and to
do so from a younger age than men, concerned children. In the event of marital break-up, the records show that women were almost invariably responsible
for their offspring. In the overall workhouse population, 90 per cent of single
parents during these years were female. Again, in the general house population,
about 6 per cent of women gave birth while inmates. For the female high-repeat
entrants, the patterns differed somewhat, however. Twenty-five of the 119 high-
repeat women – 21 per cent – gave birth a total of forty times in the house;
three women were pregnant three times; ten more gave birth two times. The
median length of time between entering the workhouse and giving birth was
two months, indicating that these women needed workhouse assistance well
before their confinements. If the high-repeat entrants made much greater use of

the workhouse in order to give birth, the situation was otherwise once children had been born. Where in the overall female population of the workhouse, nearly 24 per cent of women entered with children, only 3 per cent did so from the high-repeat group. Clearly, these women had far fewer children with them than was the case for the female house population generally, and the reasons seem grim. Of the forty children born to the high repeaters in the workhouse, five were stillborn and another twenty-one died. Only one of those who died lived long enough to see his first birthday. Yet another seven children simply disappeared from the records, possibly dying outside the house, or hopefully being cared for by others. Five more of these women were able to leave their children in the house so that the latter could be sent to the nurses in the countryside whom St Martin's employed. Why these few women were allowed to do this, when generally the parish was very suspicious of parents leaving their children in the house, was not explained. In one case, however, there was a notation in the settlement exam that Mary Stanley 'voluntarily deserted' her child 'in order to provide for herself', and it may be that the other four women did this as well.[76] High-repeat mothers, then, were far more likely to enter the house to give birth than was the case for the general female workhouse population, but conversely, were much less likely to be accompanied by children, since most of the latter disappeared within a year or so of their births.

If motherhood was a fairly fraught experience for the high repeaters, another serious problem was that of being a woman alone. Marital status was not regularly noted in the daybooks, so it is impossible to know with certainty the marital status of each woman. Nevertheless, fully eighty-three of the 119 high-repeat women – 70 per cent – always entered the workhouse alone throughout their inmate careers: they were never accompanied by spouse, children or other companions. These women also tended to have trouble making ends meet from an early age, although predictably not to the same extent as the mothers: 55 per cent (forty-six) of high-repeat women alone first entered the workhouse between the ages of sixteen and forty-four; 29 per cent (twenty-four) between forty-five and fifty-nine, and 17 per cent (fourteen) at age sixty or more. As already seen, women's trades in London suffered from low wages and a labour surplus,[77] and most women were employed in a narrow range of trades in service, the needle trades, laundry work and retail, which exacerbated the labour surplus. Typically, as seen, women earned only about 6s. a week during this period, a sum on which it would have been very difficult to live. Consequently, women needed a support system: a male breadwinner, family or friends in order to make ends meet. It is not surprising that women on their own would figure so prominently among the high repeaters.[78]

Overall, the high repeaters do seem to have been those who were most vulnerable: men who were more likely to be sick or injured than was the norm in the house, and who were edging past their prime employment years; women who were ill, pregnant or alone. In their general patterns, then, they did not differ markedly from the general workhouse population. From 1790 to 1794 sixteen of the seventeen high-repeat men were sick or injured at least once. Seven of the sixteen sick or injured men were placed in sick wards five times or more, and two more were so warded four times: more than half of the seventeen high-repeat men were sick repeatedly. Eleven of the seventeen – just under two-thirds – began entering the workhouse after age fifty, and four of these had dependants. Twelve of the high-repeat men subsequently died – seven of them were under sixty. It would seem, then, that much of the time genuine hardship caused these men to enter the workhouse repeatedly. For the high-repeat women during these years, 67 per cent (eighty) were admitted to sick wards at least once – 22 per cent of them were so warded at least three times. As seen, 26 per cent were pregnant or with children, and overall two-thirds of the high-repeat women began their workhouse careers at a younger age than men: two-thirds of these women entered the house between the ages of sixteen and forty-four. The group that was conspicuously low in numbers consisted of married women with their husbands present: there were only five such women. Of the 70 per cent of the women who always entered the house alone, three-fifths of them were entered into sick wards at least some of the time. Fifty-seven of the eighty-three women alone subsequently died, although the reasons cannot be known from these sources. Thus, much of the time, the high-repeat women seem to have entered the house from dire necessity rather than fecklessness.

Nor did this situation change during the period between 1815 and 1819. Many of these patterns are also apparent in the biographies of high repeaters between 1815 and 1819, but in attenuated form, since workhouse usage cannot be traced after 1820. In this period 45 per cent (ten) of the twenty-two high-repeat men were entered into sick wards at least once. Three of the ten had family with them; two subsequently died. Another two were more than fifty years old, and two were sent to madhouses, indicating ongoing difficulty. Aside from the ten men sent to sick wards, two more died and two more were elderly. Thus, fourteen of the twenty-two – 64 per cent – had plausible need at least some of the time. While this is lower than was the case for the 1790–4 cohort, had it been possible to trace their careers beyond 1820, the overall percentage would no doubt have been higher. Among the women, 33 per cent (fifteen) were ill or injured at least once, and 22 per cent were so three or more times. Twenty per cent of these women were pregnant (eight) or had a child but no male partner (one). Sixty-two per cent (twenty-eight) were always alone: fifteen of them were sick or injured at least once and six of them subsequently died. While the general contours were similar, there was, however, one significant difference with respect to high-repeat women. There were substantially fewer of them between 1815 and 1819: forty-five as opposed to 119 between 1790 and 1794, that is, 67 per cent of the overall number of high repeaters compared to 88 per cent in the earlier period. This fall in the number of inmates using the house at least ten times or more was not reflected in the statistics for men. As noted earlier, there were twenty-two adult male high repeaters during this five-year period, up slightly from the seventeen between 1790 and 1794, likely resulting from the demobilization of servicemen plus the falling off of war work. Why, then, was there such a noticeable drop in the number of high-repeat women? As seen earlier, things did not become easier economically for the London poor during these years, so it is very unlikely that fewer women were becoming high-repeat entrants because they were better off. Rather, the drop likely resulted in large measure from the actions of parish officers. Women, having the fewest resources, and being the most economically vulnerable, had the greatest need for the flexible deployment of resources, and consequently, they would have been particularly sensitive to changes in the institutional regime of an important resource like the workhouse. While the increasing rigidity of the workhouse regime, the ongoing search for employees willing to implement the new rules, and continuous attempts to isolate inmates more effectively likely made the workhouse a less attractive resource for all inmates, some of the changes had a disproportionate impact on women. Given that women sixteen to forty-four were especially prominent in the house, and that mothers almost always became responsible for the children, regulations targeting single mothers (the special dresses, the circumscribed liberty), single pregnant women (the prohibition on visitors), mothers whose partners were dead or absent, and mothers generally (the inability to leave the house without the children in the first year of residence) would have affected a large percentage of female inmates and made it more difficult to regain financial independence even temporarily.

Equally, the use of Sutton's City Farm in Islington from 1816 onward may well have played a crucial role in this diminution in female high-repeat numbers. Elaine Murphy has described city farms as 'open-door Bridewells' whose role was to 'mop up the misfits, the ungrateful and the undesirable' among workhouse populations.[79] City farms were also disparaged by contemporaries. The report for the Select Committee on the State of Mendicity in the Metropolis in 1816 described at least some of them as being 'much crowded and extremely filthy; nine, and ten, and eleven persons in a room; no space in the rooms when the beds were let down'.[80] At some houses, inmates were frequently hungry and sometimes cold. Whether the arrangements at Sutton's were this bad is unclear, but it is doubtful that conditions at a for-profit institution exceeded or even matched those obtaining at the parish workhouse. It is clear, however, that as was the case at Robertson's, one of the largest city farms, inmates at Islington were never allowed outside the institution. In March 1819 John Hibbert, an unemployed pauper from St Bartholomew the Great, summoned the parish officers for refusing him assistance. The beadle explained that Hibbert had been sent to

Sutton's, and after a time discharged himself, but was free to return. Hibbert in turn explained to the Guildhall court that he had no wish to be a burden on the parish 'if he could get employ; but that was quite out of the question if he went back to Mr. Sutton's; for there he was locked up from week's end to week's end and never permitted to go out to look for work'.[81] In this instance, the presiding magistrate sided firmly with Hibbert, summoning the overseers and Sutton to explain themselves. Workhouse inmates had good reason to resent and dislike incarceration at Islington, since they became trapped in the system.

Moreover, it must have been apparent to high-repeat entrants that their chances of being sent to the city farm were good, especially for women. While the number of commitments to Bridewell remained virtually unchanged, orders for the city farm rose dramatically. In all, seventy-one people were sent to the city farm between 1815 and 1819, forty-three men and twenty-eight women. While nine, or 21 per cent, of the forty-three men sent to Islington were high repeaters, ten, or more than 36 per cent, of the twenty-eight women were. Moreover, 40 per cent of the men sent to the city farm had been in the house five or more times, while 57 per cent of the women had. Clearly, the female city farm population was drawn disproportionately from repeaters and high repeaters. The anger and resentment felt towards the city farm surfaced occasionally in the daybooks. On 21 November 1820 John Erdwein, a young man of nineteen, who became a high repeater in the years following 1820, was given an order for the city farm by the board of overseers. He had previously been sent to Islington a year earlier. When leaving the house for this second tour, Erdwein tore up the order 'and threw it at the lower Porter swearing he would not go to Islington'.[82] The year before, in 1819, Eliza Johnson's protests had been more harrowing. She too became a high repeater in the years after 1820, and had also experienced the Islington regime once previously. According to the *Morning Chronicle*, on Christmas Eve morning house authorities gave her an order to be admitted to Islington, plus half-a-crown for transportation. In the evening Johnson returned to the workhouse claiming she had lost the order. Another was given to her, 'but she refused to go except a coach was provided for her, when it was ascertained that she had spent a great part of the half-crown in liquor'. According to parish officers, she became abusive and caused a disturbance, the latest in a long catalogue of such behaviour. Consequently, on Christmas Day Johnson was sent to the Public Office in Bow Street in order to be committed to Bridewell. While being held in the Public Office, she apparently gave way to despair. According to the newspaper, between 7 and 8 pm, the gaoler heard a gurgling noise and

> went into the room where she was, but found great difficulty in opening the door, arising from the woman's body hanging against it; the force he used, caused the knot to slip with which she had tied herself up to one of the iron rails of the window with her shawl, and she fell upon him and knocked him down under her. She had tied her

apron around her face, which had become completely black. A surgeon was sent for, who after a considerable time, recovered her. She was then conveyed in a hackney-coach to St Martin's workhouse, and put into a warm bed.[83]

Johnson continued to be troublesome to house authorities upon her subsequent admissions, and she may well have been an alcoholic. Aside from her Christmas drinking bout, she was brought into the house from the street twice in a state of intoxication. Johnson had been sent to Islington once before Christmas 1819, in June of that year, and had discharged herself after only one day. Although parish officers once more sent her to Bridewell in July 1822 for 'Outrageous and Violent Behaviour in this House', they never again attempted to send her to Islington. Clearly, if it was hard for paupers to use the workhouse flexibly in their battle to maintain subsistence, it was that much more difficult to use the city farm in this way.

It seems apparent that much of the time compelling need rather than feck-lessness drove the high repeaters to enter and re-enter the workhouse. They did not bear out claims for widespread degeneracy among the house population, but were rather only a small minority of workhouse inmates. Moreover, while the general tightening of regulations affected all adult inmates, the new rules concerning parenthood, especially of unaccompanied mothers, plus the greater likelihood that high-repeat women would be sent to Islington, meant that the regime was becoming particularly restrictive for women in their prime. Increas-ingly, it was difficult for women in the workhouse to learn in a timely fashion of work or the availability of other resources that might have permitted them to regain financial independence. Nor should the falling numbers of female high repeaters be seen as an indication that inmates were embracing the moral reformation so desired by authorities. Rather, there is recurring evidence that a number of house inmates, and not just high-repeat users, resisted the regime being imposed upon them, and sought instead to manipulate the poor relief sys-tem in order to gain the most advantage from it and to bend it to their needs: they were not simply passive recipients of this assistance.

This can be seen at a number of points in the relief cycle, beginning with the decision to seek this assistance in the first place. In the examination book of 1786, parish officials of St Clement Danes recorded the case of a young Irish prostitute from Jackson's Alley in Drury Lane ward. This area, on the border of St Martin's, was a neighbourhood that many prostitutes called home. Mary Brown had lived in a lodging house belonging to a Mrs Davies, who was well aware of the occupa-tion of a number of her female tenants. When Brown, who was pregnant, went into labour, Mrs Davies refused to let her remain, and recommended she go to the workhouse. When Brown pointed out she had no settlement, a conference ensued: 'Mrs. Davies ... said to the several persons about her – "We must send her to some parish, which is the Casualty Parish, send her there" ... she was answered by some of them "St Martin's." "No, no" said she, "Saint Clements's is the best casualty parish. Send her there.'"[84] Brown accepted this advice, and with the help of another young woman, concocted a story that they had lived in Greyhound Court, making her perhaps eligible for assistance. For whatever reason, the parish authorities refused to give Brown an admitting order, and the truth eventually came out. What is of interest here is not just the lie in the attempt to establish a fictitious claim, but the cool-headed assessment by Davies and company of the relative merits – that is, generosity – of the various parishes.[85]

Other women sought to gain entry to the workhouse by feigning labour. Martha Tuningley, Ann Walker and Charlotte Shrieve all claimed to be in this condition when they were admitted to the St Martin's workhouse. Indignant parish authorities recorded that their children were not born until one month, one week, and nearly two months later respectively.[86] Whether the deception resulted from moral turpitude or simply from desperate need cannot be known. Jacob Burgess had a certain éclat in his dealings with house officials. Time and again he was admitted, with variations of the phrase 'a notorious imposter' affixed to his record. In August 1805 he arrived at the house under the name of John Jones 'in a hackney coach having feigned himself ill'.[87] This kind of manipulation was not simply limited to the gaining of admission, however. Once in the house, a number of inmates sought to gain whatever advantage they could from their situation, as the overseers' minutes attest.

In 1800 Mary Downing was confined in the house penitentiary with Elizabeth Philpott for pawning house sheets and carrying away bread. Mary Chandler, in the same year, was ordered to leave the workhouse by parish authorities. She had robbed her ward of, and pledged, two sheets and a flat iron; and she had stolen a shift and a cloak from a fellow inmate.[88] In 1804 Elizabeth Stewart was taken before the magistrates at Queen's Square for pawning sheets.[89] Isabella Lidler (or Littler) was sent to Bridewell for one month in 1813 for stealing horsehair from the house.[90] In 1815 an irritated parish official recorded in the admissions register that Philip Ferguson 'has had three new shirts given him this year by the house (January 28, April 10, May 1) and has made away with them all and come in without any linen to his back'.[91] Perhaps the most notorious case that came to light, however, was that of Samuel Glasby (or Glazeby). In 1795 he was brought before the magistrates at Bow Street for stealing two sheets. According to the *Star* newspaper,

> It appeared in the course of the examination that the prisoner had long acted as a pawnbroker to the poor house, receiving the most trifling pledges from his companions, to receive and keep which in regular order, he had taken a lodging in the neighbourhood which he had converted into a warehouse. Notes and property, to a considerable amount, were found in his trunk at his lodgings the whole of which he is supposed to have scraped together in the above manner.[92]

According to the *Sun*, the property found in his lodging was worth £130.[93] If all of his goods came from the workhouse, this would certainly bespeak widespread theft by inmates or staff. Not surprisingly, workhouse officials insisted Glasby wear a badge identifying him as troublesome when he was readmitted to the house the following year.

The workhouse repeatedly had difficulty with employees, both pauper and non-pauper. In 1797 the man who looked after the 'mad ward' in the house – identified as Robinson in the overseers' minutes, and Robins in the press – was charged with purloining the provisions intended for the inmates of his ward. He was arrested in a house in Orange Court, where he had gone to sell the goods. According to press reports of another case, workhouse authorities were greatly puzzled by an apparent pudding heist in 1832. It was house practice to prepare suet puddings for Saturday dinner, and carefully to monitor their preparation by kitchen staff – composed of pauper and non-pauper workers – in order to prevent depredations. Once in their pans, the puddings were counted and then sent off to a baker's to be cooked. When Henry Williams, James Burgess and William Crooks – 'three ragged and hungry-looking "Casuals" of St Martin-in-the-Fields parish' – were spotted lurking in St Martin's Lane by a police constable, he stopped and searched them. He found a pudding on Williams, which, it was clear to workhouse officials, was one of theirs. The difficulty was that the parish had sent forty-one carefully counted puddings to the baker and received forty-one back: this was a forty-second. Officials were perplexed, until someone thought to weigh the puddings. Each of the forty-one was slightly underweight sufficient to create a forty-second. Clearly, there had been collusion between the kitchen workers in the house and the three men receiving the forty-second pudding.[94]

It is apparent that some inmates seeking admission, and some within the workhouse, were clearly manipulating or taking advantage of the system, although their motivation for doing so cannot be known. Equally apparent is their refusal of the moral reform being demanded of them by house officials. Sometimes, as Green has noted, inmate misbehaviour was not simply meant 'to squeeze more relief from ungenerous officials'. It could often involve 'symbolic forms of protest based on concepts of respectability and self esteem in the face of institutional efforts to shape the paupers' character and mould their social relations'.[95] While Green was undoubtedly correct to claim this, paupers could also attack the respectability of the house itself. In February 1817, for example, the overseers ordered John Coleman to spend twenty-four hours in the penitentiary 'for making an unfounded report (to whom was not indicated) that John Williams, a man of colour, who lately died in the house was Murdered'.[96] Paupers could also express sympathy for political views which house authorities found unacceptable. After the 15 November Spa Fields meeting in 1816 agitating for electoral reform and relief from the distress of this difficult year, part of the crowd moved through the neighbourhood near the St Martin's work-house, attacking several bakers' shops. When the crowd turned up Hemming's Row, several newspapers claimed that 'they were greeted by the old women in St Martin's work-house. The old ladies, looking eagerly through the [unclear] rail, and exclaiming – "Good luck to you my boys! Good luck to you! – Go it! Go it!"'[97] The overseers spotted the press coverage and launched enquiries. For whatever reason, the only person they could identify was Rebecca Zimmerman, a forty-year-old inmate who was employed in one of the many jobs in the house. Zimmerman had first entered the workhouse in 1813, with two children but no male partner. Her eldest child, Charlotte, died at age twelve the following year, and her illness may have been the factor that had tipped the family into des-titution. Noting that Zimmerman had confessed before 'several of the officers' – one can only speculate about the circumstances of the interview – the overse-ers decided that having 'encouraged the mob in a course of riotous proceedings', she 'be Dismissed from her Situation, and further that she be taken before a Magistrate for such Misbehaviour'.[98] Nothing seemed to have come of the last threat, and possibly as a consequence, the only further punishment available to the overseers was to order the immediate discharge from the house of Zimmer-man and her remaining child, which they did on 20 November.

Another way in which inmates resisted the ever stricter workhouse regime was in the decision to absent themselves. The decision to leave without the per-mission of workhouse authorities was often in the interest of both those who regularly depended on poor relief and were unlikely to achieve long-term sub-sistence without it, and those who were seeking to reclaim their place in the plebeian community. Table 4.3 shows adult absenters for the years 1790 to 1794 and 1815 to 1819. At first glance, the decision to absent themselves seems a puz-zling way to behave, since inmates were free to discharge themselves at any time (with the authorities' approval, of course). One reason that presents itself almost immediately, and that may have influenced the decision to absent whether or not inmates were trying to reclaim their place in the community, was fear. In some cases, inmates were absenting themselves in order to prevent their being removed to other parishes. This was apparent from the parish complaint in 1795 that sev-eral people under order of removal had escaped from the house.[99] This had been a problem in earlier years as well. In 1790, for instance, an order of 26 November instructed that Richard Turner and his wife and four children be removed. Four days later, before the order could be effected, Turner absented himself, abandon-ing his family to its fate.[100]

Table 4.3: St Martin in the Fields workhouse absenters.

	16–44	45–59	60+	NO AGE	TOTAL
MEN 1790–4					
All absenters	57	35	26	1	119
Non-returners	33	21	8	0	62 (52%)*
MEN 1815–19					
All absenters	48	31	19	0	98
Non-returners	10	7	2	0	19 (19%)*
WOMEN 1790–4					
All absenters	231	82	30	0	343
Non-returners	113	25	7	0	145 (42%)*
WOMEN 1815–19					
All absenters	48	27	22	0	97
Non-returners	10	3	1	0	14 (14%)*

*   The non-returners as a percentage of all absenters in each category.

There were, however, reasons other than fear that helped account for the decision to absent oneself. In the first place, it was difficult to get a legitimate short-term leave from the house.[101] Other absenters may simply have wanted a break – the equivalent of the modern joy ride. Between 1815 and 1819, for example, 30 per cent of people absenting themselves returned within twenty-four hours. The admission records contain a few references to people returning to the house intoxicated after a short time outside: Mary Christie, after a two-day foray in 1790, and Hannah Sitch, after four days in 1800, both returned in this condition. Whatever this says about their moral state – and the workhouse officials thought it said a lot – it was not behaviour conducive to re-attaining financial independence.

A sizable number of inmates absenting themselves did manage to stay out of the workhouse; some disappeared permanently, while others were able to cope in the community for one or more years without entering the house again. In the period from 1790 to 1794 there were 462 instances of absenting – just under 12 per cent of the 3,988 adult admissions during these years. Of the 119 adult male absenters, just over half – sixty-two, or 52 per cent – did not return to the house within a calendar year. For the 343 absenting women, the non-returning figure was 145, or 42 per cent. The absenters who did not return to the house also tended to be young. Well over three-quarters of these women were aged sixteen to forty-four, and more than half of the men fell into this age bracket. Another 17 per cent of the women and 34 per cent of the men were forty-five to fifty-nine. Given that women aged sixteen to forty-four formed a disproportionately large percentage of the workhouse population, their dominance among non-returning absenters is not surprising. Nor is it to be wondered at that proportionally more men were able to remain outside the house, since male wages were substantially higher than female and more trades were open to men. It is apparent that those with the best chance of regaining paid employment obviously were the most likely to be able to cope in the community for long periods, and were also the most likely to exercise agency through absenting.

A number of these patterns changed significantly in the period from 1815 to 1819. Most notably, there were far fewer absenters overall. Where in the first half of the nineties the 462 absenters had constituted just under 12 per cent of the adult admissions, in this second period the 195 absenters made up slightly less than 5 per cent of the 4,040 admissions. While the non-returners still tended to be young, their numbers fell sharply from 207 in the nineties – sixty-two men and 145 women – to thirty-three in the second period – nineteen men and fourteen women. The reasons for this decline were probably several. In the years from 1790 to 1794, house officials seem to have been fairly assiduous in noting whether the inmate had the right to assistance in St Martin's: 15 per cent on non-return absenters had no such right. In the second period, house authorities did not note this distinction, so it is unclear whether the numbers of those with no settlement increased, and consequently whether fears of being passed or removed might have played a bigger role in the decision to absent. One crucial difference between the two periods was the use of the city farm, which may well have siphoned off the more independently minded inmates most likely to leave of their own accord, or deterred others from entering the house at all. Finally, the continual tightening of house regulations throughout the period undoubtedly made it more difficult for inmates physically to escape the house.

The various kinds of resistance deployed by St Martin's pauper inmates do not seem to indicate that they had accepted the new notions of poor relief as a privilege rather than a right. Admittedly, the settlement and workhouse daybook records cannot prove this conclusively, but evidence a number of historians have drawn from pauper letters written to officials in distant home parishes has shown that in the 1820s and 1830s, poor relief was still regarded as a right.[102] The evidence for the St Martin's inmates seems to be of a piece with these findings. The various changes in the workhouse regime did encourage inmates to be independent, or at least not to apply for poor relief, but they did not effect the moral transformation so earnestly desired by middle- and upper-class commentators and officials. Rather, the growing inability to accommodate this formal assistance within the economy of makeshifts reinforced reliance on the resources that remained. In short, poor law reform helped promote the retention of customary culture.

5 DIFFERENT TEMPORALITIES

Having explored the lineaments of customary culture and the factors encouraging its retention – the spatiality of central neighbourhoods, employment in these areas, and the formal assistance available in times of need – it is time, finally, to focus on the ways in which various sectors of plebeian London adopted, adapted or resisted the new discourses of individualized initiative and responsibility. To this end, this chapter explores two case studies, based first on an autobiography written by a woman whose family was within the skilled sector, and second on the group that came to define disreputable plebeian life: the costermongers. In the course of doing so, the chapter attempts to address the concern expressed at the outset that a focus on factors tending to encourage certain patterns of thought and behaviour, while discouraging others, too easily segues into binary opposites: customary v. modern, collective v. individual. As pointed out in the Introduction, respectability was complicated: those who more willingly embraced the new notions being bruited about in the nineteenth century often did so on their own terms. Others who were more resistant clung tenaciously, often with good reason, to customary practices. Clearly different sectors of plebeian London were acting according to different temporalities. This chapter will examine the ways in which these impulses played out in the lives of a number of plebeian women and men.

In 1844, when she was fifty-seven, Mary Anne Ashford wrote her autobiography, *Life of a Licenced Victualler's Daughter*, a work that has featured already in this study. After being orphaned at thirteen, Ashford spent seventeen years in service, rising to the position of cook, and then was married and widowed twice. In many ways she was the embodiment of the new canons of respectability: her focus was on long-term security for herself and her family, and her relations with her neighbours, whom she often regarded as gossipy and improvident, were frequently strained. After her parents died, Ashford's relatives wished to apprentice her to a dressmaker or a milliner – genteel, respectable trades. Ashford stood against this, since she had no immediate family to support her through the slack seasons endemic to these occupations. Instead she elected to become a servant, even though her relatives made it clear they disapproved of the choice. Ashford chose her trade because it seemed to offer greater economic security than the 'genteel' trades – indeed, her focus throughout her life was on long-term security rather than on immediate appearances. She was willing to sacrifice 'face' in order to achieve this, and within her family she did so quite literally as she explained, 'if I called on any of my relations, if anyone came in, I was requested to step into another room, and kept in the background because I was a servant'.[1]

Ashford's adherence to long-term security was also made plain during a dispute over her second husband's pension. She noted that if it were not granted, 'I saw no other prospect than that of my own remnant of property being melted away ... in sustaining us ... and I might be left at an advanced age to encounter the poverty I had always endeavoured to avert'.[2] When she was first married (to her first husband), Ashford's long-term focus was also apparent: she and her husband had 'an old gentleman' put their savings in a bank in their joint names, an unusual move for people of their class – her husband being a sergeant instructor who taught shoemaking to the boys at the Royal Military Asylum. Ashford was also aware that her focus on long-term independence differentiated her from her neighbours. When her first husband's health began to fail and it became clear she was likely to be widowed with five young children, she tried to economize and to save as much as she could. She noted that 'my plan did not gain any approbation amongst those my lot was cast with; for, with very few exceptions, military people, above all others, spend all they get, be it little or much: but that I did not care a straw about'.[3]

While long-term financial independence was clearly a crucial goal for Ashford, so was provision for her family. She was left with five living children when her first husband died, and her autobiography is full of plans and schemes to ensure their present and future well-being. Indeed, Ashford married her second husband to benefit her children. She and her new husband, rather a weak man who was also a sergeant instructor at the Royal Military Asylum, had agreed that 'he could assist me in rearing his old comrade's children'.[4] This man had already outlived three wives, and Ashford observed that she had 'for the sake of my children, entered what might almost be termed a sepulchre'.[5] As was the case for so many artisanal wives, the well-being of her family was a central focus in Ashford's life.

Ashford's willingness to embrace these notions likely resulted from her own psychological predispositions as well as from structural factors in her life. Ashford's childhood undoubtedly contributed to her great concern to maintain her financial independence throughout her life, and to do so without being dependent upon others. Her natal family clung insecurely to lower-middling-sort status, and Ashford decided at a very early age to avoid credit whenever she could. Not only had her maternal grandfather been left penniless by an ill-advised decision to stand surety that left him to pay the large debt, but she had a first-hand lesson in her own life. Put out to nurse throughout her childhood with a family named

Long, Ashford clearly believed them beneath her. They were quarrelsome, and the husband was known throughout the neighbourhood as 'a profane old sot' much given to liquor.[6] Ashford's humiliation was crystallized when the Longs sent her to purchase groceries on credit, and one of her more respectable school-mates was in the shop. She said she prayed 'that I might always be able to pay for what I wanted, without asking persons to trust me'.[7]

Ashford was able to act on this wish because throughout much of her life she enjoyed far greater security than was typical. Her life as a servant on occasion was difficult – at times she was lonely; in some situations she was underfed; in others she did not feel fairly used by her employer. Nevertheless, she never had to struggle or scramble to find food and lodging. When between positions Ashford was able to stay with a family friend, Mrs Bond, or with her Great-Aunt Margaret. When she married, Ashford went to live at the Royal Military Asylum, in quarters provided to employees and their families. Indeed, so secure had her life been that when her first husband died and it was necessary to leave the asylum, she confessed that she had never before ever had to seek a lodging of her own.[8] Ashford did not just enjoy spatial security for much of her life; moreover, she also experienced a greater level of economic stability than was the norm. As noted, both of her husbands were sergeant instructors employed year round at the Royal Military Asylum to teach trade skills to the boys. Thus, they and their families were much less vulnerable to un- and underemployment brought on by seasonality and economic depression.

In all this, Ashford seems to be adopting standard notions of individualized respectability, yet elements of customary culture continued to play a role in her life. She relied repeatedly on mutuality, for example. When she became a servant, her disapproving family (with the exception of one great-aunt) made it clear, in an example of the coercive element in mutuality, that she could not look to them for help when she was out of work. In the event, Mrs Bond, the family friend, offered her shelter at any time she was out of place.[9] Shortly thereafter, she turned down one position, not simply because she was offered low wages but because the situation 'was too far from those friends who used sometimes to make me presents, to assist me while I had low wages'.[10]

The importance of mutuality is stressed repeatedly in Ashford's book. Even though as a servant, she was not able to provide much assistance to others in the form of money or goods, she nevertheless tried to find employment near her great aunt's home in Brompton after the latter had become old and infirm. This aunt was the only member of her family who had supported her decision to become a servant, and Ashford explained that 'I thought if I could get nearer to her, it would be a comfort to us both. I was not actuated by expecting anything from her, as she subsisted on an annuity, which would drop at her decease'.[11] When the aunt died, and as expected Ashford inherited nothing, she nevertheless observed,

'I had the pleasant reflection that, for the last few years of her life, protracted to extreme old age, I returned in some degree her kindness to me in early youth; and as I had never expected anything from her, I was not disappointed'.[12]

Ashford did not just deviate from orthodox notions of individualized respectability by relying on mutuality, however. Indeed, hers was not a passive acceptance of a received body of respectable ideas and codes. Rather, respectability for her became a resource, and even a weapon, often to be used against the very people most committed to it: her social superiors in the middle and upper classes. Ashford's deference was highly selective, and she was a determined campaigner for her rights even if this meant violating some of the tenets of respectability.

As pointed out in the Introduction, to explore respectability within its contested terrain, it is necessary to rethink the nature of resistance and accommodation. Using Scott's notions of public and private transcripts and Steinberg's observation that ideologies are never completely hegemonic, but always offer spaces where alternative or subversive meanings can be produced, it is possible to analyse Mary Ann Ashford's respectability. In the first place, Ashford used her respectability to gain practical rewards, if perhaps more spectacularly than most. When their royal highnesses the Duke and Duchess of Kent toured the Royal Military Asylum in 1818, they had noticed approvingly Ashford's newborn daughter, asking that she be named Victoria after the duchess. Some nine months later, just before the birth of Princess Victoria, Ashford took her daughter to Kensington Palace and returned thereafter once a year 'merely that the Duchess should remember her',[13] although she also hoped that her daughter would be taken into royal service in future. In the meantime, Ashford's daughter received an annual present from the duchess. Had the respectability of the workshop, the family's rooms[14] and Ashford herself not impressed the royal couple, she would not have been granted access to this help.

In benefiting from her respectability, Ashford seems to have been assiduous in maintaining relations with those who could help her. She managed to place one of her sons in a foundation school because an alderman, whose son was the rector of St Mary Woolnoth, had the presentation. This was Ashford's childhood parish which she had left at age thirteen. Clearly she was still well known and well thought of, since, as she explained, 'some of the inhabitants who had known me when a child, took up my cause, and got a petition to the alderman, signed by the bankers, and, indeed, all the influential gentlemen of the neighbourhood'.[15] Ashford carefully pointed out that only those who had never been in receipt of poor relief could apply to this school, thus reassuring her readers that this was not an instance of indiscriminate (and hence disreputable) charity. Ashford had been able to reach back to use her natal family's respectability in order to benefit one of her own children.

In all this, Ashford seems to be adopting standard notions of respectability. She was concerned about long-term security; she focused on providing for her children and their future; and she was decidedly proactive in her pursuit of the rewards respectability could offer. Moreover, at first glance she would seem to be a living illustration for claims that respectability undermined class solidarity. She was repeatedly critical of those in her class who did not share her values and priorities: the Longs from her childhood, her neighbours after her marriage. She also blamed her second husband's companions when, before their marriage, they – being 'of intemperate habits' – led him to drink excessively, and she complained about her neighbours' gossiping.[16]

Nevertheless, Ashford's use of respectability was more complicated than it initially seems. In the first place, her criticisms of other plebeian men and women have to be balanced against a telling life decision she made. Ashford rejected an opportunity to marry into the middle class because she had already engaged herself to the sergeant-shoemaker, whom she later admitted was 'very rough'. She refused to break her word unless her intended husband gave her 'some just cause', which he did not do. Ashford's independence and class pride were also apparent in her service days when she realized that one mistress was actually a kept woman. Ashford said, 'I prefer remaining among the "hewers of wood and drawers of water", and keeping myself'.[17] Clearly, Ashford's attitude towards class cannot simply be assumed or inferred according to her acceptance of respectability.

Respectability in Ashford's life did not mean passively accepting a received body of respectable ideas and codes. Rather, it was a resource and a weapon, often to be used against the middle and upper classes. She employed her respectability in a number of ways to resist her betters: Ashford's deference was highly selective, and she was willing to use her respectability as a weapon to pay back or defeat her enemies. Her lack of deference was made apparent early in her book. She said in the preface that she believed the 'real truth' of her life 'might offer amusement to matter-of-fact persons', and she mocked the depiction of servants in penny tracts – those cheap publications so often used by upper- and middle-class reformers to convey beliefs about and aspirations for the labouring classes. Ashford noted drily that every now and again 'a "Mary Smith" or a "Susan Jones" is introduced, in the last state of consumption, or some other lingering disease, of which they die in a heavenly frame of mind, and are duly interred'.[18] Moralistic melodramas of this sort were rejected not only in recounting her service experience, but throughout the book. Her readers were to receive the truth as she lived it.

Ashford's lack of deference to upper- and middle-class sensibilities is also apparent in the ironic, and perhaps sardonic, pseudonym she invented for the Royal Military Asylum (the RMA), the institution that employed both her husbands. She called it 'Fairy Land'.[19] With its military drills, constant drum rolls and incessant noise, the RMA was as far removed as could be from the notion of a serene and beautiful home to delicate creatures. The irony was heightened, moreover, by the behaviour Ashford repeatedly encountered at the RMA, which was arbitrary, fey and malicious – typical, seemingly, of traditional portrayals of fairy comportment. Ashford first went to the RMA as a servant to the family of the institution's clergyman. She became devoted to them and was 'utterly confounded' when her mistress suddenly notified her by letter – her employer was away from home – that she was to be fired simply because the mistress preferred to hire another servant.[20] During her second marriage, Ashford and her children were victimized and harassed by other employees who apparently wanted her husband's job and thought by vexing her to drive him out.[21] Finally, as will be seen below, Ashford regarded the behaviour of the RMA's board of commissioners as spiteful and vindictive. Fairy Land, indeed.

Ashford's irony bordered on impudence in an exchange with one of her mistresses, the penurious daughter of a Scottish earl, who tried to encourage her servant to eat less (Ashford was already seriously underfed in this position). The mistress explained, 'when I was young there was a famine, and ever since I have had such a veneration for all the necessaries of life that I cannot bear to see anything used profusely; but you never saw a famine, Mary'. To this, Ashford 'very innocently' replied, 'that I never did, but that I was sure I should always think of a famine if I thought of her place'.[22]

Ashford's lack of deference was also apparent in her dealings with the British Lying-In Hospital on Brownlow Street (or the Brownlow Street Lying-In Hospital as she called it).[23] As noted in the last chapter, applicants had to provide a marriage certificate at an interview before admission. Ashford did so, but was turned down because of a bureaucratic irregularity in the subscription payment by her sponsor. She had revenge for her humiliation by blackening the character of the board member responsible, almost certainly the Honourable Wyndham Knatchbull. Throughout her book, Ashford's strategy was to emphasize her own respectability while using the occasion to settle old scores.

She was also willing to violate some of the cardinal tenets of respectability when necessary. As noted in the last chapter, Ashford seemed to regard the charitable assistance offered by the British Lying-In Hospital as a right confirming her respectability, which certainly undercuts conventional equations between the latter and financial independence. Moreover, her second husband fell badly behind in his work; he was the sergeant tailor at the RMA and had been overly given to drink before marrying Ashford. During this period he had done little work, a fact he concealed from her until after they were married. Her response was simply to take up his work 'and in about a year he had all his numbers right'.[24] It seemed the most natural thing in the world to Ashford that she should do some of her husband's work in order to avert a crisis. Later on, when her husband – who was timid as well as weak – had trouble getting his full pension from the RMA and was refusing to fight for it in case he lost what little he did receive, Ashford simply intervened without telling him, at once abrogating notions of wifely deference to the head of the household and assumptions that public sphere concerns were not the province of women. Perhaps in deference to the expectations of respectability, Ashford did admit to being frightened and uneasy in doing this.[25]

It was in her dealings with the board of commissioners of the RMA, however, that one sees most clearly the importance of respectability as a weapon in Ashford's life. Indeed, the episode of her second husband's pension forms the climax of her book. The members of the board of commissioners were all male, and most had high military rank or connections. Initially, they approached the running of the RMA much as they would have arranged to provide for a regiment in the field. The differences in running an orphanage, however, were quickly brought home to them. In particular, as A. W. Cockerill has noted, they were confronted by the novelty of 'a barrage of questions, requests and "humble petitions" from the staff'.[26] The most cursory reading of the board's minutes reveals the discomfort and displeasure of its members with this kind of questioning. Nor did board members deal well with women. The board believed that caring for girls in the institution was an instance of 'Pure Charity', and that only the boys would be able 'to repay at a future Period the benefits they have received' – chiefly through serving Britain in the army.[27]

Given these attitudes, it is not surprising that the board did not react well to female protests. After the death of her first husband, Ashford campaigned long and hard in an attempt to receive the £4 in his pension which she believed was owed her. RMA employees in receipt of military pensions, which were normally paid four times a year, had a quarter withheld when they took up their duties at the asylum. This was to be paid when the man retired. If he died in service to the RMA, however, only partial payment of the detained quarter was made. This happened to Ashford's first husband, James Dallison, and she fought tenaciously for the full quarter's pay. Not only did the board peremptorily refuse her, but when, shortly thereafter, the board revised its policy and released the detained quarters to its employees, it still refused to pay Ashford and another widow who had been similarly protesting.[28]

With this experience under her belt, Ashford once again joined battle with the board over her second husband's pension. He had become so frail that he was medically certified as unfit to work. He was forced to retire very quickly – in less than a week – and was denied the usual pension which his service merited. Even though this meant real economic hardship for his family, as mentioned earlier, Edward Green was afraid to fight in case he lost his small military pension as well. Deciding that she had nothing to lose, Ashford, again as noted earlier, acted without her husband's knowledge. Having for years maintained a respectable way of life and made powerful connections because of it, Ashford was able to deploy this resource in order to trump the board of commissioners. The board was made up of aristocrats, gentlemen and senior officers. Ashford felt sufficiently confident to go over their heads to royalty. What she did was to write a letter of appeal to Queen Adelaide. Ashford was canny enough to wait until the court moved to Brighton, explaining that she thought 'it would stand a better chance of reaching her [the Queen], there than in town, as she might not be so taken up with visitors'.[29] Ashford was right: shortly thereafter, as a result of royal intervention, her husband received both a sizable pension and back pay which he was owed. In effect, Ashford had cashed in her respectability chips.

This dispute was not the only instance in the book in which respectability became a weapon in Ashford's hands. Indeed, a telling pattern emerges throughout her book. While there are several people from her own class who are villainized – an ill-tempered suitor from her youth, the RMA employee who persecuted her in an attempt to drive out her husband – generally speaking, the opponents Ashford attacks came from classes above hers. The miserly daughter of a Scottish earl (the mistress from service days), Wyndham Knatchbull, the RMA board of commissioners, the favourite mistress who fired her in favour of another (the latter, to Ashford's satisfaction, quit almost immediately), and the mistress who refused to give a good reference in order to retain Ashford's services, all have their arbitrary, unfair or bullying behaviour contrasted to Ashford's virtuous struggles.

Indeed, Ashford even hints that she was punished for being respectable. After the death of her first husband, rumours spread about the RMA. Ashford explained, 'some of my husband's acquaintance set about that I had got an immense sum of money; a report was raised to double and treble what I really had; but as I did not choose to gratify their curiosity, I merely said I should be very much obliged to any of them who would tell me where I could find it'. Given that her late husband had provided the RMA with sixteen years of unblemished service, that he would have been entitled to a pension had he lived to retire, and that he left a family of five young children, Ashford felt she had the right to ask the board for assistance. This, she said, 'was refused in a sneering sort of way, and I soon perceived that it was thought I had got more than I had a right to, hard as I had strived to get it together'.[30] There are two things of note in this situation. First, the exchange illustrates the fact that the upper-class board of commissioners and the plebeian woman had quite different expectations concerning respectability. If Ashford's comments are to be trusted, the board seemed to have resented her success: it was unquestioning deference rather than financial security that seems to have been most important to them. It was just this kind of presumption that Ashford resisted; for her, deference was earned through proper behaviour. Clearly, in this environment the successful pursuit of a respectable way of life did not automatically guarantee rewards and respect. It is equally apparent that this struggle over the meaning of respectability was the kind of public transcript conflict that Scott and Steinberg described.

The second thing to note from these conflicting notions was the fact that respectability offered little protection against gossip, rumour and insult. As this incident shows, one's good reputation had to be protected or negative consequences could well follow. Indeed, Ashford's book functions as a kind of public shaming ritual. Repeatedly, she gave sufficient information in her text for her targets to have been readily identifiable by her contemporary readers. She provided the address of her former mistress, the Scottish earl's daughter: City Terrace, a street with only fourteen houses. As noted earlier, Ashford admitted in her text that she was not completely sure about Sir William Knatchbull's name. She was right to be hesitant; almost certainly she meant the Hon. Wyndham Knatchbull, who is listed in the British Lying-In Hospital records as recommending the admission of a number of women at the time Ashford applied.[31] The mistress who dismissed her – the wife of the asylum's clergyman – would also have been readily identifiable, as were the members of the board of commissioners. Moreover, Ashford paid back in spades a mistress from her service days who had tried to prevent her leaving by providing poor references to prospective employers. Shortly after taking this position, Ashford came to realize that her mistress was a kept woman. In her book, Ashford not only provided this woman's address – 9 Lambeth Terrace – but identified her lover, 'a single gentleman, high in the law, and who afterwards became a judge, and sentenced Corder to death at Bury St. Edmunds for the murder of Maria Martin.'[32] This was a notorious murder so exhaustively covered in the press that many would remember Chief Baron Alexander hearing the case.

In not actually naming anyone, except Knatchbull, Ashford preserved the facade of decorum. Nevertheless, in making her targets so easily identifiable, Ashford seems to be resorting to the kind of public shaming ritual so common in eighteenth-century plebeian social relations: her book does not seem that far removed from the insults called out in the street naming transgressors and their failings. The propensity to name and shame did not die out in the nineteenth century; moreover, as Andy Croll has noted, by the late century it became one of the missions of local newspapers to identify various kinds of social transgressors.[33] Ashford's slightly more discrete book certainly seems a transitional point in this shift to print.

Ashford ends her book by comparing her struggles in life to the lines from Longfellow's poem, 'A Psalm of Life':

> Let us, then, be up and doing,
> With a heart for any fate;
> Still achieving – still pursuing,
> Learn to labour and to wait.[34]

On first reading, this seems little more than a mawkish and sentimental paean to respectable conventions of initiative, hard work, patience and endurance. In light of the pattern just identified, however, an alternative reading in Ashford's case seems more appropriate. Ashford had certainly learned to labour, but her waiting did not denote passive endurance. Rather, Mary Ann Ashford waited patiently and then served up a sweet, cold book of revenge. Respectability in her life became a resource which gave her access to people – sometimes very powerful people – who were able to provide assistance directly or to right wrongs done to Ashford. In her book she used this resource to call into question publicly the respectability of those, especially her social superiors, who had failed to behave as they ought.

Thus, respectability was not merely a code of behaviour and outward appearances: for Ashford it was a resource and a weapon. Just as friendly societies used their respectability to defend working-class autonomy in contests with parliament and the middle class generally, so at an individual level it could also be used for retribution, as well as to promote financial stability and to defend rights and interests through access to powerful patrons. Conceptualizing respectability as a discrete set of characteristics – a kind of static template to which people conformed or not – would make it difficult to slot someone like Mary Ann Ashford into the respectable category: her public shaming tactics, her selective bestowal of deference, her willingness to go behind her husband's back to rout his enemies in the public sphere all undercut received assumptions about nineteenth-century respectability. Nor can her class consciousness simply be read off her behaviour. The extent to which respectability was internalized or to which it increased or decreased class solidarity cannot be known by historians: temporal distance precludes this. If respectability's role cannot be determined with respect to overall class solidarity, it is clear, however, that in the hands of some at least, it became a weapon to be deployed in the constant quotidian struggle between the classes.

Respectability played a different sort of role in the second case study: the costermongers. This group of Londoners clung resolutely to customary predilections and practices, and they were a source of fascination to their contemporaries. Mayhew's interviews with them in *London Labour and the London Poor* were the best known and most influential examination of them, and were discussed widely at the time.[35] It is somewhat surprising, then, that the historiography of the costermongers is relatively small. They have not held the same fascination for historians that they did for their contemporaries, which may well result in part from a too-ready acceptance of Mayhew's judgements of them. While to a certain extent sympathetic to the costermongers, Mayhew also shared a number of the impulses and the moral disapproval of his class towards them. It was disapproval, moreover, that extended beyond his famous description of them as members of a wandering tribe (hence making them less civilized), and coloured much of what he said about them.[36] To give just one example, Marc Brodie has shown that coster politics were considerably more rational than Mayhew allowed, that their political stances were not simply motivated by a violent, undiscriminating hatred of policemen, and that when they called themselves Chartists, they were not just using the term as a short-hand label for rabble-rousing. Rather, they had a particular set of beliefs in mind:[37] they understood Chartism as being 'in some way opposed to unfair taxation, corrupt and brutal authority and perhaps, trade protection' (which would increase the price of food).[38] While these beliefs were not always ones that more conventional Chartists might recognize as central to the movement, they were far more rational than Mayhew allowed.

While Mayhew's depiction of them needs to be used cautiously, it is apparent that the costers were a group whose status at the mid-century was low: they were seen as 'roughness shaded into criminality', as Gareth Stedman Jones put it, and they were thought to pose a real danger to society, being 'outcast[s] who might overrun civilization'.[39] Stedman Jones goes on to note that by the late century the image of the coster had become more benign, morphing into that of the cockney, 'the good humoured, if sometimes ironic' figure, supposedly accepting 'social difference and subordination'. He says this shift occurred in part because in the aftermath of the London Dock Strike of 1889, the prospect of mob violence by the outcast seemed markedly less threatening.[40] Nevertheless, the costers were not thought benign at the mid-century, as an examination of newspaper stories about them published between 1840 and 1865 clearly indicates.

Of 212 stories carried in newspapers in these decades that focused on coster-mongers, the vast majority were negative.[41] In eighty, or 38 per cent, of the stories, costers attacked others physically. Twelve of these violent altercations were murders, in five of which the victim was the coster's wife. In another six of the eighty stories, a charge of attempted murder was laid, and in eighteen more cases, the target of the attack was a policeman. The costers also laid charges against police officers for excessive violence in four other instances. The police, for their part, clearly expected bad behaviour from the costers; in three theft cases there were no complainants, but the coster was charged anyway. Indeed, in fifty-nine, or 28 per cent, of the 212 cases, the coster was charged with some form of theft, and in thirty-seven other stories – 17 per cent – charges were laid that were work-related: cruelty to their animals (12), obstructing the street (10), using false weights and measures (8), selling spoiled food (4), and driving furiously (2).

Positive stories were few and far between in these decades. While in nine, the coster was the victim of violence – either beaten or murdered, in none was he thought innocent of provocation (and all of the victims were male). Only two of the 212 stories were unambiguously positive: in one a coster found a watch in the street that had been stolen, and turned it in to police. In the second, West-minster costers voted to keep alcohol-free the club set up for them by a lady philanthropist, much to her delight.[42] Four stories made fun of costermongers or saw them humorously, mimicking their speech or recording amusing comments, but generally the coster was too great a figure of fear for such stories to be common in these decades. Rather, the term costermonger was used to denote the lowest of the low: the coster was a 'byword for lying', and the extremes of society were characterized as ranging from the aristocrat down to the costermonger.[43] These street sellers were seen as violent people who lashed out physically at family members as well as friends, neighbours and strangers, who stole, who cheated their customers, and who were at war with the police, society's guardians of peaceable good order. The press coverage of them in the middle decades of the nineteenth century was overwhelmingly negative.[44] The violence, in particular, may have made it difficult for their social betters to think at all well of the costermongers. As Rosalind Crone has pointed out, while authorities were largely successful in eradicating public violence, this does not mean that plebeian Londoners turned against it. Violent activities shifted to locales that were more difficult for authorities to penetrate: the home, for example, as seen with the costers.[45] A number of factors – economic uncertainty, use of street space and the nature of poor relief – all helped ensure that the costers would continue to embrace their customary cultural practices.

The costermonger trade was difficult and uncertain, at once highly seasonal and low paid. With respect to seasonality, most costers varied the stock they sold according to the time of year: in January and February they sold fish principally, likely clearing 8*s.* a week. March was also difficult, but by April flower roots became available. In May things got better yet when fresh fish, and then in June new potatoes, peas and beans were sold, bringing in as much as a £1 a week. July brought cherries, while plums, greengages, apples and pears were in season in August, months that saw incomes of about 30*s.* In September the sale of apples brought in about 15*s.* October was uncertain with fish and oysters for sale, and things were even more difficult in November and December. Christmas brought a short respite, with oranges, lemons, holly and ivy for sale.[46] Street selling was a trade that was easily taken up, moreover. Little start-up capital was required, and there were no specialized skills to be learnt. While this made the trade attractive, it also resulted in a labour surplus leading to fierce competition and fluctuating income. Factors beyond the costers' control also hurt earnings. Mayhew quoted a clergyman that three days of rain could bring nearly 30,000 people to the brink of starvation. During the panic of the cholera epidemic in 1849, people stopped buying vegetables, fruit and fish, which brought great hardship to the costermongers.[47]

Some costers were able to claim a spot on the street from which to sell, and would return to it day after day unless ordered by the police to move on. Itinerant costers often had a daily round, which they traversed calling out their wares and frequently dealing with regular customers. Nevertheless, street selling was not an easy trade. As one coster noted, 'On the whole, we don't make more than enough to keep body and soul together, and our life is a hard one'.[48] Indeed, Mayhew quoted costers who estimated the average weekly income over the year in the trade to be 14*s*. 6*d*., as long as a man was able to pursue his trade regularly. Mayhew's own estimate was 10*s*.[49] The hours, moreover, were long, as James Greenwood reported in the *Journal of the Society of Arts* in 1867: 'You would find nobody, who was not bred to the business, who would undergo the hard labour of the costermonger for so little profit. A street seller of fish will be in Billingsgate at four o'clock in the morning, and is sometimes out till nine at night'.[50] Because this life was so insecure and the year-round income so low, most costers were wedded to a number of sharp practices: doctoring produce to make it look fresher, using false weights and measures, and selling spoiled goods even when a health risk. So necessary were these kinds of tricks that those born to the trade – perhaps half of the costers – did not think success likely for people who took it up as adults, and who were not privy to these practices. As one lifelong coster told Mayhew, for most out-of-work mechanics and poor women driven to street selling, it was '*only another way of starving*'.[51]

Moreover, the costs of doing business were high for the costermongers. They frequently borrowed money for stock and equipment, but never from banks, which, according to Mayhew, they did not trust.[52] Instead, the costers borrowed from one of themselves, from publicans or from nearby shopkeepers if they – the costers – had permanent pitches (and so were known by these retailers). Typically the costers paid exorbitant interest rates for these loans – 20 per cent per week being common. Thus, for every £100 borrowed, the cost was £1,040 a year, as a scandalized Mayhew noted.[53] Generally, however, the amounts borrowed at any one time were actually quite small – usually less than £1 – and they normally had to be repaid fairly promptly. Nothing was recorded on paper in these transactions, and neither security nor deposits were required. If the lender did not know the borrower, he – and normally it was a he – launched enquiries to ensure this individual really was what he claimed to be. Rarely did the borrower abscond; it would have been difficult to carry on business thereafter in this tight-knit community had he done so.[54]

It is apparent from Mayhew's interviews that the costermongers were skilled entrepreneurs who understood the logistics of buying and selling in the street and how best to turn a profit in doing so. More than this, they knew how to create demand. This can be seen in the ways in which they refashioned that most English of festivals: Guy Fawkes Day.[55] As noted, November was a slow month for street sellers, and extra money was always needed. In their endeavours, the costers downplayed the centrality of Guy Fawkes, instead constructing gigantic figures for street display with 'the guy being made to represent any celebrity who … for the moment offended against the opinions of the people'.[56] Beginning in 1844, groups of costers would parade their gigantic figures through the streets of the capital, collecting money along the route from spectators. The so-called 'Papal Aggression' – the creation of twelve Roman Catholic dioceses in 1850 – was a godsend, ensuring that Cardinal Wiseman and the Pope supplanted Guy Fawkes for several years. The press gave this apparently 'spontaneous' outbreak of anti-Catholicism a lot of coverage, ensuring free publicity for the costers. After the outbreak of the Crimean War, the Russian tsar became a favourite guy. There were limits on who could be depicted, however. When one group made a Florence Nightingale figure, this was thought inappropriate since she had done much good and the guy was meant to be a villain.[57]

Numerous groups of costermongers made these figures and paraded them around different parts of the city. Special rhymes were written and bellowed out to entertain and attract attention, and some groups even added clowns for the same purposes. The figures chosen were tailored to the neighbourhoods in which they were to be displayed. On Bond Street, along which members of parliament would stroll to their clubs, the guys were usually political. Near Lambeth Palace they were ecclesiastical, in the hopes that the Archbishop of Canterbury might give at least a half-crown. It was necessary, however, to avoid Irish neighbourhoods when the Pope or Cardinal Wiseman were the guys. Wherever the costers took their figures, it was crucial to keep moving, in part to maximize profits and in part to avoid antagonizing the police. As long as the streets weren't blocked by crowds of spectators, the police, for the most part, were tolerant, joining in the fun, although some costers still deliberately chose routes where the police were less likely to intervene.[58] The earnings could be substantial, with £1 clear for each participant being noted in several descriptions. The better guys could cost up to £3 or £4 to build and take up to six weeks of the coster's spare time to construct. To maximize profits the guys would be displayed for up to three days, not just on the fifth, and some costers took them as well to towns near London where such spectacles were rare and greatly appreciated. Some of the guys would be sold after their display – one coster got 15*s.* from a publican for his – while the more elaborate figures, or at least their component parts, would be stored for the following year.[59]

In all of this, the entrepreneurial skills of the costers are readily apparent. During a slack season they were able to manipulate a traditional festival in order to create an additional source of much-needed income and thus maintain their independence. They did not just meet, but rather created demand, playing on popular prejudices and topical events. The costers were also canny in choosing their display routes and in their advertising – the clowns, the rhymes – and they stretched the festival season to the maximum. Clearly, the costers were demonstrating behaviour the middle and upper classes thought crucial: initiative, hard work, independence and a range of entrepreneurial skills. Just as clearly, this behaviour did not rehabilitate the invidious reputation of the costermongers in mid-nineteenth-century London.

A minority of costers did manage to build up valuable businesses – Mayhew estimated that 200 to 300 costers employed as many as four boys each during the busy seasons to help sell their wares.[60] The surest way to financial success, according to Charles Knight, was to rent out equipment to other costers:

> a prince among the tribe is he who ... possesses accumulated capital in the shape of trucks which he lets out at a fixed rent to his less fortunate or less steady brethren ...
>
> Sometimes one of these wealthy truck-men will buy up on very advantageous terms large quantities of such articles as are in season, and he can sell again to the drawers of his trucks cheaper than they can buy in small quantities in the market.[61]

Commentators were generally agreed, however, that most costers were too improvident ever to achieve this measure of success, and consequently the vast majority continued to live precariously by their wits from day to day.[62]

In spite of the difficulties they faced, London costermongers did make an immense contribution to the formal economy. If Mayhew's calculations are to be believed, the approximately 45,000 London street traders did at least £2,500,000 worth of trade every year.[63] Mayhew thought that if these people were prevented from selling their wares, the poor rates would double, which would indicate that coster activity had a direct benefit for rate payers.[64] He also pointed out that the street sellers contributed through the taxes on 'their tea and sugar, their beer, gin, and tobacco, towards the expenses of a Government which exerts itself rather to injure than benefit them'.[65] More than this, the costers bought substantial amounts of food from London's authorized markets, and 'were the means by which the surplus produce remaining unsold ... was distributed'.[66] Mayhew, for example, estimated that costermongers bought up one-third of the fish available at Billingsgate.[67] Finally, costermongers performed a real, much-needed service to the poor. As John Benson noted, 'Street selling flourished in the nooks and crannies left by the shop-keepers and remained an efficient means both of clearing supplies of fresh food from the markets and of breaking bulk into the tiny units which were all that many of the poor could afford'.[68] At best, the costers were a necessary evil.

A second set of problems faced by the costers arose from spatiality: their use of the streets. As Mayhew noted, while they were exempted by legislation from paying the yearly £4 license if they sold fish, fruit or victuals or home-manufactured goods, their lives were nevertheless beset by insecurity. Itinerant costers were repeatedly punished by the police for obstructing the streets. If a coster habitually sold from a stall in a particular spot, a policeman would not generally disturb him – at least not unless an adjacent shopkeeper decided to complain, in which case it became the policeman's bounden duty to remove him.[69] This, of course, made the policeman rather than the shopkeepers the target of coster-monger ire. Mayhew believed the vibrant market in the New Cut, for instance, became a pale shadow of itself after new police regulations were instituted at the behest of local shopkeepers, outlawing market stalls in the area.[70] He spoke to one man after a number of stalls had been removed; others were allowed to stay if they paid a weekly fee to shopkeepers in front of whose premises they set up. This street seller said that nine months earlier (before the evictions) 'he would not have taken £20 for his pitch, and now he was a "regular bankrupt"'.[71] Those costers in that venue who did not pay were henceforth required to carry trays of goods or to keep moving with their barrows. If they failed to keep moving, even if they obstructed no one, they could be fined – 2*s*. 6*d*. in one instance[72] – or have their barrows of goods confiscated, a ruinous proposition for people who lived close to the margin. Given that it was the police who forced the cos-ters to move on, the latter developed an abiding hatred for the 'peelers'. As one coster put it, 'Can you wonder ... that I hate the police? They drive us about, we must move on, we can't stand here, and we can't pitch there'.[73] Not surprisingly, the costers tried to thwart the police whenever they could: for instance, when he had gone for assistance they would whip off wheels from a cart a constable was in the process of seizing and pass its stock to any costers nearby, knowing it would be returned later. The police then had to carry off the heavy cart to the jeers of onlookers.[74] While Stephen Inwood has raised doubts as to how strictly the police enforced the regulations against the costers in practice, the threat of action remained, and other authorities were far less equivocal in their opposition to street sellers.[75] Nor were the attitudes of authorities consistent: while the police could make life and profitability difficult for street sellers, parish authorities just as commonly set up their paupers with barrows in order to gain a livelihood – 'the stock which the one had provided (being) seized and confiscated by the other',[76] as Mayhew sardonically noted. It is clear that even when they were not operating at cross purposes, the authorities offered more harassment than protection to the costermongers.

In spite of the very real services costers performed for the formal economy, the professional lives of the vast majority of costers were very insecure, and there was inadequate recognition of the value of their enterprises. How, for instance, could a coster sell a valuable pitch location for a price reflecting its worth, if it was pos-sessed only on sufferance? Indeed, how could the business itself be sold for a fair price? What this insecurity meant in practical terms was a limited access to credit and little prospect for expansion. There was, in short, inadequate recognition and protection of the property rights of the costers.[77] As Mayhew noted of the costers,

> They are driven from stations to which long possession might have been thought to give them a quasi legal right; driven from them at the capricious desire of the shopkeepers

... They are bandied about at the will of a police-officer. They must 'move on' and not obstruct a throughfare which may be crammed and blocked with the carriages of the wealthy until to cross the road on foot is a danger. They are, in fine, a body numbering thousands, who are allowed to live in the prosecution of the most ancient of all trades, sale or barter in the open air, *by sufferance alone*. They are classed as unauthorized or illegal and intrusive traders, though they *'turn over' millions in a year*.[78]

The costers' rights were inadequately protected because their use of road space violated notions that streets were meant only to be traversed.

In spite of the precariousness of their lives, costermongers did not rely on poor relief to any great extent. There were relatively few costers living in St Martin's; rather, as David Green has noted, they were to be found in far greater numbers in the adjacent parish of St Giles in the Fields. Green sampled the latter parish's settlement examinations, finding that between 1830–44 street trading was the occupation of 8 per cent of the men questioned and 27 per cent of the women. In the period 1845–60, these figures rose to 12 per cent for the men, and fell to 18 per cent for the women. These patterns found paler reflections in the workhouse population. According to the 1851 census return, only 2 per cent of the male inmates were street traders, while 15 per cent of the women were. The 1861 workhouse returns for St Giles have not survived, but in 1871 5 per cent of adult male inmates were street traders and 8 per cent of the women were. At least 60 per cent of the men in both periods had been employed in the building, metal work, clothing and shoemaking trades, again a similar pattern to that in Green's settlement exam analysis. Three-quarters of the women in the workhouse came from a small number of trades – domestic service, needlework, charring and laundry work – that made up much of the restricted female labour market at this time. While the slight increase in male costers seeking poor relief may well reflect the fact that the number of street sellers was increasing, as Green thought, the fact remains that overall the costers constituted only a small percentage of the male house population, and not much more of the settlement examinees. The greater percentage of female costers is likely indicative of the high concentration of female workers in a very narrow range of trades. The coster antipathy to poor relief was apparent to Mayhew. He was told by two young women that in the aftermath of the police crackdown on costermongers in the New Cut, they had turned to prostitution rather than enter the workhouse. Mayhew went on to note that 'applications for parochial relief in consequence of these removals have been fewer than was anticipated' – only thirty families had done so at a cost of £50. He noted caustically that the assistance the parish had provided was to furnish money 'to start the (coster) trade, their expulsion from which had driven them to pauperism' in the first place.[79] The relatively small number of costers to be found in the workhouse undoubtedly resulted as well from the predilections, priorities, needs and resources existing within the coster community. The ability to act quickly on information, and the need for flexibility – changing stock rapidly, buying at the best prices, often in combination with other costers, and taking advantage of unforeseen opportunities – all made workhouse assistance particularly inappropriate for the costers.

The economic uncertainties of the trade, the spatial requirements of costers, and the inappropriateness of poor law assistance – especially the workhouse – meant that customary resources for and approaches to maintaining subsistence continued to provide the greatest likelihood of success. This was apparent in a number of ways. First, costermongers cooperated with one another. They clubbed together to buy stock in quantity and so obtain it for a lower price.[80] The entire transaction was informal and could be deeply puzzling to middle-class observers, who thought that it displayed 'a very reckless degree of confidence in each other' and that 'it is not easy to perceive by what arrangement they can divide the bargain amongst each other without serious disputes'.[81] No doubt a formal contract would have been requisite for analogous middle-class agreements. In the Guy Fawkes ventures, costers formed informal companies, with regular contributions towards costs expected from each member and a divvying-up of profits at the end of the undertaking. In one instance the coster building the guy went several times to his mates living close by, and each time they subscribed between 6*d.* and 2*s.*, depending on how well they had done selling on the day of the request.[82] As noted earlier, costers also borrowed money from each other to buy stock individually; one woman told Mayhew that the loan of a few shillings from another poor costermonger had kept her family out of the workhouse.[83] As noted earlier, they were usually punctilious about repaying such debts, and on occasion could be extraordinarily so. Mayhew records a story told by a coster who had lent to two young street sellers whom he did not know 10*s.* for stock. One of them paid off his half of the debt, and then, because his friend had absconded, volunteered to pay the second half as well.[84] Costers generally were honest with one another. They perhaps understandably relied not on the police force to protect their interests and property, but upon one another and on the informal organizations they set up among themselves. Not only did they claim never to steal from one another, but said they would 'never wink at anyone stealing from a neighbouring stall'.[85] In the owner's absence, they watched one another's stalls to prevent theft, and they punished thieves themselves, usually with a good hiding.[86]

The mutual reliance upon one another in the coster community was not just limited to work situations, however. In their own purchases, costers tried to deal with other street sellers as much as possible, priding themselves on 'sticking to their own'. They were also able to act as a community to enforce ethical standards of behaviour. Mayhew was told, 'A whole court of costermongers ... would withdraw their custom from a tradesman, if one of their body, who had influence over them, showed that the tradesman was unjust to his workpeople'.[87] To cope with the insecurity resulting from economic factors like seasonality and low income, and from spatial factors centring on street usage, the costermongers relied upon one another and on the informal organizations they set up among themselves. To help one of their number in distress, an item of his belongings would be raffled off and the money given to the needy coster. The raffles were highly organized, with cards printed to advertise the coming event and written subscription lists kept.[88] Moreover, in spite of their sharp practices, their customers trusted them. As Mayhew observed, poor people accustomed to buying from costers could not be induced to switch to shops since they were convinced that street sellers were cheaper, and in any case were 'apt to think shopkeepers are rich and street-sellers poor, and that they may as well encourage the poor'.[89] Greenwood noted that coster customers tended to be locals who did not expect to get full weight and measure in this 'recognized swindle', but appreciated the small affordable units of fresh, good-quality food the street sellers typically offered.[90]

The costers also had a strong attachment to their neighbourhood. Charles Pascoe, a middle-class writer, visited a costermonger living in an alley in Clerkenwell. According to Pascoe, the condition of the houses was wretched, privacy was non-existent, and overall the alley was 'hideously disgusting'. The costermonger was 'hardworking, thrifty, and honest' and relished life in his neighbourhood. He had got used 'to the atmosphere of the alley, loved the ways of its inhabitants, and by right of long habitation had come to be looked up to as a sort of authority on matters generally'.[91] Given the exigencies of the coster trade, status was rarely achieved through the accumulation of material wealth. Rather, it was attained through the approbation of one's neighbours and co-workers, and was marked, in the costers' case, through the possession of a kingsman – a coloured silk handkerchief tied around the neck – and good strong boots, preferably with roses, hearts or thistles decorating the upper leathers.[92] The boots were a necessity in this trade; the handkerchief, like the watches owned by other plebeian Londoners, not only brought status, but had pawnable value in times of need.

Not surprisingly, in such an insecure trade, the focus of most costermongers was resolutely short-term. According to Mayhew, even the few provident costers wanted 'an almost *immediate* return for ... outlays', distrusting 'any remote or contingent profit'. Unlike the provident few, most costers spent 'recklessly in dissipation and amusement', principally with other costers in beer shops and gambling and playing cards, although dog fights – by this time illegal – were also favoured, as were penny gaffs and 'twopenny hops', dances organized by the costers. Like most middle-class observers, Mayhew deplored many of these pastimes, not appreciating the instrumental value of sociability: that remaining on good terms with those in one's community meant having access to help in times of hardship.

These cultural priorities and patterns of behaviour were reinforced by the refusal of upper- and middle-class observers to recognize the great entrepreneurial skills many costers demonstrated. Their perceived moral failings precluded this, and consequently, their property rights were not protected. Indeed, the cohesiveness of the coster community was promoted by the moral disapprobation to which they were subjected by their social betters. The upper and middle classes during this period tended to accept claims promoted by the Evangelicals that moral rectitude had preferably to predate and certainly to underlie material success. Ambition was not to overstep righteousness; the amoral entrepreneur, utterly determined to turn a profit no matter what the means or the cost to others, was always to be condemned. In the case of the costermongers, they were thought so lacking in moral rectitude, both with respect to their personal lives and in their business affairs, that as Greenwood regretfully concluded, 'costermongering and degradation' were 'co-efficient terms'.[93] Isolated as the morally inferior 'other' whose culture was thought wholly lacking, and placed in an insecure position with respect to their ability to prosper, the costers clung resolutely to customary practices and priorities. As such, they created a moral quandary for their social betters, as Greenwood ruefully acknowledged. He said they were part of a system that was 'rotten at heart' because it was 'identical with depravity and ignorance'. Nevertheless, as seen, the costermonger system played an important role in the formal economy, distributing surplus food from the markets to the poor at prices lower than those charged in shops. Unfortunately, the work of the coster was so hard that 'No better class would take it up'. Moreover, Greenwood continued, 'if you bring the costermonger to a sense of his degradation, he would soon discover that it was inseparable from his occupation, and do his best to cease to be degraded, and, consequently, he would cease to be a costermonger. You would teach him to be something better, and the poor would, in the end, be the losers'.[94] As long as the coster was seen as a figure of moral opprobrium who was a danger of society and who could not be improved, there was no way out of this trap.

While some plebeian women and men embraced a way of life that would have been recognized as respectable by moral reformers and the affluent generally, they did so on their own terms and for their own purposes. The new tenets of respectability could become a potent weapon in the hands of someone like Mary Ann Ashford. In groups like the costermongers, who were regarded with such censure, the moral condemnation led to a great irony: it helped reinforce the very behaviour thought so objectionable, and gave the customary culture of the costermongers resilience and plausibility. Decisions whether or not to embrace the new codes had little to do with accommodation or passivity, but rather resulted from choices and predilections that were shaped in crucial ways by the factors making them more or less plausible: in this period, the degree of economic security, spatiality and the social safety net.

CONCLUSION

Customary culture persisted in many sectors of plebeian London throughout the period of this study, and indeed well into the twentieth century. The factors identified at the outset – the spatiality of neighbourhoods, economic insecurity, the forms and practices of formal assistance, and the lack of mobility – combined to create conditions that allowed customary cultural practices and priorities to remain plausible for many, if not most, plebeian Londoners. Reputation and the respectability emanating from it remained crucially important, but in this fluid urban context needed to be re-established on a daily basis. Consequently, people defended their respectability with alacrity against perceived slights and insults. As quarrelsome as they were mutually supportive, plebeian Londoners also developed strategies to try to contain violence and resolve disputes, although clearly these were not always successful. Reputation and respectability brought access to important resources in the battle to make ends meet: borrowing networks, pawning and credit were all dependent upon being well thought of by others in the neighbourhood.

The spatial configuration of the streets and houses in plebeian neighbourhoods did not lend themselves to the new codes of urban civility that posited a privatized family life centred on the home – and lived largely within it. Courts, yards and alleys remained sites of sociability, and homes all too often consisted of flimsy demarcations within subdivided houses, offering scant privacy and little comfort. Governments during this period, moreover, were unable consistently to enforce infrastructure legislation that supported the new urban codes of civility – sanitation, dust collection and pollution control all remained serious problems in nineteenth-century London. Given the capital's patchwork of governing authorities at this time, perhaps not surprisingly, effective government control was not achieved during this period. Plebeian neighbourhoods generally consisted of subdivided single-family dwellings often tucked away in close courts, alleys and yards that were active impediments to privacy as now understood. Much of life took place on the streets or in spaces open to surveillance by others. Ironically, improvement schemes involving the razing of slums worsened conditions in surrounding neighbourhoods, exacerbating overcrowding and reinforcing customary codes of behaviour. Not until well after this period did cheap public transportation offer an alternative to the spatiality of these neighbourhoods.

Economic uncertainty also helped keep customary cultural priorities and behaviour relevant. Many of the trades that were the biggest employers in central London offered scant security to the people who worked in them, and this was certainly the case in St Martin in the Fields. While there was relative stability with respect to the kinds of work done, conditions in a number of trades worsened during the period of this study. Women's work, always restricted to a small number of trades, suffered from a consequent labour surplus and low wages, and if anything was even more insecure than male employment in the capital. Adding to these woes were the pressures of the life cycle: the elderly and families with dependent children were particularly hard-pressed in their struggles to maintain subsistence, while fragmented families were almost always in trouble. When difficulties almost inevitably occurred, it was necessary to rely on family, friends and neighbours in order to make ends meet, and consequently, to be on good terms with them. In St Martin in the Fields there was also evidence of occupational clustering, which meant that neighbourhood solidarities were densely textured, constructed on both propinquity and shared workplace experience.

Both charity and poor relief were reshaped during this period in order to effect the moral reform of recipients. As charitable bodies sought to help the deserving rather than simply ministering to the needy, different collectivities within plebeian London used this kind of assistance variously. Some applicants from the most skilled sectors saw assistance from the most reputable charities as a confirmation of status, turning the objective of financial independence on its head. Attempts by charities to determine applicant worthiness, and hence to effect a moral reform of those thought most disreputable, exposed the neediness of this clientele to their neighbourhoods at large, and endangered access to borrowing networks and credit from landlords and shopkeepers.

As workhouse regulations were tightened and inmates became more isolated from other plebeian Londoners, it became more difficult to accommodate poor relief within the precarious configuration of makeshift resources through which people maintained subsistence. Consequently, workhouse inmates attempted to bend this increasingly rigid assistance to meet their needs, but there is little compelling evidence that they embraced the values being promoted by the regime. The number of high-repeat users, most of whom were clearly vulnerable and needy rather than degenerate, fell after the 1790s. High-repeat users were also disproportionately female, and a number of the new regulations targeted them particularly. Indeed, there is widespread evidence of inmate resistance, as they tried to gain advantage from the system, bend it to their needs or simply call its respectability into question. It is difficult not to conclude that the increasingly ill fit between this assistance and plebeian needs actually helped to promote the retention of customary cultural practices.

If these various factors helped customary culture remain relevant, it does need to be recognized that it remained more so for some sectors of plebeian London than others. While in the long run the urban codes of civility being promoted in the nineteenth century have been generally accepted, different sectors within plebeian London adopted them at different times and on their own terms. The meanings of respectability were at times contested, and in the hands of some could become a weapon with which to excoriate, shame and defeat errant social superiors. The adoption of new codes of respectability did not necessarily denote passivity, but could be turned to defend rights and interests. Other plebeian Londoners clung tenaciously to customary cultural practices. Where economic uncertainty remained the norm, use of the streets contested and property rights insufficiently protected, and where poor relief and charity were shaped in ways that did not meet needs, customary resources remained appealing and most likely to be successful in maintaining subsistence.

The pattern that has emerged repeatedly in this study was that moral condemnation, and the practices meant to rectify the perceived failings, gave customary culture resiliency and plausibility. Only when plebeian neighbourhoods were transformed or cheap transportation allowed these Londoners to live in new suburban estates, when work became better paid and more regular, and finally when there was a social security safety net serving needs appropriately, could the situation be otherwise.

APPENDIX

Since poor relief was often avoided, it may be that many people whose situations were highly precarious lived in streets unidentified by contemporary accounts and settlement examinations. These sources can be corroborated by the rate books of St Martin in the Fields, which provide rental information for all of the streets in the parish. St Martin's was divided into ten wards. Using the rate books to determine the median rent level for the houses in each street of each ward ought to indicate levels of affluence or poverty. There is a potential problem, however: the rate books give next to no information of lodging – the normal practice of the poor – since they indicate only the overall rent of the house. It might well be that larger houses with higher rents were in fact warrens for the poor, a situation upon which the rate books can shed no light. Indeed, the analysis of David Green and Alan Parton of the St Giles in the Fields rookery, Little Ireland, indicates that this was precisely the case in the mid-nineteenth century.[1]

The Statistical Society of London (later the Royal Statistical Society), in its 1836 investigation of the state of the poor in a district near Gray's Inn, also claimed that very high densities were the norm: 'Several families – in one instance 11 – live in one house. Generally each family occupies only one room, and that sometimes a cellar or kitchen underground'.[2] In 1840 in St Margaret and St John's, a parish adjacent to St Martin's, the society found that 'Many of the houses in the district visited were sub-divided into single rooms, and each room contained frequently a separate family'.[3] Three years later it found in St George's, Hanover Square, (another adjacent parish), that 'Some houses were ... tenanted by ten, eleven, and twelve separate families, being one family to each room'.[4] Potentially, lodging – particularly where it was very intense – could render the rate book information all but useless. It is impossible to tell how pervasive very intense lodging actually was, but given the upper-class propensity to concentrate on the most sensational and extreme, these claims should be taken cautiously. Certainly, with respect to the Statistical Society material, ignoring the descriptive comments and concentrating on the figures the society provided quickly shows that intensive lodging patterns were not the norm, or even very common. In the Gray's Inn district, the society's figures show that there were 2.4 families per house on average. In St Margaret's and St John's, again, an average of only 2.4 families per house was found, according to society figures. In St George's, the average was even lower: 2.1 families per house. This is particularly telling, since the society claimed only to have visited working-class homes. It would seem, then, that a small number of houses in the areas investigated were rented out to ten or twelve families. In particularly notorious slums like Little Ireland, very high densities undoubtedly were the norm, but such areas were not typical of plebeian life in the capital, and as seen from the densities given earlier, not typical of St Martin in the Fields either.

Nevertheless, this does not address the basic problem in the rate books: the invisibility of the lodgings into which many houses were subdivided. While this problem cannot be addressed directly, it is possible to test the general proposition that there is a direct relationship between rent and income levels. This can be done by referring to the assessed taxation material from the period. In 1798 the government had the collectors of the assessed taxes complete returns providing information concerning their respective areas.[5] Those for St Martin's, however, have not survived. Rather, what can be found is a large manuscript page for part of the Strand taxation ward (Helmet Court, Angel Court, Swan Yard, Wych Street, Little Drury Lane, Catherine Street, the Strand and Drury Lane). This area was immediately adjacent to St Martin's Drury Lane ward. The document is of particular interest because of the range of data it contains: names, addresses, occupations, estimates of income, and descriptions of poverty or affluence are provided for most of the thirty-four entries (see Table A.1). Thus, it should be possible to see whether there is a relationship between income and rent levels, since several of these streets were described in contemporary literature as poor and disreputable, and presumably contained substandard housing.

Table A.1: Strand taxation ward rent and income data.

N	Rent Level £s	Median Rent £s	Median Income £s	% of Income Paid in Rent*	% of Group Called Poor†
0	0–9	–	–	–	–
5	10–19	15	50	30	80
8	20–9	22	100	22	58.5
7	30–9	36	200	18	40
5	40–9	44.10.0	175	25.4	0
5	50–74‡	60	400	15	0
4	75–99‡	95	350	27.1	0§

N = 33 (for one other entry there was no income given).
* (median rent/median income)* 100.
† Entries were either described as 'poor', as having difficulty paying their taxes, or, in one instance, as having a 'large family' – presumably denoting difficulty.
‡ Because of the very small number of members, these groups have been left with the larger number of intervals, but have been corrected for overlap.
§ One entry in this group was described as 'rather distressed'. Since the income listed was £300, and the rent £46, it did not seem that this person should be included in the 'poor' category, however.

The tax collector divided the entries into seven classes according to the amount of rent paid: £0–£10, £10–£20, £20–£30, £30–£40, £40–£50, £50–£75 and £75–£100.[6] Generally speaking, as incomes increased, so did rent levels. At the same time, the percentage of income spent on rent tended to fall, while the percentage of the group described as poor also decreased. This accords with Jeremy Boulton's findings that the proportion of income spent on rent tended to increase as earnings declined.[7] All five families whose rents were between £10 and £19 were described as being very poor, unable to pay taxes or a large family. The tax collector noted generally that 'a great number in this class in similar circumstances many of whom have great difficulty to live'.[8] In the third class paying rents of £20 to £29, four of the eight families were described as being poor, and in the fourth paying £30 to £39, two of the seven families were poor. There are, however, anomalies – particularly with respect to groups five and seven. The break in the upward progression in income may be due to the very small numbers in each group: possibly it would not be disturbed if a larger sample were available. As well, it may be that once a certain income level was attained, the relationship between rent and income became more flexible. The amount of money left to live on after rent may have been at least as crucial as income and the percentage of it going towards rent. In other words, once enough money was left (after rent) to ensure a certain standard of living, it may be that greater flexibility in rent as a percentage of income was permissible. Thus, everyone paying more than £40 in rent had at least £110 left over (with only one exception),[9] and none was described as poor. Of those paying £10 to £39 and who were described as poor, on the other hand, none had more than £80 left after rent. Since the anomalies occur in the higher classes where there was no poverty, this greater flexibility may in part explain them. In any case, these aberrations do not refute the overall relationship between rent and income – a relationship, moreover, which seems to hold in spite of the practice of lodging. At the lower end of the economic scale particularly, the relationship appears clear-cut – at least according to the Strand ward taxation data.[10]

This evidence, although based on a small number of families, seems to indicate that a general relationship does exist between rent and income, and hence, that the rate books should be able to help make poor neighbourhoods visible. Another problem concerns the determination of a rental level below which people can be considered poor. Such a level can only be provisional and does not take into account factors like family size. Given that a general relationship does seem to exist between income and rent, however, such a marker should be able to give a general idea of the areas in St Martin's where the poor lived. The question is how might this level be found? It is already apparent from the assessed tax records that in the £10 to £19 group, 80 per cent were experiencing financial difficulty. Indeed, the collector noted that there were 'a great number in this class in similar circumstances many of whom have great difficulty to live'.[11] For a more precise identification within the £10 to £19 rent range, however, other sources must be considered.

Johnstone's *London Commercial Guide & Street Directory* for 1817 is particularly useful, since its entries are grouped according to street as well as by name and trade. This directory sought to include 'the Name of every Firm, Establishment, Professional Man, Merchant and Tradesman of respectability resident in London and its environs'.[12] By comparing the streets of St Martin's with those included in the directory, a list of parish streets on which no 'respectables' were to be found can be compiled. Median rent levels on these streets can then be examined to see if any useful information or patterns emerge. Two approaches can be pursued: either the overall median rent level of all unlisted streets can be determined, or, alternatively, the median rental levels of each of the unlisted streets can be identified to see whether there is clustering below a particular point.

In the first instance, in calculating the median rent levels of all the unlisted St Martin's streets, the midpoint of the series is £12, and in the second, until the £17 median rent level is reached, more than 80 per cent of the streets are not listed in Johnstone's *Directory*. At this point the situation begins to shift markedly. Only 63 per cent of streets with median rent levels of £20 or less are unlisted, for instance. While it remains to be proven that these figures are indicators of financial hardship, they do point the way to a provisional figure that can be tested. If £12 is the median rent level of the unlisted streets, and £17 is the turning point at which streets assume a much more respectable character, then possibly the midpoint between them – £14.10.0 – can be taken as a provisional figure denoting financial hardship. While this is a fairly arbitrary choice, the fact that £14.10.0 is also the midpoint of the Strand tax ward £10–£19 rental group that was described as having difficulty living also adds credence to its use.

This figure can be tested by trying to determine what it meant to the labourers of Westminster – a group whose ability to achieve subsistence was precarious. Schwarz estimated that labourers at this time were earning approximately ten shillings a week, or £26 a year. While this figure is too low in that it does not take into account the contribution made by women and children to the economy of the family, it is probably also too high, for as Schwarz noted of one typical trade, bricklaying,

> Making allowances for Sundays and public holidays, a bricklayer's labourer would, if fully employed, be earning £30 p.a. in the 1770's and 1780's and about the same amount, in real terms, by 1815. If he were unemployed for only one-sixth of the year, or for less than nine weeks, he would be earning less than 10s. a week on average; most labourers would earn less.[13]

At best, without making labourers' wages a study in itself, the 10*s.* amount can be used as a working figure. Similarly, labourers' rental levels can be estimated.

Schwarz thought that labourers were spending approximately 16 per cent of their income on rent, which meant they were paying £4.3.2 annually. Richard Rodger, on the other hand, has estimated that the working class often spent as much as 25 per cent of its income on rent.[14] If their putative annual wage is divided by four – which still may be a conservative estimate of the percentage[15] – then London labourers were paying £6.10.0 in annual rent.

But labourers did not as a rule rent whole houses, and this is apparent from the 1841 census data for St Martin's.[16] By this time, there were on average 9.5 people in a house in St Martin's. Since the average family size for the parish was only 4.2, lodging does seem to have been prevalent. If, as noted earlier, it is assumed that two-thirds of the houses in St Martin's contained lodgers, then the average rental for these houses (using Schwarz's and Rodger's percentages) would fall between £9.19.7 and £15.12.0. As will be seen, work was irregular for labourers, so they were likely paying the higher percentage of income for rent. Thus, the poverty line for house rentals undoubtedly falls nearer the higher of these two amounts. Exactly where it falls it problematic, however, because wage and rent information cannot be known precisely. In light of these surmises, the £14.10.0 figure arrived at above does seem to be a reasonable poverty line.

With this figure in hand, two kinds of information have been elicited from the records of St Martin's parochial rates: first, the median rent level of every street in each ward has been determined to see whether there was a geography of poverty; and second, streets whose inhabitants experienced high degrees of difficulty in paying the rates have been identified. If there is any significant correspondence between the two, this would be additional evidence that these sources do indeed indicate poor districts. Medians are preferable because unlike averages, they are not skewed by one or two very high or low rent levels on a particular street. As well, many of the streets in St Martin's were too short and houses too few for there to be a modal point. While overall there was an average of 16.2 houses per street in the parish, it was not unusual to find streets with only five or six houses, and in many instances there was no single rental amount which was more common than any other. By using the median, these kinds of problems can be avoided.

Once the median rent levels had been determined for every street, or section thereof in each ward, they were grouped according to these levels. The findings are shown in Table A.2. It is apparent from this table that the vast majority of the streets of St Martin's had median rent levels which fell below £30 – 84.4 per cent in fact, and half of these streets had median rent levels which fell into the £10–19 grouping. There were also geographic patterns with respect to median rent levels in St Martin's: the three wards of Drury Lane, Long Acre and Bedfordbury had the lowest range of median rent levels. Indeed, the quartile deviation – a measure of homogeneity – shows that these wards were made up of streets whose median rent levels were uniformly low. None was above £30 a year, in fact. A large quartile deviation indicates that street median rent levels were widely scattered, while a low deviation figure means that the rent levels were concentrated around the median for the ward overall. While the streets of the three wards of Bedford-bury, Long Acre and Drury Lane had uniformly low median levels, those found in the wards of Exchange, Strand, and Charing Cross I and II showed much greater heterogeneity in their median rent levels, and hence a much greater range in the amounts of rent being paid.

Table A.2: St Martin's streets grouped by median rent levels and percentage having difficulty paying rates.

Rental Group	Frequency	% of Total Number of Streets	% Having Difficulty Paying Rates
£110–19	1	0.5	0
£100–9			
£90–9			
£80–9			
£70–9	3	1.6	0
£60–9	1	0.5	5.9
£50–9	5	2.6	7.9
£40–9	7	3.7	5.2
£30–9	13	6.8	6.7
£20–9	50	26.3	7.1
£10–19	80	42.1	14.7
£0–9	30	15.8	20.8

N = 190

There were in most wards, moreover, particular areas that had especially low medians according to the provisional definition given above of a rental median of £14.10.0 or less per annum. In the three wards with the lowest quartile deviations, there were a number of areas that had particularly low medians. In Drury Lane Ward, the small courts near St Martin's burial ground (on Drury Lane near Little Russell Street), those in the very northeast corner of the parish, and those near Exeter Street had especially low rental medians. In Long Acre Ward, the courts near Charles Street and Drury Lane had particularly low levels. In Bed-fordbury, by far the largest of the three wards, the courts and alleys in the area contained by Chandos Street, St Martin's Lane and New Street – the neighbour-hood of Bedfordbury – also had low rental median levels.

Aside from these three wards, there were also pockets with low median levels in many of the wards with greater quartile deviations. In Strand Ward, the courts and alleys south of Covent Garden, and north of the Strand between Bedford and Exeter Streets had low median levels. In New Street Ward there was a similar pocket located north of New Street, and west of Leg Alley which surrounded Long Acre. In Spur Alley Ward, the courts and alleys around Hungerford Market (as well as the market itself) had low levels, as did the Suffolk Street Ward courts running off Whitcomb Street below Coventry Street. There were two small low-level pockets in Exchange Ward, one north of the Strand consisting of Church Lane and Old Round Court, and one south of the Strand consisting of Off and George Alleys. Finally, in Charing Cross Ward II, Long's Court and Moor's Yard had low levels. Thus, as defined, the streets with low median income levels were not simply scattered haphazardly throughout the parish, but, were, to a great extent, clustered. Moreover, the arc of poverty, which showed up in the settlement examinations, is also apparent here, as are the three other areas of poverty previously discussed.

The reliability of low median rent levels as an indication of poverty can be further corroborated by rate book entries indicating the degree of difficulty people had in paying the parish rates, since one would generally expect lower-income earners to find the rates most burdensome. Returning to the rate books and dividing those who had difficulty, according to the groupings established, shows that a pattern does exist. The category of 'those having difficulty' has been defined as those who paid no rates, who made only partial payment, or who owed arrears. Those who made less than complete payment because they moved during the year have been excluded. Table A.2 shows the percentage of ratepayers having difficulty by rental median group. The relationship between those who had difficulty, and the median rental level on the street on which they lived is readily apparent. While the £50–9 and the £70–9 groupings are anomalous, this may in part result from the smallness of these groups. In any case, they do not disturb the overall pattern. The seven highest rental-median groups (for which there are entries) all have difficulty-in-payment rates of less than 8 per cent. The bottom two groups, however, reveal much higher percentages of those having difficulty. Thus, there is a general pattern in that the lower the annual median house rent on a street, the greater the likelihood its inhabitants would have difficulty paying the parish rates.

If the streets where the highest percentages of those having difficulty lived are mapped, the pattern which emerges is strikingly similar to the areas of low rental medians. In defining 'high percentages of difficulty', any street whose percentage was greater than 20.8 was included, since this was the degree of difficulty experienced by the lowest rental group. Streets with high difficulty percentages tend to be found in the same areas as those with low rental medians. Indeed, more than a quarter of the streets – 28 per cent – share both characteristics, which is particularly telling since the number of streets on which there was difficulty in paying the rates was far fewer than the number with low medians. If they are examined alone, slightly more than 60 per cent of the streets on which there was difficulty paying rates had medians which fell below £14.10.0. Another 17 per cent of these streets had medians below £20. Thus, more than three-quarters of the streets on which there was trouble paying the rates fell into the category in which people generally had difficulty making ends meet (according to the Strand taxation ward data). It is not unreasonable, then, to see difficulty in paying parish rates as an indication of financial hardship. The similarity in geographic patterns in turn lends validity to a link between rent levels and poverty and affluence. Parish records, settlement examinations and rate books, bolstered and corroborated by other kinds of evidence – assessed taxation records, *Johnstone's Directory* – identify the streets in St Martin's that sheltered the poor.

NOTES

Introduction

1. See especially R. Shoemaker, 'Decline of the Public Insult in London, 1660–1800', *Past and Present*, 169 (2000), pp. 97–131; 'Male Honour and the Decline of Public Violence in Eighteenth-Century London', *Social History*, 26:2 (May 2001), pp. 190–208; 'The Taming of the Duel: Masculinity, Honour and Ritual Violence in London, 1660–1800', *Historical Journal*, 45:3 (2002), pp. 525–45; and 'Public Spaces, Private Disputes? Fights and Insults on London's streets, 1660–1800', in T. Hitchcock and H. Shore (eds), *The Streets of London* (London: Rivers Oram Press, 2003), pp. 54–68.
2. R. Shoemaker, *The London Mob* (London: Hambledon and London, 2004), p. 297.
3. Ibid., pp. 151–2.
4. Ibid., pp. 295–6.
5. By plebeian, I mean women and men of the labouring and lower middle classes.
6. Shoemaker, it should be noted, explicitly rejects Elias's notion of the civilizing process, on the grounds that it works 'from the top down, emanating from the growing powers of the state or the cultural practices of the aristocracy and the gentry'; Shoemaker, *The London Mob*, p. 290.
7. N. Rogers, 'London's Marginal Histories', *Labour/Le Travail*, 60 (Fall 2007), pp. 217–34, on p. 230.
8. J. Carter Wood, *Violence and Crime in Nineteenth-Century England* (London: Routledge, 2004), pp. 3–4.
9. Ibid., p. 141. For a discussion of violence, see especially P. Spierenburg (ed.), *Men and Violence: Gender, Honor, and Rituals in Modern Europe and America* (Columbus, OH: Ohio State University Press, 1998); and M. Wiener, *Men of Blood: Violence, Manliness, and Criminal Justice in Victorian England* (Cambridge: Cambridge University Press, 2006).
10. J. Lawrence, 'Review', *Journal of Victorian Culture*, 11:2 (Autumn 2006), pp. 376–81.
11. A. Twells, *The Civilising Mission and the English Middle Class, 1792–1850* (Basingstoke: Palgrave Macmillan, 2009).
12. N. Elias, *The Civilizing Process* (Oxford: Blackwell, 2000).
13. For a critique of Elias's history, see R. J. Robinson, '"The Civilizing Process": Some Remarks on Elias's Social History', *Sociology*, 21:1 (February 1987), pp. 1–17; E. Dunning, 'A Response to R. J. Robinson's "The Civilizing Process": Some Remarks on Elias's Social History', *Sociology*, 23:2 (1989), pp. 299–307; and R. Van Krieken, 'Violence,

Self-Discipline and Modernity: Beyond the "Civilizing Process", *Sociological Review*, 37:2 (1989), pp. 193–218.

14. *A Tale of Two Britains*, BBC Four, 25 October 2009.

15. P. Willmott and M. Young, *Family and Kinship East London* (London: Routledge and Kegan Paul, 1963); and M. Bulmer, *Neighbours: The Work of Philip Abrams* (Cambridge: Cambridge University Press, 1986), p. 91.

16. E. W. Soja, 'Author's Response', *Progress in Human Geography*, 30 (December 2006), pp. 817–20, on p. 818.

17. E. W. Soja, *Postmodern Geographies: The Reassertion of Space in Critical Social Theory* (London: Verso, 1989), pp. 10–11.

18. D. R. Green, *From Artisans to Paupers* (Aldershot: Scolar Press, 1995).

19. Bulmer, *Neighbours*, p. 92.

20. G. Sims, *How the Poor Live* (London: Chatto and Windus, 1883), p. 13.

21. C. Lis and H. Soly, 'Neighbourhood and Social Change in West European Cities Sixteenth to Nineteenth Centuries', *International Review of Social History*, 38 (1993), pp. 1–30, on p. 29. Also see C. Lis, *Social Change and the Labouring Poor: Antwerp, 1770–1860* (New Haven, CT: Yale University Press, 1986).

22. J. C. Scott, *Domination and the Arts of Resistance* (New Haven, CT: Yale University Press, 1990), p. 151.

23. Green, *From Artisans to Paupers*, p. 93.

24. Ibid., p. 94.

25. Ibid.

26. D. Cannadine, *The Rise and Fall of Class in Britain* (New York: Columbia University Press, 1999), pp. 19–20.

27. G. Eley and K. Nield, *The Future of Class* (Ann Arbor, MI: University of Michigan Press, 2007), pp. 197 and 200.

28. Ibid., p. 13.

29. G. Best, *Mid-Victorian Britain, 1851–1870* (Glasgow: Fontana-Collins, 1982), pp. 282–4; F. M. L. Thompson, *The Rise of Respectable Society* (Cambridge, MA: Harvard University Press, 1988), pp. 113, 195, 353–4, 360. More recently Woodruff Smith, in an examination of upper-class respectability, has argued that it was the impetus for consumption, that is, that the consumption of certain appropriate goods, became an important and even crucial part of respectable social identity. See W. Smith, *Consumption and the Making of Respectability 1600–1800* (New York: Routledge, 2002); G. Crossick, 'The Labour-Aristocracy and its Values: A Study in Mid-Victorian Kentish London', *Victorian Studies*, 19:3 (March 1976), pp. 301–28, and *The Labour Aristocracy and its Values* (Bloomington, IN: Indiana University Press, 1976); R. Q. Gray, *The Labour Aristocracy in Nineteenth-Century Britain, 1850–1900* (London: Macmillan, 1981); N. Kirk, *The Growth of Working Class Reformism in Mid-Victorian England* (Urbana, IL: University of Illinois Press, 1985), ch. 5, pp. 174–240; and R. J. Wegs, 'Working-Class Respectability: The Viennese Experience', *Journal of Social History*, 15:4 (1982), pp. 621–35.

30. Kirk, *The Growth of Working Class Reformism*, pp. 229 and 227.

31. E. Ross, "'Not the Sort that Would Sit on the Doorstep": Respectability in Pre-World War I London Neighbourhoods', *International Labour and Working-Class History*, 27 (Spring 1985), pp. 39–59, on p. 46.

32. J. Davis, 'Jennings' Buildings and the Royal Borough: The Construction of the Under-Class in Mid-Victorian England', in D. Feldman and G. Stedman Jones (eds), *Metropolis*

London: Histories and Representations since 1800 (London: Routledge, 1989), pp. 11–39, on pp. 31–2.

33. See Ross, 'Not the Sort that Would Sit on the Doorstep', p. 42.

34. P. Bailey, '"Will the Real Bill Banks Please Stand Up?" Towards a Role Analysis of Mid-Victorian Working-Class Respectability', *Journal of Social History*, 12:3 (1979), pp. 336–53, on pp. 343–4; I. McCalman, 'Unrespectable Radicalism: Infidels and Pornography in Early Nineteenth-Century London', *Past and Present*, 104 (1984), pp. 74–110, on pp. 104–5.

35. M. J. Maynes, 'Autobiography and Class Formation in Nineteenth-Century Europe: Methodological Considerations', *Social Science History*, 16:3 (Fall 1992), pp. 517–37, on p. 522.

36. Scott, *Domination and the Arts of Resistance*, pp. 187–92.

37. Ibid., p. 105. Some of the difficulties in employing Scott's ideas in a European context have been discussed in J. Braddick and J. Walter, 'Grids of Power: Order, Hierarchy and Subordination', in J. Braddick and J. Walter (eds), *Negotiating Power in Early Modern Society* (Cambridge: Cambridge University Press, 2001), pp. 1–42.

38. M. Steinberg, 'The Dialogue of Struggle: The Contest over Ideological Boundaries in the Case of the London Silk Weavers in the Early Nineteenth Century', *Social Science History*, 18:4 (Winter 1994), pp. 505–42, on p. 506. See also Steinberg's 'The Roar of the Crowd: Repertoires of Discourse and Collective Action among the Spitalfields Silk Weavers in Nineteenth-Century London', in M. Traugott (ed.), *Repertoires and Cycles of Collective Action* (Durham, NC: Duke University Press, 1995), pp. 57–87; '"The Labour of the Country is the Wealth of the Country": Class Identity, Consciousness, and the Role of Discourse in the Making of the English Working Class', *International and Working-Class History*, 49 (Spring 1996), pp. 1–25; 'The Talk and Back Talk of Collective Action: A Dialogic Analysis of Repertoires of Discourse among Nineteenth-Century English Cotton Spinners', *American Journal of Sociology*, 105:3 (November 1999), pp. 736–80; and *Fighting Words: Working-Class Formation, Collective Action and Discourse in Early Nineteenth-Century England* (Ithaca, NY: Cornell University Press, 1999).

39. Steinberg, 'The Dialogue of Struggle', p. 513.

40. Ibid., p. 511.

41. See the *International Journal of Historical Archaeology*, 3:1 and 3:2 (1999).

42. B. Frazer, 'Reconceptualizing Resistance in the Historical Archaeology of the British Isles: An Editorial', *International Journal of Historical Archaeology*, 3:1 (1999), pp. 1–10, on pp. 5 and 7.

43. S. Cordery, 'Friendly Societies and the Discourse of Respectability in Britain, 1825–1875', *Journal of British Studies*, 34 (January 1995), pp. 35–58, on p. 40. See also S. Cordery, *British Friendly Societies, 1750–1914* (Basingstoke: Palgrave Macmillan, 2003).

44. P. Colquhoun, *A Treatise on Indigence* (London: Hatchard, 1806), p. 17.

45. Ibid., pp. 17–18.

46. See for instance Green, *From Artisans to Paupers*, ch. 3; and I. Prothero, *Artisans and Politics* (Folkestone: Dawson, 1979), pp. 27–8.

47. A. Kidd, *State, Society and the Poor in Nineteenth-Century England* (Basingstoke: Macmillan, 1999), pp. 10 and 168.

48. Green, *From Artisans to Paupers*, p. 44.

49. Kidd, *State, Society and the Poor*, p. 46.

50. C. Cook and J. Stevenson, *The Longman Handbook of Modern British History 1714–2001* (Harlow: Longman, 2001), p. 151.

51. P. J. Corfield, *The Impact of English Towns 1700–1800* (Oxford: Oxford University Press, 1982), p. 2.

52. B. Weinreb and C. Hibbert, *The London Encyclopaedia* (London: Macmillan, 1987), 'Population', p. 613.

53. Cook and Stevenson, *The Longman Handbook of Modern British History*, p. 153.

54. Ibid., p. 71.

55. Ibid., p. 73.

56. See for instance D. Andrew, *Philanthropy and Police: London Charity in the 18th Century* (Princeton, NJ: Princeton University Press, 1989); and S. Macfarlane, 'Social Policy and the Poor in the Later Seventeenth Century', in A. L. Beier and R. Finlay (eds), *London 1500–1700* (Harlow: Longman, 1986), pp. 252–77.

57. R. Horwood, *The A to Z of Regency London* (London: London Topographical Society, 1985), plates 13 and 23. This volume contains Richard Horwood's map of the metropolis in 1813.

58. C. Dickens, 'The Devil's Acre', *Household Words*, 1:13 (22 June 1850), pp. 297–301, on p. 297.

59. Green, *From Artisans to Paupers*, pp. 26–32.

60. Ibid., p. 34.

61. R. Dennis, *Cities in Modernity* (Cambridge: Cambridge University Press, 2008), p. 143.

62. Ibid.

63. This is the first reliable indicator. In Appendix III B of *London Life in the Eighteenth Century*, M. D. George includes an earlier estimation of London's population which was compiled by the Convocation of the Church of England, but she warns on p. 412 that much of the information is 'clearly exaggerated'. See M. D. George, *London Life in the Eighteenth Century* (Chicago, IL: Academy Chicago Publishers, 1984).

64. *British Parliamentary Papers*, Accounts and Papers 1833, Vol. XXXVI, pp. 374–5.

65. A. Wohl, *The Eternal Slum* (New Brunswick, NJ: Transaction Publishers, 2009), p. 26.

66. Colquhoun gives a figure of 8.41 people per house in 1801 and 8.95 per house in 1811 for Westminster overall; see P. Colquhoun, *A Treatise on the Wealth, Power and Resources of the British Empire* (London: J. Mawman, 1814), p. 45.

67. See George, *London Life in the Eighteenth Century*, pp. 118–19.

68. Mortality rates in general were falling in London, as M. K. Matossian has shown in her article 'Death in London', in the *Journal of Interdisciplinary History*, 16:2 (Autumn 1985), pp. 183–97. Nevertheless, according to the Abstract of Answers and Responses to the Population Act in 1811, deaths outnumbered births by 4,100 in Westminster during the years 1801 to 1810 inclusive; *British Parliamentary Papers*, House of Commons, 1812, Vol. XI, p. 639.

69. L. D. Schwarz, 'Income Distribution and Social Structure in London in the Late Eighteenth Century', *Economic History Review*, 2nd ser., 32:2 (1979), pp. 250–9, on p. 258.

70. Schwarz relied on returns collected from assessed taxation commissioners in 1797. Unfortunately the returns for St Martin's have not survived, though many of the other Westminster parishes are well represented. At best, then, one can construct a probable picture for St Martin's.

71. H. Mayhew, *The Morning Chronicle Survey of Labour and the Poor: The Metropolitan Districts*, 6 vols (Firle: Caliban Books, 1980), vol. 1, 'Letter XI, Friday, November 23, 1849', pp. 221–46, and vol. 2, 'Letter XV, Friday, December 7, 1849', pp. 66–9.

72. K. Wrightson, 'Mutualities and Obligations: Changing Social Relationships in Early Modern England', *Proceedings of the British Academy*, 139 (2006), pp. 157–94, on pp. 184–6.

73. A. Clark, *The Struggle for the Breeches* (Berkeley, CA: University of California Press, 1997).

1 Borrowing a Warm

1. K. Thomas, *The Ends of Life* (Oxford: Oxford University Press, 2009), p. 182.
2. Ibid., p. 183.
3. Corfield, *The Impact of English Towns*, p. 68.
4. P. Horden and N. Purcell, *The Corrupting Sea* (Oxford: Wiley-Blackwell, 2000), p. 500.
5. D. R. Green and A. Parton, 'Slums, and Slum Life in Victorian England: London and Birmingham at Mid-Century', in, S. M. Gaskell (ed.), *Slums* (Leicester: Leicester University Press, 1990), pp. 17–91, on p. 79.
6. Ibid., p. 81.
7. George, *London Life in the Eighteenth Century*, p. 103.
8. Anon., *Low Life or One Half of the World Knows Not How the Other Half Live* (London: John Lever, 1764), p. 17.
9. G. Godwin, *Town Swamps and Social Bridges* (1859; Leicester: Leicester University Press, 1972), p. 92.
10. See L. Gowing, 'Language, Power and the Law: Women's Slander Litigation in Early Modern London', in J. Kermode and G. Walker (eds), *Women, Crime and the Courts* (Chapel Hill, NC: University of North Carolina Press, 1994), pp. 26–47; and L. Gowing, *Domestic Dangers: Women, Words and Sex in Early Modern London* (Oxford: Clarendon Press, 1996).
11. Hart against Aaron, December 1785, London Metropolitan Archives, Consistory Court Depositions (hereafter LMA, CCD) X19/147, p. 193.
12. Palmer against Williams, December 1782, LMA, CCD X19/146, p. 368.
13. Nowlan against Rose, January 1793, LMA, CCD X19/150, p. 347.
14. Goulee against Shadd, May 1805, LMA, CCD X19/214, p. 652.
15. Jones against Parker, February 1805, LMA, CCD X19/151, pp. 143–51.
16. Rose against Graham, May 1794, LMA, CCD X19/150, pp. 412 and 419.
17. In the remaining three cases, it was not clear where the disputants lived.
18. J. A. Sharpe has found that sexual reputation had been the concern of both sexes in the seventeenth century and that men were far more likely to bring charges, especially in the early 1600s, than was the case in the late eighteenth century. In 1590 males brought 49 per cent of the cases; by 1690 this had fallen to 24 per cent. Sharpe suggests this may reflect the growth of a double standard. See J. A. Sharpe, *Defamation and Sexual Slander in Early Modern England: The Church Courts at York*, Borthwick Papers No. 58 (York, 1980), pp. 27–8.
19. McAlister against Seeley, February 1811, LMA, CCD X19/217, pp. 260–7; and Meek against Puzey, February 1816, LMA, CCD DL/C/298.
20. Gowing, 'Language, Power and the Law', p. 30.
21. Jarman against Sanders, May 1789, LMA, CCD X19/148, pp. 565–9.
22. Meek against Puzey, February 1816, LMA, CCD DL/C/298.
23. Jennings against Palmer, February 1801, LMA, CCD X19/151, pp. 153–9.
24. Palmer against Williams, December 1782, LMA, CCD X19/146, p. 347.
25. Nowlan against Ross, January 1793, LMA, CCD X19/150, p. 347.
26. Cairns against Moss, January 1814, LMA, CCD X19/215, pp. 401–13.
27. Sefton against Taylor, December 1783, LMA, CCD X19/147, pp. 468–9.
28. Spence against Heberley, December 1783, LMA, CCD X19/147, p. 461.
29. Robinson against Mills, July 1811, LMA, CCD X19/153, pp. 215–18.
30. Palmer against Williams, December 1782, LMA, CCD X19/146, p. 349.

31. Jones against Parker, February 1805, LMA, CCD, X19/151, pp. 143–52.

32. G. Litton Fox, "'Nice Girl': Social Control of Women through a Value Construct', *Signs*, 2:4 (1977), pp. 805 and 811.

33. Powley against Maddeson, December 1780, LMA, CCD X19/146, p. 322.

34. Dinnis against Groves, February 1789, LMA, CCD X19/148, pp. 204–5.

35. White against Bower, February 1789, LMA, CCD X19/148, p. 684.

36. Cairns against Moss, January 1814, LMA, CCD X19/215, pp. 402 and 409.

37. Jennings against Palmer, February 1891, LMA, CCD X19/151, p. 156.

38. Rose against Graham, May 1794, LMA, CCD X19/150, p. 419.

39. Spence against Heberley, December 1783, LMA, CCD X19/147, p. 461.

40. The gossip among neighbours is not recounted in sufficient detail to permit an in-depth analysis of it, so it is difficult to know whether it bears out M. Gluckman's claims that gossip maintains 'the unity, morals and values of social groups'; M. Gluckman, 'Gossip and Scandal', *Current Anthropology*, 4:3 (1963), p. 307. See also M. Gluckman, 'Psychological, Sociological and Anthropological Explanations and Gossip: A Clarification', *Man*, new ser., 3 (1968), pp. 20–34. For critiques of Gluckman, see R. Paine, 'What is Gossip About? An Alternative Hypothesis', *Man*, new ser., 2 (1967), pp. 278–85; and P. J. Wilson, 'Filcher of Good Names: An Enquiry into Anthropology and Gossip', *Man*, new ser., 9 (1974), pp. 93–102.

41. Cairns against Moss, January 1814, LMA, CCD X19/215, p. 403.

42. Child against Lacey, June 1785, LMA, CCD X19/147, p. 100.

43. M. Tebbutt, *Women's Talk: A Social History of 'Gossip' in Working Class Neighbourhoods, 1880–1960* (Aldershot: Scolar Press, 1997), p. 11.

44. Ibid., p. 3.

45. B. Capp, *When Gossips Meet* (Oxford: Oxford University Press, 2003), p. 60.

46. J. Pitt-Rivers, 'Honour and Social Status', in J. G. Peristiany (ed.), *Honour and Shame* (Chicago, IL: University of Chicago Press, 1966), pp. 19–77, on p. 27.

47. Goulee against Shadd, May 1805, LMA, CCD X19/214, p. 652.

48. Robinson against Mills, July 1811, LMA, CCD X19/153, p. 217.

49. Powley against Maddeson, December 1780, LMA, CCD X19/146, p. 321.

50. Palmer against Williams, December 1782, LMA, CCD X19/146, p. 357.

51. Dinnis against Groves, February 1789, LMA, CCD X19/148, p. 200.

52. Sefton against Taylor, December 1783, LMA, CCD X19/147, p. 466.

53. Jones against Parker, February 1805, LMA, CCD X19/151, p. 146.

54. Palmer against Williams, December 1782, LMA, CCD X19/146, p. 354.

55. Graves against Walls, March 1813, LMA, CCD X19/215, p. 272.

56. Palmer against Williams, December 1782, LMA, CCD X19/146, p. 359.

57. Jarman against Sanders, May 1789, LMA, CCD X19/148, p. 566.

58. Goulee against Shadd, May 1805, LMA, CCD X19/214, pp. 652–3.

59. Palmer against Williams, December 1782, LMA, CCD X19/146, p. 359–66.

60. P. Earle, *A City Full of People* (London: Methuen, 1994), pp. 186–7.

61. Jarman against Sanders, May 1789, LMA, CCD X19/148, pp. 565–6.

62. Dinnis against Groves, February 1789, LMA, CCD X19/148, pp. 208-9.

63. Goulee against Shadd, May 1805, LMA, CCD X19/214, p. 254.

64. P. Hudson and L. Hunter (eds), 'The Autobiography of William Hart, Cooper, 1776–1857, a Respectable Artisan in the Industrial Revolution', Part I, *London Journal*, 7:2 (1981), pp. 144–60, on p. 157.

65. E. P. Thompson and E. Yeo (eds), *The Unknown Mayhew* (Harmondsworth: Penguin, 1974), letter VII, 9 November 1849, pp. 161–2.
66. V. A. C. Gatrell, *The Hanging Tree* (New York: Oxford University Press, 1994), pp. 132–3 and 144.
67. Ibid., p. 144.
68. Pitt-Rivers, 'Honour and Social Status', p. 21.
69. Ibid., pp. 22–3.
70. Prothero, *Artisans and Politics*, p. 28.
71. Thomas, *The Ends of Life*, p. 160.
72. Thomas, incidentally, gives examples right up to the very end of the eighteenth century to back these claims; ibid., p. 164.
73. Horden and Purcell, *The Corrupting Sea*, p. 490; and J. K. Campbell, *Honour, Family and Patronage* (Oxford: Oxford University Press, 1964). See also F. H. Stewart, *Honor* (Chicago, IL: University of Chicago Press, 1994).
74. It is true that the consistory court defamation cases constitute a small sample, for, as noted earlier, the courts were falling into desuetude: there are twenty-one cases clearly involving labouring-class people between 1780 and 1820. Nevertheless, the work of S. M. Waddams, focusing on internal changes in the consistory courts and the continuing popularity of the summary courts as arenas in which to air disputes, weakens claims that there was a shift in plebeian attitudes. Anna Clark has also noted that defamation case records, consisting largely of the written depositions from local witnesses, still illuminate the details, disagreements and tensions in neighbourhood life in ways that few other sources can achieve. They are a rich (if diminishing) source. See S. M. Waddams, *Sexual Slander in Nineteenth-Century England: Defamation in the Ecclesiastical Courts, 1815–1855* (Toronto: University of Toronto Press, 2000); Gowing, 'Language, Power and the Law'; A. Clark, *The Struggle for the Breeches*, p. 52; and A. Clark, 'Whores and Gossips: Sexual Reputation in London 1770–1825', in A. Angerman et al. (eds), *Current Issues in Women's History* (London: Routledge and Kegan Paul, 1989), pp. 231–48, on pp. 235–8.
75. Clark, 'Whores and Gossips', p. 239. Also see Clark, *The Struggle for the Breeches*, p. 52.
76. White against Bower, February 1789, LMA, CCD X19/148, p. 684.
77. Powley against Maddeson, December 1780, LMA, CCD X19/146, pp. 318–21.
78. C. de Saussure, *A Foreign View of England in the Reigns of George I and George II* (London: John Murray, 1902), letter of 7 February 1727, p. 180.
79. Anon., *The Dens of London* (London: Thompson and Alfred, 1835), pp. 85–7.
80. P. Grosley, *A Tour to London, New Observations on England* (London: Lockyer Davis, 1772), p. 64.
81. For a discussion of violence, see S. D'Cruze, *Crimes of Outrage* (Dekalb, IL: Northern Illinois University Press, 1998); and Carter Wood, *Violence and Crime in Nineteenth-Century England*.
82. Earle, *A City Full of People*, p. 173.
83. Anonymous navvy, in J. Burnett (ed.), *Useful Toil* (London: Routledge, 1984), p. 62.
84. E. Ross, 'Survival Networks: Women's Neighbourhood Sharing in London Before World War One', *History Workshop Journal*, 15 (Spring 1983), pp. 4–27; and Ross, 'Not the Sort that Would Sit on the Doorstep'.
85. H. Medick, 'Plebeian Culture in the Transition to Capitalism', in R. Samuel and G. Stedman Jones (eds), *Culture, Ideology and Politics* (London: Routledge and Kegan Paul, 1982), pp. 84–113, on p. 92.

86. D. Vincent, *Bread, Knowledge and Freedom* (London: Europa, 1981), p. 66.
87. Medick, 'Plebeian Culture in the Transition to Capitalism', p. 91.
88. M. Tebbutt, *Making Ends Meet: Pawnbroking and Working-Class Credit* (Leicester: University of Leicester Press, 1983), p. 19.
89. Vincent, *Bread, Knowledge and Freedom*, p. 200.
90. T. Carter, *Memoirs of a Working Man* (London: Charles Knight and Co., 1845), p. 18.
91. Ibid., p. 21.
92. Ibid., p. 42.
93. Ibid., pp. 94–5.
94. Ibid., p. 194.
95. Ibid., p. 152.
96. Ibid., pp. 144–6.
97. Ibid., p. 186.
98. Ibid., p. 144.
99. W. E. Hickson, quoted in [C. R. Lushington], *The Practice of the Mendicity Society* (London: John Murray, 1847), p. 17.
100. That is, the pawning was mentioned in passing while some other reason was cited as the main cause of the apparent theft.
101. This claim is based on a close reading of the cases in which the accused gave defence statements for the five years from 1780 to 1784. The cases making up the percentages include those where either the accused or a witness indicated that the goods had been pawned with permission, that they had been lent in order to be pawned, that the accused had intended to redeem them, or that the accused had pawned the goods in order to settle an outstanding debt (usually wages that the prosecutor had failed to pay). The actual percentages of women in 1780, 1781, 1782, 1783 and 1784 respectively were as follows: 19 per cent, 16 per cent, 12 per cent, 11 per cent and 15 per cent. For men, they were 2 per cent, 1 per cent, 3 per cent, 2 per cent and 3 per cent.
102. Proceedings of the Old Bailey, Case 127, Ann Friend, 23 February 1780, and Case 341, Ann Powell, 28 June 1780, at www.oldbaileyonline.org [accessed 15 June 2011].
103. Ibid., Case 516, Sarah Skettles, 11 September 1782.
104. Ibid., Case 155, Martha Ray, 14 January 1784.
105. Ibid., Case 504, Margaret Rowe, 11 September 1782.
106. Ibid., Case 761, Elizabeth Bland 14 September 1785.
107. Ibid., Case 276, Ann Mitchell, 20 February 1782.
108. Ibid., Case 859, Elizabeth Gosling, 12 September 1787.
109. Ibid., Case 112, Elizabeth Cooper, 14 December 1785.
110. Ibid., Case 119, Jane Williams, 9 January 1788.
111. Ibid., Case 336, Mary Robinson, 30 May 1781.
112. Ibid., Case 705, Catherine Knock, 29 June 1785.
113. Ibid., Case 179, Ann Wood, 5 April 1780.
114. Ibid., Case 198, Mary Williams, 25 April 1781.
115. Ibid., Case 67, Susanna Kelly, 4 December 1782.
116. Ibid., Case 565, Elizabeth Green, 12 September 1781.
117. Ibid., Case 642, Jane Curtey, 29 June 1785.
118. Ibid., Case 10, Elizabeth Jones, 10 January 1781.
119. Ibid., Case 204, Mary Hughes, 25 April 1781.
120. Ibid., Case 444, Jenny Mead, 25 June 1788.
121. Medick, 'Plebeian Culture in the Transition to Capitalism', p. 92.

122. Tebbutt also advances some non-monetary reasons for the popularity of pawning. The shop was far more secure than most labouring-class homes, and so could be used as a kind of safety deposit. As well, items not in use at certain times of the year could in effect be stored at the pawn shop by pledging them. See M. Tebbutt, *Making Ends Meet*, p. 19.

123. Ibid., p. 13.

124. J. H. Treble, *Urban Poverty in Britain* (New York: St Martin's Press, 1979), p. 132.

125. Tebbutt, *Making Ends Meet*, p. 27.

126. F. Place, *The Autobiography of Francis Place*, ed. M. Thale (Cambridge: Cambridge University Press, 1972), p. 117.

127. Tebbutt, *Making Ends Meet*, p. 22.

128. A. Tomkins, 'Pawnbroking and the Survival Strategies of the Urban Poor in 1770s York', in S. King and A. Tomkins (eds), *The Poor in England, 1700–1850* (Manchester: Manchester University Press, 2003), pp. 166–98, on p. 183.

129. Ibid., pp. 180–1.

130. Proceedings of the Old Bailey, Case 104, Ann Braidy, 10 January 1781, at www.oldbaileyonline.org [accessed 15 June 2011].

131. Martha White, 21 September 1796, St Martin's Overseers Minutes, Westminster Public Archives (hereafter WPA), F 2075; Eleanor Evans, 16 November 1796, WPA, F 2075; and Mary Draper, 25 October 1814, WPA, F 2077.

132. See B. Lemire, 'Peddling Fashion: Salesmen, Pawnbrokers, Taylors, Thieves and the Second-hand Clothes Trade in England, c. 1700–1800', *Textile History*, 22:1 (1991), pp. 67–82; and B. Lemire, 'Petty Pawns and Informal Lending: Gender and the Transformation of Small-Scale Credit in England, circa 1600–1800', in K. Bruland and P. K. O'Brien (eds), *From Family Firms to Corporate Capitalism* (Oxford: Clarendon Press, 1998), pp. 112–38.

133. G. Stedman Jones, *Outcast London* (Harmondsworth: Penguin, 1971), pp. 87–8.

134. Place, *Autobiography*, p. 117.

135. Anon., *Low Life*, quoted in D. Davis, *Fairs, Shops and Supermarkets: A History of English Shopping* (Toronto: University of Toronto Press, 1966), p. 216.

136. H. and L. H. Mui, *Shops and Shopkeeping in Eighteenth Century England* (London: Routledge, 1989), p. 207.

137. Tebbutt, *Making Ends Meet*, p. 16.

138. Mui and Mui, *Shops and Shopkeeping*, p. 212.

139. Ibid., p. 218.

140. Ibid., p. 289.

141. C. Muldrew and S. King, 'Cash, Wages and the Economy of Makeshifts in the Economy of England, 1650–1800', in P. Scholliers and L. Schwarz (eds), *Experiencing Wages* (New York: Berghahn Books, 2003), pp. 155–82, on p. 171.

142. For a discussion of this tactic, see J. Kok, K. Mandemakers and H. Wals, 'City Nomads: Changing Residence as a Coping Strategy, Amsterdam, 1890–1940', *Social Science History*, 29:1 (Spring 2005), pp. 15–43.

143. Muldrew and King, 'Cash, Wages and Makeshifts', p. 174.

2 Mazy Courts and Dark Abodes

1. H. Lefebvre, *The Production of Space* (Oxford: Blackwell, 1991).

2. Soja, *Postmodern Geographies*, p. 11.

3. Ibid., p. 23.

4.   S. Zukin, 'Postmodern Urban Landscapes: Mapping Culture and Power', in S. Lash and J. Friedman (eds), *Modernity and Identity* (Oxford: Blackwell, 1992), pp. 221–47, on p. 224.

5.   F. Mort and M. Ogborn address these concerns in 'Transforming Metropolitan London, 1750–1960', the introductory essay to a special issue of the *Journal of British Studies*, 43:1 (January 2004), pp. 1–14.

6.   J. Marriott, 'The Spatiality of the Poor in Eighteenth-Century London', in Hitchcock and Shore (eds), *The Streets of London*, pp. 119–34, on p. 122.

7.   P. J. Corfield, 'Walking the City Streets: The Urban Odyssey in Eighteenth-Century England', *Journal of Urban History*, 16:2 (February 1990), pp. 132–74, on pp. 132–3.

8.   L. Simond, *Journal of a Tour and Residence in Great Britain during the Years 1810 and 1811* (London: Archibald Constable and Co., 1815), p. 21.

9.   M. J. Daunton, *House and Home in the Victorian City* (London: E. Arnold, 1983), p. 12. See also M. J. Daunton, 'Public Place and Private Space: The Victorian City and the Working-Class Household', in D. Fraser and A. Sutcliffe (eds), *The Pursuit of Urban History* (London: E. Arnold, 1983), pp. 212–33, on pp. 214–15.

10. Daunton, *House and Home*, p. 12.

11. Daunton, 'Public Place and Private Space', p. 214.

12. V. Thompson, 'Telling "Spatial Stories": Urban Space and Bourgeois Identity in Early Nineteenth-Century Paris', *Journal of Modern History*, 75 (September 2003), pp. 523–56, on pp. 538 and 547.

13. C. Otter, 'Making Liberalism Durable: Vision and Civility in the Late Victorian City', *Social History*, 27:1 (January 2002), pp. 1–15, on p. 1.

14. M. Foucault, 'Governmentality', in M. Foucault, *Power*, ed. J. Faubion, Vol. 3 (New York: New Press, 1994), p. 291.

15. The phrase 'indirect mechanisms' is taken from P. Miller and N. Rose, 'Governing Economic Life', in M. Gane and T. Johnson (eds), *Foucault's New Domains* (London: Routledge, 1993), p. 76.

16. Otter, 'Making Liberalism Durable', p. 1.

17. Ibid., p. 2.

18. Ibid., p. 3.

19. Ibid.

20. T. Beames, *The Rookeries of London*, 2nd edn (London: Thomas Bosworth, 1852), p. 153. While political fears were an important component in the calls for reform of plebeian behaviour, it is difficult to see them as the central motivating force given the more common focus on morality. For a dissenting view, see Lis and Soly's discussion of the campaign against drinking in 'Neighbourhood and Social Change in Western European Cities', p. 19.

21. See for example A. Robey, '"All Asmear with Filth and Fat and Blood and Foam": The Social and Architectural Reformation of Smithfield Market during the 19th Century', *Transactions of the Ancient Monuments Society*, 42 (1998), pp. 1–12.

22. J. Winter, *London's Teeming Streets, 1830–1914* (London: Routledge, 1993), p. 20.

23. M. Ogborn, *Spaces of Modernity: London's Geographies 1680–1780* (New York: Guildford Press, 1998), pp. 6–28.

24. Marriott, 'The Spatiality of the Poor', p. 134.

25. See for instance Corfield, 'Walking the City Streets'; Hitchcock and Shore (eds), *The Streets of London*; C. Brant and S. Whyman, *Walking the Streets of Eighteenth-Century London: John Gay's Trivia* (Oxford: Oxford University Press, 2007); and A. O'Byrne,

'The Art of Walking in London: Representing Urban Pedestrianism in the Early Nineteenth Century', *Romanticism*, 14:2 (2008), pp. 94–107.

26. A thoughtful antidote to this mindset is Ogborn's *Spaces of Modernity*.
27. H. Mayhew, *London Labour and the London Poor*, 4 vols (New York: Dover, 1968) (hereafter *LLLP*), vol. 2, p. 195.
28. R. Turvey, 'Street Mud, Dust and Noise', *London Journal*, 21:2 (1996), pp. 131–48, on p. 134.
29. A. Tanner, 'Dust-O! Rubbish in Victorian London, 1860–1900', *London Journal*, 31:2 (November 2006), pp. 157–78, on p. 168.
30. See for instance the Proceedings of the Old Bailey, available at www.oldbaileyonline.org. Throughout the 1780s, defendants regularly explained their presence in suspicious places by claiming they were 'easing' themselves.
31. J. Peller Malcolm, *Anecdotes of the Manners and Customs of London during the Eighteenth Century* (London: Longman, Hurst, Rees and Orme, 1808), p. 473.
32. H. Gavin, *Sanitary Ramblings* (London: Cass, 1971), p. 80.
33. J. Gage, 'The Rise and Fall of the St. Giles Rookery', *Camden History Review*, 12 (1984), pp. 17–24, on p. 23.
34. J. Clifford, 'Some Aspects of London Life in the Mid-18th Century', in P. Fritz and D. Williams (eds), *City and Society in the Eighteenth Century* (Toronto: Hakkert, 1975), p. 27.
35. W. Guy, 'On the Health of Nightmen, Scavengers, and Dustmen', *Journal of the Statistical Society of London*, 11:1 (March 1848), pp. 72–81, on p. 73.
36. Paving Committees oversaw street lighting and dust collection as well as paving; St Martin in the Fields Committee for Paving, Lighting, etc., Minutes, 6 April 1781, WPA, F 2532.
37. H. Phillips, *Mid Georgian London* (London: Collins, 1964) p. 221.
38. C. P. Moritz, *Journeys of a German in England in 1782*, trans. and ed. R. Nettel (New York: Holt, Rinehart and Winston, 1965), p. 189.
39. Peller Malcolm, *Anecdotes of the Manners and Customs of London*, p. 473. According to Tanner, dust consisted mainly of coal breeze (small cinders) and ash; 'Dust-O! Rubbish in Victorian London', p. 159.
40. H. Gavin, *Unhealthiness of London* (New York: Garland, 1985), p. 6.
41. Gavin, *Sanitary Ramblings*, p. 80.
42. Peller Malcolm, *Anecdotes of the Manners and Customs of London*, p. 472.
43. St Martin's Paving Committee, 2 July 1780, WPA, F 2532.
44. Ibid., 21 July 1780, WPA, F 2532.
45. Tanner, 'Dust-O! Rubbish in Victorian London', p. 160.
46. St Martin's Paving Committee, 13 April 1781, WPA, F 2532.
47. Tanner, 'Dust-O! Rubbish in Victorian London', p. 166.
48. Grosley, *A Tour to London*, p. 36.
49. J. Gay, *Trivia* (Dublin: George Risk, 1727), p. 17.
50. Grosley, *A Tour to London*, p. 115. Corfield, 'Walking the City Streets', makes a similar point on p. 143.
51. R. Mudie, quoted in R. Allen, 'Observing London Street-Life: G. A. Sala and A. J. Munby', in Hitchcock and Shore (eds), *Streets of London*, pp. 198–214, on p. 200.
52. J. Badcock, quoted in J. Rendall, 'Displaying Sexuality: Gendered Identities and the Early Nineteenth-Century Street', in N. Fyfe (ed.), *Images of the Street* (London: Routledge, 1998), pp. 74–91, on p. 80.

53. De Saussure, *A Foreign View of England*, p. 168.
54. C. Harvey, E. Green and P. J. Corfield, 'Continuity, Change, and Specialization within Metropolitan London: The Economy of Westminster, 1750–1820', *Economic History Review*, 52:2 (1999), pp. 469–93, on p. 474; and J. White, *London in the Nineteenth Century* (London: Vintage, 2008), p. 15.
55. M. Jenner, 'Circulation and Disorder: London Streets and Hackney Coaches, c. 1640–1740', in Hitchcock and Shore (eds), *The Streets of London*, pp. 40–53, on p. 42.
56. Jenner, 'Circulation and Disorder', p. 53.
57. J. Grant, *Lights and Shadows of London Life*, Vol. 1 (London: G. Routledge, 1846), pp. 243–4.
58. Moritz, *Journeys of a German in England*, p. 12.
59. Anon., *Low Life*, p. 33.
60. Simond, *Journal of a Tour and Residence in Great Britain*, p. 22.
61. Grosley, *A Tour to London*, p. 47.
62. Ibid., p. 48.
63. Ibid., pp. 48–50.
64. P. Brimblecombe, *The Big Smoke* (London: Methuen, 1987).
65. J. Lettsom, quoted in George, *London Life in the Eighteenth Century*, p. 102.
66. Gavin, *Unhealthiness of London*, pp. 42–3.
67. F. Place, quoted in George, *London Life in the Eighteenth Century*, p. 113.
68. Brimblecombe, *The Big Smoke*, p. 85.
69. Simond, *Journal of a Tour and Residence in Great Britain*, p. 38.
70. Otter, 'Making Liberalism Durable', p. 3.
71. S. Mosley, 'Fresh Air and Foul: The Role of the Open Fireplace in Ventilating the British Home, 1837–1910', *Planning Perspectives*, 18 (2003), pp. 1–21, on p. 9.
72. Ibid., p. 3.
73. Brimblecombe, *The Big Smoke*, pp. 109–15.
74. T. Miller, *Picturesque Sketches of London* (London: Office of the National Illustrated Library, 1852), p. 247.
75. Ibid.
76. M. Falkus, 'Lighting in the Dark Ages of English Economic History: Town Streets before the Industrial Revolution,' in D. C. Coleman and A. H. John (eds), *Trade, Government and Economy in Pre-Industrial England* (London: Littlehampton Book Services Ltd, 1976), pp. 248–73, on p. 261.
77. The parish had sought to save money by eliminating some of its lamps. When the inspector went round to do so, he realized that the contractor had listed – and presumably was charging for – more lamps than had actually been put up. Hence, the census. St Martin's Paving Committee Minutes, 13 October 1782, WPA, F 2532.
78. Ibid., 27 January 1813, WPA, F 2534.
79. Clifford, 'Some Aspects of London Life', p. 32.
80. St Martin's Paving Committee Minutes, 19 October 1814, WPA, F 2534.
81. Falkus, 'Lighting in the Dark Ages of English Economic History', p. 262.
82. Peller Malcolm, *Anecdotes of the Manners and Customs of London*, p. 463.
83. Moritz, *Journeys of a German in England*, p. 15.
84. Grosley, *A Tour to London*, p. 44.
85. Otter, 'Making Liberalism Durable', p. 6.
86. St Martin's Paving Committee Minutes, 8 December 1780, WPA, F 2532.
87. Ibid., 2 December 1801, WPA, F 2533.

88. Ibid., 27 January 1813, WPA, F 2534.

89. J. H. MacMichael, *Charing Cross and its Immediate Neighbourhood* (London: Chatto and Windus, 1906), p. 80.

90. P. Cunningham, *A Handbook of London Past and Present* (London: John Murray, 1849), p. xxxvii.

91. Falkus, 'Lighting in the Dark Ages of English Economic History', p. 267.

92. Grosley, *A Tour to London*, p. 62.

93. De Saussure, *A Foreign View of England*, pp. 294–5.

94. See Jenner, 'Circulation and Disorder'.

95. Moritz, *Journeys of a German in England*, p. 32.

96. E. Beresford Chancellor, *Annals of Covent Garden* (London: Hutchinson and Co., 1930), p. 198.

97. Grant, *Lights and Shadows of London Life*, p. 245.

98. P. Grosley, quoted in Peller Malcolm, *Anecdotes of the Manners and Customs of London*, p. 220.

99. See R. Shoemaker, 'Streets of Shame? The Crowd and Public Punishments in London 1700–1820', in S. Devereux and P. Griffiths (eds), *Penal Practice and Culture* (Basingstoke: Palgrave Macmillan, 2004), pp. 232–57; and Shoemaker, *The London Mob*, ch. 4. Greg Smith is much more concerned with the shift in attitudes of the authorities and the middle and upper classes, in G. Smith, 'Civilized People Don't Want to See That Kind of Thing: The Decline of Public Physical Punishment in London, 1760–1840', in C. Strange (ed.), *Qualities of Mercy* (Vancouver: University of British Columbia Press, 1996), pp. 21–51.

100. M. White, '"Rogues of the Meaner Sort"? Old Bailey Executions and the Crowd in the Early Nineteenth Century', *London Journal*, 33:2 (July 2008), pp. 135–53, on p. 148.

101. Ibid., p. 139.

102. Ibid., p. 149.

103. In 1859 4,000 Kentish residents, mostly women and children, attended an execution, and in 1863 some 6,000 watched a murderer hang; C. Conley, *The Unwritten Law: Criminal Justice in Victorian Kent* (Oxford: Oxford University Press, 1991), p. 47.

104. Miller, *Picturesque Sketches of London*, p. 183.

105. Ibid., p. 184.

106. Ibid., p. 190.

107. St Martin's Paving Committee Minutes, 12 November 1806 and 11 August 1813, WPA, F 2534.

108. For an analysis of this print, see S. Shesgreen, *Images of the Outcast: The Urban Poor in the Cries of London* (New Brunswick, NJ: Rutgers University Press, 2002), pp. 90–117.

109. B. Assael, 'Music in the Air', in Hitchcock and Shore (eds), *The Streets of London*, pp. 183–97, on p. 183.

110. St Martin's Paving Committee Minutes, WPA, F 2532–4.

111. Proceedings of the Old Bailey, Case 669, John Hyde, September 1783, at www.oldbaileyonline.org [accessed 10 May 2011].

112. Ibid., Case 809, Edward Robinson, September 1784.

113. Ibid., Third Session commencing 19 February 1800 and Seventh Session commencing 17 September 1800.

114. J. Davis, 'Prosecutions and their Context: The Use of the Criminal Law in Later Nineteenth-Century London', in D. Hay and F. Snyder (eds), *Policing and Prosecution in Britain, 1750–1850* (Oxford: Clarendon Press, 1989), pp. 397–426, on p. 425.

115. Peller Malcolm, *Anecdotes of the Manners and Customs of London*, p. 466.

116. St Martin's Paving Committee Minutes, 12 August 1812, WPA, F 2534.

117. H. Fielding, *An Enquiry into the Causes of the Late Increase of Robbers*, 2nd edn (London: M. Cooper, 1751), p. 116.

118. As Daunton has noted, 'There was an ambiguous boundary, an uncertain threshold, between the private and the public'; *House and Home*, p. 12.

119. L. Pollock, 'Living on the Stage of the World: The Concept of Privacy among the Elite of Early Modern England', in A. Wilson (ed.), *Rethinking Social History* (Manchester: Manchester University Press, 1993), pp. 78–96; L. Klein, 'Gender and the Public/Private Distinction in the Eighteenth Century: Some Questions about Evidence and Analytic Procedure', *Eighteenth-Century Studies*, 29:1 (1995), pp. 97–109, on p. 104; and J. Bailey, '"I Dye [sic] by Inches": Locating Wife Beating in the Concept of a Privatization of Marriage and Violence in Eighteenth-Century England', *Social History*, 31:3 (August 2006), pp. 273–9.

120. A. Vickery, *Behind Closed Doors* (New Haven, CT: Yale University Press, 2009), p. 27.

121. Pollock, 'Living on the Stage of the World', p. 89.

122. Vickery, *Behind Closed Doors*, pp. 25–48.

123. L. Cowen Orlin, *Locating Privacy in Tudor London* (Oxford: Oxford University Press, 2007), p. 173.

124. Ibid., p. 174.

125. Ibid.

126. A. Vickery, 'An Englishman's Home is his Castle? Thresholds, Boundaries and Privacies in the Eighteenth-Century London House', *Past and Present*, 199 (May 2008), pp. 147–73, on p. 158; and Vickery, *Behind Closed Doors*, p. 33.

127. H. J. Dyos, 'The Objects of Street Improvement in Regency and Early Victorian London', in *Exploring the Urban Past: Essays in Urban History by H. J. Dyos*, ed. D. Cannadine and D. Reeder (Cambridge: University of Cambridge, 1982), p. 84.

128. T. Hunt, *Building Jerusalem* (London: Phoenix, 2004), p. 395.

129. Gage, 'The Rise and Fall of the St. Giles Rookery', p. 23.

130. *British Parliamentary Papers*, Accounts and Papers 1833, Vol. XXXVI, pp. 374–5; Wohl, *The Eternal Slum*, pp. 29–30.

131. Lis and Soly, 'Neighbourhood and Social Change in West European Cities', p. 27.

132. Wohl, *The Eternal Slum*, p. 27.

133. Ibid., p. 6.

134. Ibid., p. 29.

135. J. Hollingshead, *Ragged London in 1861* (London: Smith, Elder and Co., 1861), p. 121.

136. Gage, 'The Rise and Fall of the St. Giles Rookery', p. 23.

137. R. Dennis, '"The Geography of Victorian Values: Philanthropic Housing in London, 1840–1900', *Journal of Historical Geography*, 15:1 (January 1989), pp. 40–54, on pp. 43–5. For a more positive assessment of model dwellings, see S. Morris, 'Market Solutions for Social Problems: Working-Class Housing in Nineteenth-Century London', *Economic History Review*, 54:3 (2001), pp. 525–45.

138. Wohl, *The Eternal Slum*, p. 24.

139. D. Olsen, *The Growth of Victorian London* (London: Batsford, 1976), p. 270.

140. Dyos, 'The Objects of Street Improvement', p. 141.

141. Hollingshead, *Ragged London in 1861*, p. 116.

142. Gage, 'The Rise and Fall of the St. Giles Rookery', p. 23.

143. J. McEwan, 'The Lodging Exchange: Space, Authority and Knowledge in Eighteenth-Century London', in J. McEwan and P. Sharpe (eds), *Accommodating Poverty* (Basingstoke: Palgrave Macmillan, 2011), pp. 50–68, on p. 54.

144. Godwin, *Town Swamps and Social Bridges*, p.18.

145. George, *London Life in the Eighteenth Century*, p. 100.

146. Cowen Orlin, *Locating Privacy in Tudor London*, p. 170.

147. G. Godwin, *London Shadows: A Glance at the 'Homes' of the Thousands* (London : G. Routledge and Co., 1854), p. 6.

148. Ibid.

149. Anon., *The Dens of London*, pp. 10–11.

150. Ibid., pp. 26–7.

151. For a fuller discussion of this, see L. D. Schwarz, 'Hanoverian London: The Making of a Service Town', in P. Clark and R. Gillespie (eds), *Two Capitals: London and Dublin 1500–1840* (Oxford: Oxford, University Press, 2001), pp. 93–110, on p. 107.

152. These figures are based on the County of London as established by the 1888 Local Government Act. See Weinreb and Hibbert, *The London Encyclopaedia*, p. 614.

153. R. Phillips, *Modern London* (London: C. Mercier, 1804), p. 113.

154. The assessed taxation returns that have survived for this part of London indicate that the following percentages of assessed houses contained lodgers: in St Clement Danes, 70 per cent; in St Margaret's, 66 per cent; in St Anne's, 67 per cent; in St George Hanover Square, 59 per cent; and in St Paul Covent Garden, 72 per cent; Assessed Taxation Returns, Chatham Papers, National Archives, PRO 30/8/281.

155. Phillips, *Mid Georgian London*, p. 100.

156. Hollingshead, *Ragged London in 1861*, p. 113.

157. MacMichael, *Charing Cross*, p. 165.

158. Anon., *The London Guide and Strangers' Safeguard against the Cheats, Swindlers and Pickpockets that Abound within the Bills of Mortality* (London: J. Bumpus, 1818), p. 107.

159. Moritz, *Journeys of a German in England*, p. 6.

160. Hollingshead, *Ragged London*, pp. 113–14.

161. G. Sala, *Twice Round the Clock* (New York: Humanities Press, 1971), p. 145.

162. E. Beresford Chancellor, *Annals of the Strand* (London: Chapman and Hall, 1912), p. 95.

163. Godwin, *Town Swamps and Social Bridges*, p. 91.

164. MacMichael, *Charing Cross*, p. 144.

165. George, *London Life in the Eighteenth Century*, p. 92.

166. Phillips, *Mid Georgian London*, p. 126.

167. B. Jonson, quoted in MacMichael, *Charing Cross*, p. 144.

168. Phillips, *Mid Georgian London*, p. 126.

169. Ibid.

170. George, *London Life in the Eighteenth Century*, p. 92.

171. Beresford Chancellor, *Annals of the Strand*, p. 43.

172. Gay, *Trivia*, p. 37.

173. Anon., *Low Life*, p. 89.

174. J. Fielding, quoted in George, *London Life in the Eighteenth Century*, p. 338.

175. E. J. Burford, *Wits, Wenchers and Wantons* (London: R. Hale, 1986), p. 230.

176. *The Times*, quoted in T. Henderson, *Disorderly Women in Eighteenth-Century London* (London: Longman, 1999), p. 59.

177. Godwin, *London Shadows*, p. 53.

178. J. McMaster, *A Short History of the Royal Parish of St. Martin in the Fields* (London: G. Holder and Sons, 1916), p. 230.

179. St Martin in the Fields Vestry Minutes, 29 June 1787, WPA, F 2031.

180. G. Walker, *Gatherings from Graveyards* ((London: Longman and Co., 1839), p. 163.

181. Burford, *Wits, Wenchers and Wantons*, p. 225.

182. Godwin, *Town Swamps and Social Bridges*, p. 42.

183. Ibid.

184. Ibid.

185. Beresford Chancellor, *Annals of Covent Garden*, p. 100.

186. Ibid.

187. F. Tristan, *The London Journal of Flora Tristan 1842: The Aristocracy and the Working Class of England* (London: Virago, 1989).

188. The settlement examinations between February 1795 and October 1816 have not survived. An analysis of the first five years in the 1790s shows that the parish examined fewer people than was the case from 1816 onward, and provided addresses for only a small minority. In 1790 317 people were examined, for whom 28 addresses were provided. In 1791 273 people were examined, and 21 addresses given; in 1792 243 were examined and 23 addresses provided. In 1793 the figures were 243 and 27 respectively, and in 1794, 172 and 11 respectively. See St Martin in the Fields Settlement Examinations, WPA, F 5073–4, and the Rough Examination Book (no accession number).

189. The number of people examined from Charles Court was undoubtedly higher than these figures indicate. There were three Charles Courts in St Martin's, and it is often unclear from the examinations which one was the individual's address. I have counted only those instances where the court was clearly identified as being south of the Strand.

190. Otter, 'Making Liberalism Durable', p. 4.

3 The Daily Grind

1. M. Ball and D. Sunderland, *An Economic History of London, 1800–1914* (London: Routledge, 2001). Few historians have characterized nineteenth-century London as 'backward', for instance, as the authors do on p. 9.

2. For an optimistic interpretation, see for instance P. Lindhert and J. Williamson, 'English Workers' Living Standards during the Industrial Revolution: A New Look', *Economic History Review*, 2nd ser., 36 (February 1983), pp. 1–25; and J. Williamson, *Did British Capitalism Breed Inequality?* (Boston, MA: Allen and Unwin, 1985).

3. L. D. Schwarz, *London in the Age of Industrialisation* (Cambridge: Cambridge University Press, 1992), p. 75.

4. See for instance L. Hollen Lees, 'Review', *Journal of Social History*, 31:4 (Summer 1998), pp. 967–70, on p. 967.

5. Green, *From Artisans to Paupers*, p. 176.

6. L. D. Schwarz, 'Review', *Journal of Historical Geography*, 23:1 (January 1997), pp. 81–2.

7. D. R. Green, 'The Nineteenth-Century Metropolitan Economy: A Revisionist Interpretation', *London Journal*, 21:1 (1996), pp. 9–26, on p. 16.

8. Schwarz, *London in the Age of Industrialisation*, p. 12.

9. L. D. Schwarz, 'The Standard of Living in the Long Run: London 1700–1860', *Economic History Review*, 2nd ser., 38:1 (1985), pp. 24–41, on p. 25.

10. Green, *From Artisans to Paupers*, p. 48.

11. Ibid., p. 58.

12. Ibid., p. 55.
13. Ibid., p. 40.
14. Stedman Jones, *Outcast London*, p. 54.
15. R. Floud, *The People and the British Economy, 1830–1914* (Oxford: Oxford University Press, 1997), p. 24.
16. C. Booth, *Labour and the Life of the People*, Vol. 2 (London: Williams and Norgate, 1889), p. 21.
17. See M. Anderson, 'What Can the Mid-Victorian Censuses Tell Us about Variations in Married Women's Employment?', in N. Goose (ed.), *Women's Work in Industrial England* (Hatfield: Local Population Studies, 2007), pp. 182–208. See as well E. Higgs, 'The Tabulation of Occupations in the Nineteenth-Century Census, with Special Reference to Domestic Servants', in Goose (ed.), *Women's Work in Industrial England*, pp. 250–9; and M. Anderson, 'Mis-Specification of Servant Occupations in the 1851 Census: A Problem Revisited', in Goose (ed.), *Women's Work in Industrial England*, pp. 260–8.
18. Muldrew and King, 'Cash, Wages and Makeshifts', p. 156.
19. Though obviously deriving from later sources, this scheme was also adopted by J. Boulton in *Neighbourhood and Society* (Cambridge: Cambridge University Press, 1987), his study of seventeenth-century Southwark. A detailed description of the scheme can be found in W. A. Armstrong, 'The Use of Information about Occupation', in E. A. Wrigley (ed.), *Nineteenth Century Society* (Cambridge: Cambridge University Press, 1971), pp. 191–253.
20. Westminster Election Poll Book, London Metropolitan Archives, WR/PP 1802; and Anon., *Westminster Poll Book* (London: J. Stockdale, 1818).
21. This accords with the claims of Harvey, Green and Corfield, that generally speaking there was 'broad continuity' in Westminster's economy between 1750 and 1820, although they noted a 'gradual process of job diversification'; 'Continuity, Change and Specialization', pp. 478 and 482.
22. Street Indexes to the 1841 Census, Book 12, Parish of St Martin in the Fields, National Archives, HO 107/739–740; and *British Parliamentary Papers*, Accounts and Papers, 1833, Vol. XXXVI, pp. 374–5.
23. Rough Examination Book, St Martin's in the Fields, WPA (no accession number).
24. Norma Landau's very interesting contention that the settlement laws were used to control migration in Kent is unlikely to have been the case in Westminster. From 1790 to 1794 inclusive, the percentage of the parish population subjected to examination ranged from 0.7 per cent to 1.2 per cent annually. In 1816–17 this rose to 1.4 per cent. Given that migration was very high at this time, one would have expected a far greater number of examinations had this been the case in Westminster. See N. Landau, 'The Settlement Laws and the Surveillance of Migration in Eighteenth-Century Kent', *Continuity and Change*, 3 (1988), pp. 391–420.
25. With the addition of nine seamen (overall a small trade in St Martin's), these are the most numerous occupations in the settlement examination list.
26. George, *London Life in the Eighteenth Century*, p. 159.
27. Stedman Jones, *Outcast London*, p. 59.
28. R. Campbell, *The London Tradesman* (Newton Abbot: David and Charles, 1969), p. 338.
29. George, *London Life in the Eighteenth Century*, p. 204.
30. H. Mayhew, 'The Boot and Shoemakers', in Thompson and Yeo (eds), *The Unknown Mayhew*, p. 295.

31. L. D. Schwarz, 'Conditions of Life and Work in London, c. 1770–1820, with Special Reference to East London' (unpublished D.Phil. thesis, University of Oxford, 1976), p. 86.

32. H. Mayhew, in Thompson and Yeo (eds), *The Unknown Mayhew*, p. 281.

33. M. D. George, in *London Life in the Eighteenth Century*, p. 199, says this was the case as early as 1761.

34. Campbell, *The London Tradesman*, p. 193.

35. J. Rule, *The Experience of Labour in Eighteenth Century English Industry* (New York: St Martin's Press, 1981), p. 51.

36. C. R. Weld, 'On the Condition of the Working Classes in the Inner Ward of St. George's Parish, Hanover Square', *Royal Statistical Society, London Journal*, ser. A, 6:1 (April 1843), pp. 17–23, on p. 18.

37. Green, *From Artisans to Paupers*, p. 160.

38. B. Taylor, *Eve and the New Jerusalem* (London: Virago, 1983), p. 102.

39. Ibid., p. 104.

40. Green, *From Artisans to Paupers*, p. 162.

41. Campbell, *The London Tradesman*, p. 193.

42. Weld, 'On the Condition of the Working Classes', p. 18.

43. See for instance the articles in Goose (ed.), *Women's Work in Industrial England*; and E. Higgs, 'Women, Occupations and Work in the Nineteenth Century Censuses', *History Workshop Journal*, 23 (Spring 1987), pp. 59–80, on pp. 63–8.

44. See Anderson, 'What Can the Mid-Victorian Censuses Tell Us', and 'Mis-Specification of Servant Occupations in the 1851 Census'; A. Erickson, 'Married Women's Occupations in Eighteenth-Century London', *Continuity and Change*, 23:2 (2008), pp. 267–307; and A. August, *Poor Women's Lives* (Cranbury, NJ: Associated University Presses, 1999), pp. 102–19.

45. August, *Poor Women's Lives*, p. 103.

46. See for instance Anderson, 'What Can the Mid-Victorian Censuses Tell Us', p. 207.

47. Ibid., p. 208.

48. In the Parliamentary Papers, the Westminster occupational returns are broken down into four subgroups: males under twenty, those twenty and upward, females under twenty, and finally, those twenty and upward. The parish of St Martin in the Fields contained a little more than one-tenth of the Westminster population, and, as will be seen below, the overall female occupational breakdown was fairly similar for both the parish and the city. See 'Occupational Abstract', (MDCCCXLI), Part I, England and Wales, *House of Commons Parliamentary Papers*, 1844, Vol. XXVII, pp. 188–285, mf 48.224.

49. Place, *Autobiography*, p. 111.

50. S. Horrell and J. Humphries, 'The Origins and Expansion of the Male Breadwinner Family: The Case of Nineteenth-Century Britain', *International Review of Social History*, 42 (1997), pp. 25–64, on pp. 30–5, and 'Women's Labour Force Participation and the Transition to the Male Breadwinner Family, 1790–1865', *Economic History Review*, 48:1 (1995), pp. 89–117, on pp. 100–5.

51. For work segregation, see J. Humphries, '"...The Most Free from Objection..." The Sexual Division of Labor and Women's Work in Nineteenth-Century England', *Journal of Economic History*, 47:4 (December 1987), pp. 929–49.

52. M. A. Ashford, *Life of a Licensed Victualler's Daughter* (London: Saunders and Otley, 1844), p. 22.

53. Ibid., p. 23.

54. Ibid., p. 41.
55. Francis Place's wife also had fairly similar experiences while in service. Like Ashford, she held a number of positions. Her duties varied, occasionally encompassing more than domestic labour, and on at least one occasion she had difficulty collecting her wages. Finally, like Ashford, she left service upon marriage. See Place, *Autobiography*, pp. 96–102.
56. Humphries, '"...The Most Free from Objection..."', pp. 935 and 947.
57. S. Alexander, A. Davin and E. Hostettler, 'Labouring Women: A Reply to Eric Hobsbawm', *History Workshop Journal*, 8 (Autumn 1979), pp. 174–82, on p. 178.
58. Dressmaker/milliners, seamstresses, bonnet makers, straw hat makers, embroiderers and shirtmakers.
59. S. Alexander, 'Women's Work in Nineteenth Century London; A Study of the Years 1820–50', in A. Oakley and J. Mitchell (eds), *The Rights and Wrongs of Women* (Harmondsworth: Penguin, 1983), pp. 59–111, on p. 87.
60. Ibid., p. 86.
61. Ibid., p. 105.
62. Ibid.
63. The many references in the contemporary literature to the fact that needlework was one of the most respectable trades for women is borne out by the addresses of those engaged in it in St Martin's. For the most part, they lived on the bigger and not the poorest streets in the parish. There were many needlewomen around Leicester Square, on the better streets in Bedfordbury, and on the residential streets south of the Strand (especially towards Hungerford). They were also found on Long Acre and the streets running into it – on Mercer Street especially – and in the bigger courts of Drury Lane. Very few needlewomen were found in the warren of courts north of the Strand. Laundresses, on the other hand, had a marked tendency to live on the poorest streets in the parish.
64. I. Pinchbeck, *Women Workers and the Industrial Revolution, 1750–1850* (London: Virago, 1981), p. 295.
65. Alexander, Davin and Hostettler, 'Labouring Women', p. 178.
66. Pinchbeck, *Women Workers and the Industrial Revolution*, p. 295.
67. Davis, *Fairs, Shops and Supermarkets*, p. 216.
68. Mui and Mui, *Shops and Shopkeeping*, p. 138. Shops run by wives may well have had lower incomes if they were only operated part-time. But even half this amount – £25 – would have constituted a substantial increase in a family's income.
69. Ibid., p. 138.
70. Pinchbeck, *Women Workers and the Industrial Revolution*, p. 300.
71. Vincent, *Bread, Knowledge and Freedom*, p. 97.
72. Alexander, 'Women's Work in Nineteenth Century London', p. 73.
73. Schwarz, 'The Standard of Living in the Long Run', p. 32.
74. E. Gilboy, *Wages in Eighteenth Century England* (Cambridge, MA: Harvard University Press, 1934), p. 254; Alexander, 'Women's Work in Nineteenth Century London', p. 74.
75. Horrell and Humphries, 'The Origins and Expansion of the Male Breadwinner Family', p. 35.
76. Alexander, 'Women's Work in Nineteenth Century London', p. 77.
77. J. Burnette, 'An Investigation of the Female-Male Wage Gap during the Industrial Revolution in Britain', *Economic History Review*, 50 (1997), pp. 257–81, and *Gender, Work, and Wages in Industrial Revolution Britain* (Cambridge: Cambridge University Press, 2008). For responses, see also A. Froide, C. Goldin, J. Humphries, P. Sharp and J. Bur-

nette, 'Special Section: Debating Gender, Work, and Wages: A Roundtable Discussion', *Social Science History*, 33:4 (Winter 2009), pp. 459–504.

78. J. S. Taylor, *Poverty, Migration and Settlement in the Industrial Revolution* (Palo Alto, CA: Society for the Promotion of Science and Scholarship, 1989), pp. 128 and 133.

79. P. Earle, 'The Female Labour Market in London in the Late Seventeenth and Early Eighteenth Centuries', *Economic History Review*, 2nd ser., 42:3 (1989), pp. 328–53, on p. 343.

80. D. A. Kent has shown that 40 per cent of yearly hired servants were thirty and over, and has claimed that service offered single women a measure of economic independence. He based this on settlement examinations for St Martin's between 1750 and 1760. The parish examined such a small percentage of its population, however, that it is not clear how typical these people were. See D. A. Kent, 'Ubiquitous but Invisible: Female Domestic Servants in Mid-Eighteenth Century London', *History Workshop Journal*, 28 (Autumn 1989), pp. 111–28.

81. Alexander, 'Women's Work in Nineteenth Century London', p. 98.

82. See for instance P. Kirby, 'Debate: How Many Children Were "Unemployed" in Eighteenth- and Nineteenth-Century England?', *Past and Present*, 187 (May 2005), pp. 187–202; and H. Cunningham, 'Reply', *Past and Present*, 187 (May 2005), pp. 203–15. See as well J. Humphries, *Childhood and Child Labour in the British Industrial Revolution* (Cambridge: Cambridge University Press, 2010); K. Honeyman, *Child Workers in England, 1780–1820: Parish Apprentices and the Making of the Early Industrial Labour Force* (Aldershot: Ashgate, 2007); P. Kirby, *Child Labour in Britain, 1750–1870* (Basingstoke: Palgrave Macmillan, 2003), and 'A Brief Statistical Sketch of the Child Labour Market in Mid-Nineteenth-Century London', *Continuity and Change* 20:2 (2005), pp. 229–45; and H. Cunningham, 'The Employment and Unemployment of Children in England c.1680–1851', *Past and Present*, 126 (February 1990), pp. 115–50.

83. Kirby, 'A Brief Statistical Sketch', p. 232.

84. Ibid., p. 230.

85. Cunningham, 'The Employment and Unemployment of Children'.

86. Anon., *Sketch of the State of the Children of the Poor in the Year 1756 and of the Present State and Management of All Poor in the Parish of St. James, Westminster in January 1797* (London: J. Stockdale, 1797), p. 11.

87. St Martin's Register of Apprentices, 1767–1842, WPA, F 4309–10.

88. Place, *Autobiography*, pp. 127, 137 and 150.

89. See for instance Horrell and Humphries, 'Women's Labour Force Participation', for a recapitulation of the historiography of this question, especially pp. 89–96.

90. The settlement examinations have survived only for the years 1790 through to February 1795, and for 1816–17, So 1790 is one of the few years in which a direct comparison is possible.

91. Anon., *The First Report of the Society Established in London for the Suppression of Mendicity* (London: J. W. Whiteley, 1819); Anon., *The Second Report of the Society Established in London for the Suppression of Mendicity* (London: F. Warr, 1820); Anon., *The Fourth Report of the Society Established in London for the Suppression of Mendicity* (London: F. Warr, 1822); Anon., *The Sixth Report of the Society Established in London for the Suppression of Mendicity* (London: F. Warr, 1824); Anon., *The Ninth Report of the Society Established in London for the Suppression of Mendicity* (London: F. Warr, 1827); Anon., *The Eleventh Report of the Society Established in London for the Suppression of Mendicity* (London: F. Warr, 1829); Anon., *The Twelfth Report of the Society Established in London for the Suppression of Mendicity* (London: F. Warr, 1830).

92. This seems especially likely, for as will be seen, the society stressed the importance of moral reform, which may well have predisposed it to view its clients as feckless if their reasons for begging could not be demonstrably proven (i.e. widowhood, infirmity, etc.).

93. Vincent, *Bread, Knowledge and Freedom*, p. 68.

94. Thompson and Yeo (eds), *The Unknown Mayhew*, pp. 585 and 592.

95. Place, *Autobiography*, p. 106.

96. This category includes victuallers, licenced victuallers, and hotel and inn keepers.

97. This category includes green grocers, cheesemongers and tea dealers, as well as grocers.

98. For example, coach makers and jewellers especially: according to R. Campbell, the apprentice fees in these trades were higher (a minimum of £50 and £20 respectively) than was the case for tailors and shoemakers (£5 minimum). In addition, it was expensive to set up as a master: a minimum of £500 for a coach maker, and £100 to £500 for a jeweller. Both of these factors meant that these trades could, in most cases, provide a more comfortable life for their practitioners.

4 Using Charity and Poor Relief

1. For a general discussion of friendly societies, see Kidd, *State, Society and the Poor*, pp. 109–59; E. Hopkins, *Working-Class Self-Help in Nineteenth-Century England* (New York: St Martin's Press, 1995); P. H. J. H. Gosden, *The Friendly Societies in England 1815–75* (New York: Barnes and Noble, 1974); and Cordery, *British Friendly Societies 1750–1914*.

2. *British Parliamentary Papers*, 1803–04, Vol. XIII, pp.724–5, mf 4.84.

3. B. Harris and P. Bridgen, 'Introduction', in B. Harris and P. Bridgen (eds), *Charity and Mutual Aid in Europe and North America since 1800* (New York: Routledge, 2007), p. 3.

4. M. Gorsky, 'The Growth and Distribution of English Friendly Societies in the Early Nineteenth Century', *Economic History Review*, 51:3 (1998), pp. 489–511, on pp. 493–7 and 507.

5. For a discussion of the restrictions and limitations of early nineteenth-century societies, see P. H. J. H. Gosden, *Self Help* (New York: Barnes and Noble, 1974), pp. 16–17.

6. Prothero, *Artisans and Politics*, p. 30.

7. B. Harris, 'Charity and Poor Relief in England and Wales, circa 1750–1914', in Harris and Bridgen (eds), *Charity and Mutual Aid*, pp. 20–3.

8. M. Dean, *The Constitution of Poverty* (London: Routledge, 1991), p. 13. See as well L. Hollen Lees, *The Solidarities of Strangers* (Cambridge: Cambridge University Press, 1998), pp. 135–45.

9. A. Kidd, 'The "Liberal State": Civil Society and Social Welfare in Nineteenth-Century England', *Journal of Historical Sociology*, 15:1 (March 2002), pp. 114–19, on p. 117.

10. Harris and Bridgen, 'Introduction', p. 7.

11. A. Tanner, 'The Casual Poor and the City of London Poor Law Union, 1837–1869', *Historical Journal*, 42 (1999), pp. 183–206.

12. R. Dyson, 'Who Were the Poor of Oxford in the Late Eighteenth and Early Nineteenth Centuries?', in A. Gestrich, S. King and L. Raphael (eds), *Being Poor in Modern Europe* (Bern: Peter Lang, 2006), pp. 43–67, on p. 48.

13. D. Owen, *English Philanthropy, 1660–1960* (Cambridge, MA: Belknap Press, 1964), p. 112.

14. Ibid.

15. This was an uncatalogued collection in the Manuscripts Room of the British Library which, at the time I examined it, possessed no accession or folio numbers.
16. See L. MacKay, 'A Culture of Poverty? The St. Martin in the Fields Workhouse, 1817', *Journal of Interdisciplinary History*, 26:2 (Autumn, 1995), pp. 209–31.
17. M. Martin, *Substance of a Letter, Dated Poet's Corner, Westminster, 3 March, 1803, to the Rt. Hon. Lord Pelham, on the State of Mendicity in the Metropolis* (London: Society for Bettering the Condition of the Poor, 1811), pp. 22–4.
18. Anon., *Fourth Report for the Suppression of Mendicity*, p. 21.
19. [Lushington], *The Practice of the Mendicity Society*, p. 41.
20. Anon., *The Mendicity Society Unmasked* (London W. C. Wright, 1825), pp. 24–5.
21. Anon., *Ninth Report for the Suppression of Mendicity*, p. 44.
22. Letter to Lord Spencer from J. Stephens, Assistant Manager of the Mendicity Office, 17 August 1829, Althorp Papers, British Library Manuscripts Room, MS Add. 75969/ G155.
23. For an in-depth analysis of the Mendicity Society clientele, see L. MacKay, 'The Mendicity Society and its Clients: A Cautionary Tale', *Left History*, 5:1 (1997), pp. 39–64.
24. Mayhew, *LLLP*, vol. 1, 'Street Sellers of Stationery, Literature, and the Fine Arts', pp. 322–3.
25. Thompson and Yeo (eds), *The Unknown Mayhew*, letter XI, 23 November 1849, p. 209.
26. Ibid., p. 216.
27. A. Kidd, 'Philanthropy and the "Social History Paradigm"', *Social History*, 21:2 (May 1996), pp. 180–92, on p. 187.
28. Ashford, *Life of a Licenced Victualler's Daughter*, p. 66.
29. Ibid., p. 65.
30. Ibid., p. 67.
31. See A. Tomkins, *The Experience of Urban Poverty, 1723–82: Parish, Charity and Credit* (Manchester and New York: Manchester University Press, 2006), pp. 7–8, for a discussion of the historiography of this disagreement; and J. R. Poynter, *Society and Pauperism* (London: Routledge and Kegan Paul, 1969), pp. xviii–xix for the contemporary debate.
32. Hudson and Hunter (eds), 'The Autobiography of William Hart, Cooper', Part I, p. 152.
33. Ibid., p. 153.
34. St Martin in the Fields Workhouse Standing Orders, No. 15, 1817, WPA, F3 903.
35. The amounts were provided in the 1819 summaries of 2 and 17 April, 1, 15 and 29 May, 12 and 26 June, 10 July, 7 August and 4 September, and in the 1820 summaries of 1, 15 and 29 April. No information was provided for winter months. St Martin in the Fields Workhouse Daybooks, 1819–20, WPA, F 4028.
36. St Martin in the Fields Overseers Minutes, 12 June 1793, WPA, F 2074.
37. St Martin in the Fields, *Report on the Subject of the Casual Poor Admitted by Relief Tickets into the Workhouse of the Parish of St. Martin in the Fields* (London: J. Smith, 1839), p. 3.
38. For example, according to Frederick Eden, in 1796 the parish spent £886 on out relief and £171 on the casual poor; F. Eden, *The State of the Poor*, Vol. 2 (London: Cass, 1966), pp. 440–4.
39. R. Dyson, 'Welfare Provision in Oxford during the Latter Stages of the Old Poor Law, 1800–1834', *Historical Journal*, 52:4 (2009), pp. 943–62, on pp. 948–9.
40. Dyson, 'Who Were the Poor of Oxford', p. 55.
41. D. R. Green, *Pauper Capital* (Farnham: Ashgate, 2010), p. 38.
42. See E. Murphy, 'The Metropolitan Pauper Farms', *London Journal*, 27:1 (2002), pp. 1–18.

43. W. Carey, *Strangers' Guide through London, or a View of the British Metropolis in 1809* (London: Albion, 1809), p. 253.
44. The dates of the censuses were 7 June in 1841, 30 March in 1851 and 7 April for 1861. This means that the 1841 figures are lower than they would have been in March–April. The summary figures are taken from the nearest statement to the period 30 March to 7 April.
45. D. R. Green, 'Icons of the New System: Workhouse Construction and Relief Practices in London under the Old and New Poor Law', *London Journal*, 34:3 (2009), p. 264–84.
46. St Martin in the Fields Workhouse Standing Orders, No. 15, 1817, WPA, F 3903.
47. Anon., *Rules and Regulations for the Government of the Workhouse of the Parish of St. Martin in the Fields and of the Infant Poor at Highwood Hill* (London: J. Smith, 1828), p. 8.
48. St Martin in the Fields Workhouse Report of Subcommittees, 28 November 1817, WPA, F 3914.
49. Anon., *Rules and Regulations for the Government of the Workhouse*, p. 9.
50. St Martin's Overseers Minutes, 20 February 1799, WPA, F 2075.
51. St Martin's Overseers Minutes, 3 June 1818, WPA, F 2077; and St Martin in the Fields Workhouse Report of Subcommittees, November 1820, WPA, F 3914.
52. From the 5 November 1817 entry in the Subcommittee Reports, it is clear that men, women and children worked together in the hair shed, and though reasons are not given, that the state of morals was thought very bad. Earlier in the 24 September 1817 entry, there had been a recommendation that men and boys engaged in shoemaking be separated, and that the boys be supervised. St Martin in the Fields Workhouse Report of Subcommittees, WPA, F 3914.
53. St Martin in the Fields Workhouse Standing Orders, No. 15, 1817, WPA, F 3903.
54. St Martin's Overseers Minutes, 30 January 1805, WPA, F 2076.
55. These were introduced in 1805, done away with in 1808, and reintroduced in 1814. The reasons for these decisions are not given in the Overseers Minutes.
56. St Martin's Overseers Minutes, 20 April 1796 and 28 October 1812, WPA, F 2075 and WPA, F 2076.
57. St Martin's Overseers Minutes, 30 January 1805, WPA, F 2076.
58. St Martin's Overseers Minutes, 1805, WPA, F 2076, *passim*.
59. St Martin in the Fields Workhouse Standing Orders, No. 15, 1817, WPA, F 3903.
60. St Martin's Overseers Minutes, 2 December 1795, WPA, F 2075.
61. Anon., *Rules and Regulations for the Government of the Workhouse*, p. 39.
62. Ibid., p. 22. This does not always seem to have been observed in practice.
63. Ibid., p. 7.
64. In the St Marylebone workhouse, for instance, whipping was permitted. See A. R. Neate, *St. Marylebone Workhouse* (Westminster: St Marylebone Society, 2003), p. 16.
65. See Murphy, 'The Metropolitan Pauper Farms', p. 7. City farms were not agrarian undertakings, but were owned by 'farmers' in the same sense as tax farmers. St Martin's Overseers Minutes, 8 May 1816, WPA, F 2075.
66. Anon., *Rules and Regulations for the Government of the Workhouse*, p. 11.
67. Eden, *The State of the Poor*, p. 438.
68. St Martin in the Fields Workhouse Standing Orders, No. 15, 1817, WPA, F 3903, p. 29. It was common to expect inmates to work. In the parish of St James Westminster, for example, 43 inmates were nurses or their assistants, 17 inmates were employed in making and mending linen, 29 in 'petty offices', 10 minding children, 11 on the 'house account' and 156 in 'various works for money'. Thus, 266 of the 713 inmates were employed in

various works (the other 447 were infirm, elderly, ill or handicapped). See Anon., *Sketch of the State of the Children of the Poor*, pp. 16–17. While paupers did much of the work in the house, there were a number of positions – usually managerial – that were filled by non-inmates. The master (paid £50 p.a.), the matron (£20 p.a.), the apothecary (£120 p.a.), the surgeon (£120 p.a.), the chaplain (£30 p.a.) and the overseer's clerk (£150 p.a.) certainly all fell into this category. Eden gives a list of house establishment with salaries, but does not distinguish pauper from non-pauper labour; see *The State of the Poor*, p. 444.

69. St Martin in the Fields Workhouse Standing Orders, No. 15, 1817, WPA, F 3903, p. 18.
70. Green, 'Icons of the New System', p. 269.
71. St Martin's Overseers Minutes, August 1794, 4 November 1795, 19 October 1796, 14 June 1797, 22 October 1794, 23 August 1797, 15 November 1797, 2 September 1801, 26 October 1803, 10 September 1812 and 13 September 1816, WPA, F 2075-2076.
72. St Martin's Workhouse Daybooks, 1780–1820, WPA, F 4020–7.
73. To be sure, as Boulton and Schwarz have noted, the workhouse did provide important medical services, but in the period under examination here, it was not the primary focus of workhouse assistance. J. Boulton and L. Schwarz, 'The Parish Workhouse, the Parish and Parochial Medical Provision in Eighteenth-Century London: Challenges and Possibilities', *Pauper Lives in Georgian London and Manchester*, Working Papers, at http://research.ncl.ac.uk/pauperlives/workhousemedicalisation.pdf [accessed 19 October 2012].
74. Anon., 'The St. Martin in the Fields Infirmary', *Lancet*, 86:2193 (9 September 1865), pp. 296–8.
75. For a discussion of this issue, see Dyson, 'Who Were the Poor of Oxford', pp. 43–4. As he found for the Oxford parishes he examined, the causes were intertwined in London, as well.
76. St Martin in the Fields Settlement Examinations, 12 February 1790, WPA, F 5073.
77. For this period, see for instance Alexander, 'Women's Work in Nineteenth-Century London'; and Schwarz, *London in the Age of Industrialisation*, pp. 14–22 and 45–50.
78. Gilboy, *Wages in Eighteenth Century England*, p. 254; and Alexander, 'Women's Work in Nineteenth-Century London', p. 74.
79. Murphy, 'The Metropolitan Pauper Farms', p. 14.
80. *Report from the Select Committee on the State of Mendicity in the Metropolis* (London: House of Commons, 28 May 1816), p. 6.
81. 'Law Intelligence', *Morning Chronicle*, 1 March 1819, p. 3.
82. St Martin in the Fields Workhouse Daybook, 21 November 1820, WPA, F 4026.
83. 'Public Office, Bow St.', *Morning Chronicle*, 27 December 1819, p. 3.
84. St Clement Danes Examination Books, WPA, B 1187, 26 January 1786, pp. 147–50.
85. My thanks to Nick Rogers for bringing this story to my attention.
86. St Martin's Vestry Minutes, 31 May 1807, WPA, F 2009; 21 July and 20 August 1813, WPA, F 2010.
87. St Martin's Workhouse Daybooks, Admissions, 24 August 1805, WPA, F 4024. Burgess or Jones was also admitted in 1790 and 1810.
88. Ibid., Discharges, 31 October 1800, WPA, F 4023.
89. St Martin's Overseers Minutes, 13 June 1798, 5 March 1800, 6 June 1804, F 2075; and 13 October 1813, WPA, F 2076.
90. St Martin's Vestry Minutes, 14 October 1813, WPA, F 2010.
91. St Martin's Workhouse Daybooks, Admissions, 12 May 1815, WPA, F 4026.

92. 'Samuel Glasby', *Star*, 29 August 1795, p. 4.
93. 'Public Office, Bow St.', *Sun*, 29 August 1795, p. 3.
94. 'Police', *Morning Chronicle*, 30 August 1832, p. 4.
95. D. R. Green, 'Pauper Protests: Power and Resistance in Early Nineteenth-Century London Workhouses', *Social History*, 31:2 (May 2006), pp. 137–59, on p. 159.
96. St Martin's Overseers Minutes, 21 February 1817, WPA, F 2077.
97. 'Meeting in Spa Fields', *Liverpool Mercury*, 22 November 1816, p. 2; 'Meeting in Spa Fields', *Aberdeen Journal*, 27 November 1816, p. 4.
98. St Martin's Overseers Minutes, 16 November 1816, WPA, F 2077.
99. St Martin's Overseers Minutes, 25 February 1795, WPA, F 2075.
100. The case is indicative of parish determination to be rid of expensive relief recipients. After noting that Turner's absence prevented his family being removed (the reason was not given), the parish passed Martha and her children as vagrants. St Martin's Removal Orders, 26 November 1790, WPA, F 6076.
101. In 1790 slightly more than 6 per cent of the total workhouse population was granted leave. Thereafter, never more than 3.5 per cent of the inmates were given this privilege.
102. There is a burgeoning literature based on pauper letters. See especially S. King, 'Negotiating the Law of Poor Relief in England, 1800–1840', *History*, 96:324 (2011), pp. 410–35, and '"I Fear You Will Think Me Too Presumtuous in My Demands but Necessity Has No Law": Clothing in English Pauper Letters 1800–1834', *International Review of Social History*, 54:2 (2009), pp. 207–36; as well as T. Sokoll, *Essex Pauper Letters, 1731–1837* (Oxford: Oxford University Press, 2001).

5 Different Temporalities

1. Ashford, *Life of a Licenced Victualler's Daughter*, p. 40.
2. Ibid., p. 84.
3. Ibid., p. 71.
4. Ibid., p. 76.
5. Ibid., p. 77.
6. Ibid., p. 13.
7. Ibid., p. 14.
8. Ibid., p. 72.
9. Ibid., p. 21.
10. Ibid., p. 24.
11. Ibid., pp. 48–9.
12. Ibid., p. 53.
13. Ibid., p. 70.
14. While A. W. Cockerill indicates that before 1815 sergeant instructors and their families did not normally live at the institution, it is apparent from Ashford's book that as the wife of both Dallison and Green she lived at the RMA. See A. W. Cockerill, 'The Royal Military Asylum (1803–15)', *Journal for the Society of Army Historical Research*, 79 (2001), pp. 25–44, on p. 35. See also A. W. Cockerill, *The Charity of Mars* (Cobourg: Black Cat Press, 2002).
15. Ashford, *Life of a Licensed Victualler's Daughter*, p. 75.
16. Ibid., pp. 71, 76 and 72.
17. Ibid., pp. 63, 61 and 38.
18. Ibid., p. iv.

19. It should be noted that the modern usage of the word 'fairy', meaning a homosexual, did not emerge until the very late nineteenth century.
20. Ashford, *Life of a Licensed Victualler's Daughter*, p. 56.
21. Ibid., pp. 77–8.
22. Ibid., p. 29.
23. See H. Lambert, 'The British Lying In Hospital', *Origins*, 18 (1994), pp. 91–3; and D. Andrew, 'Two Medical Charities in Eighteenth-Century London: The Lock Hospital and the Lying-In Charity for Married Women', in J. Barry and C. Jones (eds), *Medicine and Charity before the Welfare State* (New York: Routledge, 1994), pp. 82–97.
24. Ashford, *Life of a Licensed Victualler's Daughter*, p. 79.
25. Ibid., pp. 87–8.
26. Cockerill, 'The Royal Military Asylum', p. 39. Although her focus is somewhat different, Patricia Lin also demonstrates the RMA's discomfort with women; see P. Y. C. E. Lin, 'Citizenship, Military Families, and the Creation of a New Definition of "Deserving Poor" in Britain, 1793–1815', *Social Politics*, 7:1 (2000), pp. 5–46.
27. Royal Military Asylum, Board of Commissioners, National Archives, PRO WO 143/8, p. 39.
28. Ashford, *Life of a Licensed Victualler's Daughter*, pp. 85–8.
29. Ibid., p. 88.
30. Ibid., pp. 72 and 73.
31. According to Debrett's, Knatchbull was in his eighties, and never inherited the family baronetcy. See W. Courthope (ed.), *Debrett's Baronetage of England* (London: J. G. and F. Rivington, 1835), p. 59.
32. Ashford, *Life of a Licensed Victualler's Daughter*, p. 36.
33. A. Croll, 'Naming and Shaming in Late Victorian and Edwardian Britain', *History Today*, 47:5 (1997), pp. 3–6.
34. Ashford, *Life of a Licensed Victualler's Daughter*, p. 91. She seems not to have realized that Longfellow was the author, claiming to have seen the verse in a newspaper.
35. See for instance Anon., 'London Street-folk – Coster Life', *Eliza Cook's Journal*, 5 (April–October 1851), pp. 329–32; Anon., 'London's Costermongers', *Baptist Reporter and Missionary Intelligencer*, 25 (1851), pp. 111–12; W. C., 'Costers and their Donkeys', *Chambers's Journal*, 727 (1 December 1877), pp. 753–5; and Anon., 'The London Costermongers', *Ladies' Repository*, 12 (1852), pp. 192–3.
36. Mayhew, *LLLP*, vol. 1, p. 2.
37. M. Brodie, 'Free Trade and Cheap Theatre: Sources of Politics for the Nineteenth-Century London Poor', *Social History* 28:3 (October 2003), pp. 346–60. Brodie deals with coster politics in the late nineteenth century in '"Jaunty Individualists" or Labour Activists? Costermongers, Trade Unions, and the Politics of the Poor', *Labour History Review*, 66:2 (Summer 2001), pp. 147–64.
38. Brodie, 'Free Trade and Cheap Theatre', p. 353.
39. G. Stedman Jones, 'The Cockney and the Nation, 1780–1988', in Feldman and Stedman Jones (eds), *Metropolis London*, pp. 301–28, on pp. 294 and 305.
40. Ibid., pp. 314 and 305.
41. Newspapers in the British Library's *British Newspapers 1600–1900* database were searched for the decades, using the search term 'costermonger'. Stories in which costers were merely mentioned have been ignored.
42. 'The Police Courts: Southwark', *Daily News*, 2 September 1863, p. 3; 'Club House Sobriety: Drinking Habits of the Working Class', *Glasgow Herald*, 23 April 1864, p. 2.

43. 'Our London Correspondent and the Whig', *Belfast News-Letter*, 29 January 1863, p. 3; 'The Debarcation and the Reception of the Princess Alexandra', *Era*, 8 March 1863, p. 4; 'An American View of Englishmen', *Hampshire Telegraph and Sussex Chronicle*, 10 October 1863, p. 7.

44. My thanks to Kylie Stasila, my research assistant, for this research.

45. Crone has shown that the representation of violence in the press and on the stage, for example, was bloody, angry and turbulent. A 'culture of violence' was embraced with gusto and used to create new solidarities among audiences and to resist the new codes of respectability while promoting a customary mentality, if only symbolically. See R. Crone, *Violent Victorians* (Manchester: Manchester University Press, 2012), pp. 15–38.

46. A. Ogilvy, 'Poor Brother Jack', *Once a Week* (7 December 1867), pp. 668–72, on p. 670.

47. Mayhew, *LLLP*, vol. 1, p. 57.

48. Ogilvy, 'Poor Brother Jack', p. 670.

49. Mayhew, *LLLP*, vol. 1, pp. 55–6.

50. J. Greenwood, 'Proceedings of the Society: Food Committee', *Journal of the Society of Arts*, 16 (27 December 1867), pp. 91–5, on p. 94.

51. Mayhew, *LLLP*, vol. 1, p. 7.

52. Ibid., vol. 1, p. 57.

53. Ibid., vol. 1, p. 29.

54. Ibid., vol. 1, p. 30.

55. For Guy Fawkes celebrations, see R. Storch, '"Please to Remember the Fifth of November": Conflict, Solidarity and Public Order in Southern England, 1815–1900', in R. Storch (ed.), *Popular Culture and Custom in Nineteenth-Century England* (London: Croom Helm, 1982), pp. 71–99; and J. A. Sharpe, *Remember Remember the Fifth of November: Guy Fawkes and the Gunpowder Plot* (London: Profile, 2006).

56. Mayhew, *LLLP*, vol. 3, p. 64.

57. Ibid., vol. 3, p. 68.

58. Ibid., vol. 3, pp. 66–7.

59. Ibid., vol. 3, p. 70.

60. Ibid., vol. 1, p. 35.

61. C. Knight, *London*, Vol. 6 (London: Charles Knight and Co., 1851), p. 143.

62. See for example Mayhew, *LLLP*, vol. 1, p. 58.

63. Mayhew, *LLLP*, vol. 2, p. 2.

64. Ibid., vol. 2, p. 3.

65. Ibid., vol. 2, p. 4.

66. D. Revest, 'Street Trading *versus* Street Traffic in Victorian and Edwardian London', *Cycnos*, 19:1 (June 2008), at http://revel.unice.fr/cycnos/index.html?id=1263, [accessed 17 July 2012], p. 4.

67. Mayhew, *LLLP*, vol. 1, p. 5.

68. J. Benson, *The Penny Capitalists* (New Brunswick, NJ: Rutgers University Press, 1983), p. 102.

69. Mayhew, *LLLP*, vol. 1, p. 58.

70. Ibid., vol. 1, p. 10. Mayhew may have exaggerated the impact. Certainly, according to Jerry White, the New Cut was still vibrant and chaotic in the 1860s; see *London in the Nineteenth Century*, 'The New Cut: On the Edge', pp. 197–222. White also claims in passing that a coster's pitch was real estate that could be sold or bequeathed. Unfortunately, there is no citation for this statement, and Mayhew's costermongers indicate that this was not guaranteed; see ibid., p. 208.

71. Mayhew, *LLLP*, vol. 1, p. 60.
72. Ibid., vol. 1, p. 103.
73. Ibid., vol. 1, p. 20.
74. Ibid.
75. S. Inwood, 'Policing London's Morals: The Metropolitan Police and Popular Culture, 1829–1850', *London Journal*, 15:2 (1990), pp. 129–46.
76. Mayhew, *LLLP*, vol. 1, p. 101.
77. For a discussion of property rights, see R. Congost, 'Property Rights and Historical Analysis: What Rights? What History?', *Past and Present*, 181 (2003), pp. 73–106, on p. 80; and J. Getzler, 'Theories of Property and Economic Development', *Journal of Interdisciplinary History*, 25:4 (Spring 1996), pp. 639–69. The costers bear many similarities to the workers in the informal sector in Peru that Hernando de Soto has identified; see H. De Soto, *The Other Path* (New York: Harper and Row, 1989).
78. Mayhew, *LLLP*, vol. 2, p. 3.
79. Ibid., vol. 1, p. 60.
80. Ibid., vol. 1, p. 68.
81. Knight, *London*, p. 142.
82. Mayhew, *LLLP*, vol. 3, p. 70.
83. Ibid., vol. 1, p. 92.
84. Ibid., vol. 1, p. 32.
85. Ibid., vol. 1, p. 26.
86. Ibid., vol. 1, pp. 26 and 31.
87. Ibid., vol. 1, pp. 51–2.
88. Ibid., vol. 1, p. 58.
89. Ibid., vol. 1, p. 60.
90. Greenwood, 'Proceedings of the Society', pp. 92 and 95.
91. C. E. Pascoe, 'About London XI Seven Dials', *Appleton's Journal*, 15 (1876), pp. 816–18, on p. 816.
92. Mayhew, *LLLP*, vol. 1, p. 51.
93. Greenwood, 'Proceedings of the Society', p. 94.
94. Ibid.

Appendix

1. Green and Parton, 'Slums, and Slum Life in Victorian England', p. 66.
2. Anon., 'Moral Statistics of a District near Gray's Inn', *Royal Statistical Society, London Journal*, ser. A, 1:9 (January 1839), pp. 541–2.
3. Anon., 'Report of a Committee of the Statistical Society of London, on the State of the Working Classes in the Parishes of St. Margaret and St. John, Westminster', *Royal Statistical Society, London Journal*, ser. A, 3:1 (April 1840), pp. 14–24, on p. 14.
4. Weld, 'On the Condition of the Working Classes', p. 18.
5. As Schwarz has pointed out, returns survive for only a few parts of England, but London is well represented, with information from parishes encompassing more than 75 per cent of the metropolitan population; Schwarz, 'Income Distribution and Social Structure in London', p. 251.
6. The overlap is found in the original document, and I have corrected for it in the figures that follow.

7. J. Boulton, "'Turned into the Street with My Children Destitute of Every Thing"; The Payment of Rent and the London Poor, 1600–1850', in McEwan and Sharpe (eds), *Accommodating Poverty*, pp. 25–49, on p. 34.

8. Assessed Taxation Returns, National Archives, PRO 30/8/281.

9. Samuel Woodhead, a Strand pawnbroker, paid £44 rent, while his income was estimated at only £100. This gave him only £66 to live on, which in every other entry guaranteed poverty. It seems likely that Woodhead had some kind of undeclared support, or his income had been underestimated, or perhaps that the collector had neglected to enter a comment concerning his financial state; Assessed Taxation Returns, National Archives, PRO 30/8/281.

10. Using data from the same 1798 assessment, the Muis have found the same general relationship between rent and income for various parts of London; see *Shops and Shopkeeping*, pp. 111–21 and 137–40.

11. Assessed Taxation Returns, National Archives, PRO 30/8/281, fol. 59.

12. A. Johnstone, *Johnstone's London Commercial Guide & Street Directory* (London: Barnard and Farley, 1817), p. xi. While the directory does not give a clear definition of the term 'respectable', some idea of its meaning can be gleaned from an examination of the extent of its application. One can do this by considering the self-employment percentages given in Schwarz's breakdown of London's social structure. Using Rudé's figures, which Schwarz quotes, approximately 0.6 per cent of the upper income class would have been in high finance or large-scale trade. By definition, the 17 to 21 per cent comprising the 'middling classes' should be considered as self-employed, since they were described as encompassing both 'moderately wealthy merchants and small employers working in their own shop with only two or three men under them'; Schwarz, 'Income Distribution and Social Structure in London', p. 254. Finally, Schwarz says approximately 10 per cent of the 75 per cent of the working population, or 7.5 per cent, were self-employed; ibid., p. 258. Added together, the total percentage of those self-employed comes to between 25.1 and 29.1 per cent.

    Johnstone's *Directory* has 1,376 entries for St Martin's. The 1811 census says there were 6,297 families in the parish (and considers them as occupational units). Thus, the directory contains listings for 21.9 per cent of these family/occupational units. Since it is highly likely that these entries consist of business owners and masters, this percentage can be compared to that for self-employment. In the event, the Johnstone's figure is the lower by 3.3 to 7.3. It is tempting to conclude that this discrepancy results from the exclusion of the 7.5 per cent of the working population, but whatever one's suspicions, Johnstone's figure does seem to be fairly exhaustive, and to warrant use in this kind of exercise.

13. L. D. Schwarz, 'Occupations and Incomes in Late Eighteenth-Century London', *East End Papers*, 14:2 (December 1972), pp. 87–100, on p. 95.

14. R. Rodger, *Housing in Urban Britain 1780–1914* (Basingstoke: Macmillan, 1989), p. 10.

15. Rodger thinks the very poor may have been spending as much as 30 per cent of their income on rent; ibid.

16. It will be recalled that according to the assessed taxation data, just under two-thirds of the houses in Westminster contained lodgers.

WORKS CITED

Primary Sources

Althorp Papers, British Library Manuscripts Room, MS Add. 75969/G155.

Assessed Taxation Returns, Chatham Papers, National Archives, PRO 30/8/281.

Consistory Court Depositions, London Metropolitan Archives, X19/146-298.

British Parliamentary Papers, 1803–04, Vol. XIII, pp. 724–5, mf 4.84.

British Parliamentary Papers, House of Commons, 1812, Vol. XI.

British Parliamentary Papers, Accounts and Papers 1833, Vol. XXXVI.

'Occupational Abstract', (MDCCCXLI), Part I, England and Wales, *House of Commons Parliamentary Papers*, 1844, Vol. XXVII, pp. 188–285, mf 48.224.

Proceedings of the Old Bailey, at www.oldbaileyonline.org

Report from the Select Committee on the State of Mendicity in the Metropolis (London: House of Commons, 28 May 1816).

Royal Military Asylum, Board of Commissioners, National Archives, PRO WO 143/8–10.

St Clement Danes Examination Books, Westminster Public Archives, B 1187.

St Martin in the Fields Overseers Minutes, Westminster Public Archives, F 2075–7.

St Martin in the Fields Committee for Paving, Lighting, etc. Minutes, Westminster Public Archives, F 2532–4.

St Martin in the Fields Register of Apprentices, 1767–1842, Westminster Public Archives, F 4309–10.

St Martin in the Fields Removal Orders, Westminster Public Archives, F 6076.

St Martin in the Fields Settlement Examinations, Westminster Public Archives, F 5073–4 and the Rough Examination Book (no accession number).

St Martin in the Fields Vestry Minutes, Westminster Public Archives, F 2031.

St Martin in the Fields Workhouse Daybooks, 1780–1820, Westminster Public Archives, F 4020–6.

St Martin in the Fields Workhouse Registers, 1780–1819, at www.LondonLives.org

St Martin in the Fields Workhouse Report of Subcommittees, Westminster Public Archives, F 3914.

St Martin in the Fields Workhouse Standing Orders, No. 15, 1817, Westminster Public Archives, F 3903.

Street Indexes to the 1841 Census, Book 12, Parish of St Martin in the Fields, National Archives, HO 107/739–740.

Westminster Election Poll Book, London Metropolitan Archives, WR/PP 1802.

Newspapers

Aberdeen Journal

Belfast News-Letter

Daily News

Era

Glasgow Herald

Hampshire Telegraph and Sussex Chronicle

Liverpool Mercury

Morning Chronicle

Star

Sun

Secondary Sources

A Tale of Two Britains, BBC Four, 25 October 2009.

Alexander, S., 'Women's Work in Nineteenth Century London; A Study of the Years 1820–50', in A. Oakley and J. Mitchell (eds), *The Rights and Wrongs of Women* (Harmondsworth: Penguin, 1983), pp. 59–111.

Alexander, S., A. Davin and E. Hostettler, 'Labouring Women: A Reply to Eric Hobsbawm', *History Workshop Journal*, 8 (Autumn 1979), pp. 174–82.

Allen, R., 'Observing London Street-Life: G. A. Sala and A. J. Munby', in T. Hitchcock and H. Shore (eds), *The Streets of London* (London: Rivers Oram Press, 2003), pp. 198–214.

Anderson, M., 'Mis-Specification of Servant Occupations in the 1851 Census: A Problem Revisited', in N. Goose (ed.), *Women's Work in Industrial England* (Hatfield: Local Population Studies, 2007), pp. 260–8.

—, 'What Can the Mid-Victorian Censuses Tell Us about Variations in Married Women's Employment?', in N. Goose (ed.), *Women's Work in Industrial England* (Hatfield: Local Population Studies, 2007), pp. 182–208.

Andrew, D., *Philanthropy and Police: London Charity in the 18th Century* (Princeton, NJ: Princeton University Press, 1989).

—, 'Two Medical Charities in Eighteenth-Century London: The Lock Hospital and the Lying-In Charity for Married Women', in J. Barry and C. Jones (eds), *Medicine and Charity before the Welfare State* (New York: Routledge, 1994), pp. 82–97.

Anon., *Low Life or One Half of the World Knows Not How the Other Half Live* (London: John Lever, 1764).

Anon., *Sketch of the State of the Children of the Poor in the Year 1756 and of the Present State and Management of All Poor in the Parish of St. James, Westminster in January 1797* (London: J. Stockdale, 1797).

Anon., *The London Guide and Strangers' Safeguard against the Cheats, Swindlers and Pickpockets that Abound within the Bills of Mortality* (London: J. Bumpus, 1818).

Anon., *Westminster Poll Book* (London: J. Stockdale, 1818).

Anon., *The First Report of the Society Established in London for the Suppression of Mendicity* (London: J. W. Whiteley, 1819).

Anon., *The Second Report of the Society Established in London for the Suppression of Mendicity* (London: F. Warr, 1820).

Anon., *The Fourth Report of the Society Established in London for the Suppression of Mendicity* (London: F. Warr, 1822).

Anon., *The Sixth Report of the Society Established in London for the Suppression of Mendicity* (London: F. Warr, 1824).

Anon., *The Ninth Report of the Society Established in London for the Suppression of Mendicity* (London: F. Warr, 1827).

Anon., *The Eleventh Report of the Society Established in London for the Suppression of Mendicity* (London: F. Warr, 1829).

Anon., *The Twelfth Report of the Society Established in London for the Suppression of Mendicity* (London: F. Warr, 1830).

Anon., *The Mendicity Society Unmasked* (London: W. C. Wright, 1825).

Anon., *Rules and Regulations for the Government of the Workhouse of the Parish of St. Martin in the Fields and of the Infant Poor at Highwood Hill* (London: J. Smith, 1828).

Anon., *The Dens of London* (London: Thompson and Alfred, 1835).

Anon., 'London Street-folk – Coster Life', *Eliza Cook's Journal*, 5 (April–October 1851), pp. 329–32.

Anon., 'London's Costermongers', *Baptist Reporter and Missionary Intelligencer*, 25 (1851), pp. 111–12.

Anon., 'The London Costermongers', *Ladies' Repository*, 12 (1852), pp. 192–3.

Anon., 'The St. Martin in the Fields Infirmary', *Lancet*, 86:2193 (9 September 1865), pp. 296–8.

Anon., 'Report of a Committee of the Statistical Society of London, on the State of the Working Classes in the Parishes of St. Margaret and St. John, Westminster', *Royal Statistical Society, London Journal*, ser. A, 3:1 (April 1840), pp. 14–24.

Anon., 'Moral Statistics of a District near Gray's Inn', *Royal Statistical Society, London Journal*, ser. A, 1:9 (January 1839), pp. 541–2.

Armstrong, W. A., 'The Use of Information about Occupation', in E. A. Wrigley (ed.), *Nineteenth Century Society* (Cambridge: Cambridge University Press, 1972), pp. 191–253.

Ashford, M. A., *Life of a Licenced Victualler's Daughter* (London: Saunders and Otley, 1844).

Assael, B., 'Music in the Air', in T. Hitchcock and H. Shore (eds), *The Streets of London* (London: Rivers Oram Press, 2003), pp. 183–97.

August, A., *Poor Women's Lives* (London: Associated University Presses, 1999).

Bailey, J., '"I Dye [sic] by Inches": Locating Wife Beating in the Concept of a Privatization of Marriage and Violence in Eighteenth-Century England', *Social History*, 31:3 (August 2006), pp. 273–94.

Bailey, P., *Leisure and Class in Victorian England: Rational Recreation and the Contest for Control* (London: Routledge, 1978).

—, '"Will the Real Bill Banks Please Stand Up?" Towards a Role Analysis of Mid-Victorian Working-Class Respectability', *Journal of Social History*, 12:3 (1979), pp. 336–53.

Ball, M., and D. Sunderland, *An Economic History of London, 1800–1914* (London: Routledge, 2001).

Beames, T., *The Rookeries of London*, 2nd edn (London: Thomas Bosworth, 1852).

Benson, J., *The Penny Capitalists* (New Brunswick, NJ: Rutgers University Press, 1983).

Beresford Chancellor, E., *Annals of the Strand* (London: Chapman and Hall, 1912).

—, *Annals of Covent Garden* (London: Hutchinson and Co., 1930).

Best, G., *Mid-Victorian Britain, 1851–1870* (Glasgow: Fontana-Collins, 1982).

Booth, C., *Labour and the Life of the People*, Vol. 2 (London: Williams and Norgate, 1889).

Boulton J., *Neighbourhood and Society* (Cambridge: Cambridge University Press, 1987).

—, '"Turned into the Street with My Children Destitute of Every Thing"; The Payment of Rent and the London Poor, 1600–1850', in J. McEwan and P. Sharpe (eds), *Accommodating Poverty* (Basingstoke: Palgrave Macmillan, 2011), pp. 25–49.

Boulton, J., and L. Schwarz, 'The Parish Workhouse, the Parish and Parochial Medical Provision in Eighteenth-Century London: Challenges and Possibilities', in *Pauper Lives in Georgian London and Manchester*, Working Papers, at http://research.ncl.ac.uk/pauperlives/workhousemedicalisation.pdf [accessed 19 October 2012].

Braddick, J., and J. Walter, 'Grids of Power: Order, Hierarchy and Subordination', in J. Braddick and J. Walter (eds), *Negotiating Power in Early Modern Society* (Cambridge: Cambridge University Press, 2001), pp. 1–42.

Brant, C., and S. Whyman, *Walking the Streets of Eighteenth-Century London: John Gay's Trivia* (Oxford: Oxford University Press, 2007).

Brimblecombe, P., *The Big Smoke* (London: Methuen, 1987).

Brodie, M., '"Jaunty Individualists" or Labour Activists? Costermongers, Trade Unions, and the Politics of the Poor', *Labour History Review*, 66:2 (Summer 2001), pp. 147–64.

—, 'Free Trade and Cheap Theatre: Sources of Politics for the Nineteenth-Century London Poor', *Social History*, 28:3 (October 2003), pp. 346–60.

Bulmer, M., *Neighbours: The Work of Philip Abrams* (Cambridge: Cambridge University Press, 1986).

Burford, E. J., *Wits, Wenchers and Wantons* (London: R. Hale, 1986).

Burnett, J. (ed.), *Useful Toil* (London: Routledge, 1994).

Burnette, J., 'An Investigation of the Female-Male Wage Gap during the Industrial Revolution in Britain', *Economic History Review*, 50 (1997), pp. 257–81.

—, *Gender, Work, and Wages in Industrial Revolution Britain* (Cambridge: Cambridge University Press, 2008).

Campbell, J. K., *Honour, Family and Patronage* (Oxford: Oxford University Press, 1964).

Campbell, R., *The London Tradesman* (Newton Abbot: David and Charles, 1969).

Cannadine, D., *The Rise and Fall of Class in Britain* (New York: Columbia University Press, 1999).

Capp, B., *When Gossips Meet* (Oxford: Oxford University Press, 2003).

Carey, W., *Strangers' Guide through London, or a View of the British Metropolis in 1809* (London: Albion, 1809).

Carter, T., *Memoirs of a Working Man* (London: Charles Knight and Co., 1845).

Carter Wood, J., *Violence and Crime in Nineteenth-Century England* (London: Routledge, 2004).

Clark, A., 'Whores and Gossips: Sexual Reputation in London 1770–1825', in A. Angerman et al. (eds), *Current Issues in Women's History* (London: Routledge and Kegan Paul, 1989), pp. 231–48.

—, *The Struggle for the Breeches* (Berkeley, CA: University of California Press, 1997).

Clifford, J., 'Some Aspects of London Life in the Mid-18th Century', in P. Fritz and D. Williams (eds), *City and Society in the Eighteenth Century* (Toronto: Hakkert, 1975), pp. 19–38.

Cockerill, A. W., 'The Royal Military Asylum (1803–15)', *Journal for the Society of Army Historical Research*, 79 (2001), pp. 25–44.

—, *The Charity of Mars* (Cobourg: Black Cat Press, 2002).

Colquhoun, P., *A Treatise on Indigence* (London: Hatchard, 1806).

—, *A Treatise on the Wealth, Power and Resources of the British Empire* (London: J. Mawman, 1814).

Congost, R., 'Property Rights and Historical Analysis: What Rights? What History?', *Past and Present*, 181 (2003), pp. 73–106

Conley, C., *The Unwritten Law: Criminal Justice in Victorian Kent* (Oxford: Oxford University Press, 1991).

Cook, C., and J. Stevenson, *The Longman Handbook of Modern British History 1714–2001* (Harlow: Longman, 2001).

Cordery, S., 'Friendly Societies and the Discourse of Respectability in Britain, 1825–1875', *Journal of British Studies*, 34 (January 1995), pp. 35–58.

—, *British Friendly Societies, 1750–1914* (Basingstoke: Palgrave Macmillan, 2003).

Corfield, P. J., *The Impact of English Towns 1700–1800* (Oxford: Oxford University Press, 1982).

—, 'Walking the City Streets: The Urban Odyssey in Eighteenth-Century England', *Journal of Urban History*, 16:2 (February 1990), pp. 132–74.

Courthope, W. (ed.), *Debrett's Baronetage of England* (London: J. G. and F. Rivington, 1835).

Cowen Orlin, L., *Locating Privacy in Tudor London* (Oxford: Oxford University Press, 2007).

Croll, A., 'Naming and Shaming in Late Victorian and Edwardian Britain', *History Today*, 47:5 (1997), pp. 3–6.

Crone, R., *Violent Victorians* (Manchester: Manchester University Press, 2012).

Crossick, G., 'The Labour-Aristocracy and its Values: A Study in Mid-Victorian Kentish London', *Victorian Studies*, 19:3 (March 1976), pp. 301–28.

—, *The Labour Aristocracy and its Values* (Bloomington, IN: Indiana University Press, 1976).

Cunningham, H., 'The Employment and Unemployment of Children in England c.1680–1851', *Past and Present*, 126 (February 1990), pp. 115–50.

—, 'Reply', *Past and Present*, 187 (May 2005), pp. 203–15.

Cunningham, P., *A Handbook of London Past and Present* (London: J. Murray, 1849.)

Daunton, M. J., *House and Home in the Victorian City* (London: E. Arnold, 1983).

—, 'Public Place and Private Space: The Victorian City and the Working-Class Household', in D. Fraser and A. Sutcliffe (eds), *The Pursuit of Urban History* (London: E. Arnold, 1983), pp. 212–33.

Davis, D., *Fairs, Shops and Supermarkets: A History of English Shopping* (Toronto: University of Toronto Press, 1966).

Davis, J., 'Jennings' Buildings and the Royal Borough: The Construction of the Under-Class in Mid-Victorian England', in D. Feldman and G. Stedman Jones (eds), *Metropolis London: Histories and Representations since 1800* (London: Routledge, 1989), pp. 11–39.

—, 'Prosecutions and their Context: The Use of the Criminal Law in Later Nineteenth-Century London', in D. Hay and F. Snyder (eds), *Policing and Prosecution in Britain, 1750–1850* (Oxford: Clarendon Press, 1989), pp. 397–426.

D'Cruze, S., *Crimes of Outrage* (Dekalb, IL: Northern Illinois University Press, 1998).

de Saussure, C., *A Foreign View of England in the Reigns of George I and George II* (London: John Murray, 1902).

De Soto, H., *The Other Path* (New York: Harper and Row, 1989).

Dean, M., *The Constitution of Poverty* (London: Routledge, 1991).

Dennis, R., 'The Geography of Victorian Values: Philanthropic Housing in London, 1840–1900', *Journal of Historical Geography*, 15:1 (January 1989), pp. 40–54.

—, *Cities in Modernity* (Cambridge: Cambridge University Press, 2008).

Dickens, C., 'The Devil's Acre', *Household Words*, 1:13 (22 June 1850), pp. 297–301.

Dunning, E., 'A Response to R. J. Robinson's "The Civilizing Process": Some Remarks on Elias's Social History', *Sociology*, 23:2 (1989), pp. 299–307.

Dyos, H. J., 'The Objects of Street Improvement in Regency and Early Victorian London', in *Exploring the Urban Past: Essays in Urban History by H. J. Dyos*, ed. D. Cannadine and D. Reeder (Cambridge: University of Cambridge, 1982).

Dyson, R., 'Who Were the Poor of Oxford in the Late Eighteenth and Early Nineteenth Centuries?', in A. Gestrich, S. King and L. Raphael (eds), *Being Poor in Modern Europe* (Bern: Peter Lang, 2006), pp. 43–67.

—, 'Welfare Provision in Oxford during the Latter Stages of the Old Poor Law, 1800–1834', *Historical Journal*, 52:4 (2009), pp. 943–62.

Earle, P., 'The Female Labour Market in London in the Late Seventeenth and Early Eighteenth Centuries', *Economic History Review*, 2nd ser., 42:3 (1989), pp. 328–53.

—, *A City Full of People* (London: Methuen, 1994).

Eden, F., *The State of the Poor*, Vol. 2 (London: Cass, 1966).

Eley, G., and K. Nield, *The Future of Class* (Ann Arbor, MI: University of Michigan Press, 2007).

Elias, N., *The Civilizing Process* (Oxford: Blackwell, 2000).

Erickson, A., 'Married Women's Occupations in Eighteenth-Century London', *Continuity and Change*, 23:2 (2008), pp. 267–307.

Falkus, M., 'Lighting in the Dark Ages of English Economic History: Town Streets before the Industrial Revolution', in D. C. Coleman and A. H. John (eds), *Trade, Government and Economy in Pre-Industrial England* (London: Littlehampton Book Services Ltd, 1976), pp. 248–73.

Feldman, D., and G. Stedman Jones (eds), *Metropolis London: Histories and Representations since 1800* (London: Routledge, 1989).

Fielding, H., *An Enquiry into the Causes of the Late Increase of Robbers*, 2nd edn (London: M. Cooper, 1751).

Floud, R., *The People and the British Economy, 1830–1914* (Oxford: Oxford University Press, 1997).

Fontaine, L., and J. Schlumbohm (eds), *Household Strategies for Survival 1600–2000: Fission, Faction and Cooperation* (Cambridge: Cambridge University Press, 2000).

Foucault, M., *Power*, ed. J. Faubion, Vol. 3 (New York: New Press, 1994).

Frazer, B., 'Reconceptualizing Resistance in the Historical Archaeology of the British Isles: An Editorial', *International Journal of Historical Archaeology*, 3:1 (1999), pp. 1–10.

Froide, A., C. Goldin, J. Humphries, P. Sharp and J. Burnette, 'Special Section: Debating Gender, Work, and Wages: A Roundtable Discussion', *Social Science History*, 33:4 (Winter 2009), pp. 459–504.

Gage, J., 'The Rise and Fall of the St. Giles Rookery', *Camden History Review*, 12 (1984), pp. 17–24.

Garrioch, D., *Neighbourhood and Community in Paris, 1740–1790* (Cambridge: Cambridge University Press, 2002).

Gatrell, V. A. C., *The Hanging Tree* (New York: Oxford University Press, 1994).

Gavin, H., *Sanitary Ramblings* (London: Cass, 1971).

—, *Unhealthiness of London* (New York: Garland, 1985).

Gay, J., *Trivia* (Dublin: George Risk, 1727).

George, M. D., *London Life in the Eighteenth Century* (Chicago, IL: Academy Chicago Publishers, 1984).

Getzler, J., 'Theories of Property and Economic Development', *Journal of Interdisciplinary History*, 25:4 (Spring 1996), pp. 639–69.

Gilboy, E., *Wages in Eighteenth Century England* (Cambridge, MA: Harvard University Press, 1934).

Gluckman, M., 'Gossip and Scandal', *Current Anthropology*, 4:3 (1963), pp. 307–16.

—, 'Psychological, Sociological and Anthropological Explanations and Gossip: A Clarification', *Man*, new ser., 3 (1968), pp. 20–34.

Godwin, G., *London Shadows: A Glance at the 'Homes' of the Thousands* (London: G. Routledge and Co., 1854).

—, *Town Swamps and Social Bridges* (1859; Leicester: Leicester University Press, 1972).

Golby, J. M., and A. W. Purdue, *The Civilisation of the Crowd: Popular Culture in England 1750–1900* (London: Batsford, 1984).

Goose, N. (ed.), *Women's Work in Industrial England* (Hatfield: Local Population Studies, 2007).

Gorsky, M., 'The Growth and Distribution of English Friendly Societies in the Early Nineteenth Century', *Economic History Review*, 51:3 (1998), pp. 489–511.

Gosden, P. H. J. H., *Self Help* (New York: Barnes and Noble, 1974).

—, *The Friendly Societies in England 1815–75* (New York: Barnes and Noble, 1974).

Gowing, L., 'Language, Power and the Law: Women's Slander Litigation in Early Modern London', in J. Kermode and G. Walker (eds), *Women, Crime and the Courts* (Chapel Hill, NC: University of North Carolina Press, 1994), pp. 26–47.

—, *Domestic Dangers: Women, Words and Sex in Early Modern London* (Oxford: Clarendon Press, 1996).

Grant, J., *Lights and Shadows of London Life*, Vol. 1 (London: G. Routledge, 1846).

Gray, R. Q., *The Labour Aristocracy in Nineteenth-Century Britain, 1850–1900* (London: Macmillan, 1981).

Green, D. R., ' Street Trading in London : A Case Study of Casual Labour, 1830–60', in J. H. Johnson and C. G. Pooley (eds), *The Structure of 19th Century Cities* (London: Croom Helm, 1982), pp. 129–52.

—, *From Artisans to Paupers* (Aldershot: Scolar Press, 1995).

—, 'The Nineteenth-Century Metropolitan Economy: A Revisionist Interpretation', *London Journal*, 21:1 (1996), pp. 9–26.

—, 'Pauper Protests: Power and Resistance in Early Nineteenth-Century London Workhouses', *Social History*, 31:2 (May 2006), pp. 137–59.

—, 'Icons of the New System: Workhouse Construction and Relief Practices in London under the Old and New Poor Law', *London Journal*, 34:3 (2009), p. 264–84.

—, *Pauper Capital* (Farnham: Ashgate, 2010).

Green, D. R., and A. Parton, 'Slums, and Slum Life in Victorian England: London and Birmingham at Mid-Century', in S. M. Gaskell (ed.), *Slums* (Leicester: Leicester University Press, 1990), pp. 17–91.

Greenwood, J., 'Proceedings of the Society: Food Committee', *Journal of the Society of Arts*, 16 (27 December 1867), pp. 91–5.

Grosley, P., *A Tour to London, New Observations on England* (London: Lockyer Davis, 1772).

Guy, W., 'On the Health of Nightmen, Scavengers, and Dustmen', *Journal of the Statistical Society of London*, 11:1 (March 1848), pp. 72–81.

Harris, B., 'Charity and Poor Relief in England and Wales, circa 1750–1914', in B. Harris and P. Bridgen (eds), *Charity and Mutual Aid in Europe and North America since 1800* (New York: Routledge, 2007), pp. 19–42.

Harris, B., and P. Bridgen, 'Introduction', in B. Harris and P. Bridgen (eds), *Charity and Mutual Aid in Europe and North America since 1800* (New York: Routledge, 2007), pp. 1–18.

Harvey, C., E. Green and P. J. Corfield, 'Continuity, Change, and Specialization within Metropolitan London: The Economy of Westminster, 1750–1820', *Economic History Review*, 52:2 (1999), pp. 469–93.

Henderson, T., *Disorderly Women in Eighteenth-Century London* (London: Longman, 1999).

Higgs, E., 'Women, Occupations and Work in the Nineteenth Century Censuses', *History Workshop Journal*, 23 (Spring 1987), pp. 59–80.

—, 'The Tabulation of Occupations in the Nineteenth-Century Census, with Special Reference to Domestic Servants', in N. Goose (ed.), *Women's Work in Industrial England* (Hatfield: Local Population Studies, 2007), pp. 250–9.

Hitchcock, T., and H. Shore (eds), *The Streets of London* (London: Rivers Oram Press, 2003).

Hollen Lees, L., 'Review', *Journal of Social History*, 31:4 (Summer 1998), pp. 967–70.

—, *The Solidarities of Strangers* (Cambridge: Cambridge University Press, 1998).

Hollingshead, J., *Ragged London in 1861* (London: Smith, Elder and Co., 1861).

Honeyman, K., *Child Workers in England, 1780–1820: Parish Apprentices and the Making of the Early Industrial Labour Force* (Aldershot: Ashgate, 2007).

Hopkins, E., *Working-Class Self-Help in Nineteenth-Century England* (New York: St Martin's Press, 1995).

Horden, P., and N. Purcell, *The Corrupting Sea* (Oxford: Wiley-Blackwell, 2000).

Horrell, S., and J. Humphries, 'Women's Labour Force Participation and the Transition to the Male Breadwinner Family, 1790–1865', *Economic History Review*, 48:1 (1995), pp. 89–117.

—, 'The Origins and Expansion of the Male Breadwinner Family: The Case of Nineteenth-Century Britain', *International Review of Social History*, 42 (1997), pp. 25–64.

Horwood, R., *The A to Z of Regency London* (London: London Topographical Society, 1985).

Hudson, P., and L. Hunter (eds), 'The Autobiography of William Hart, Cooper, 1776–1857, a Respectable Artisan in the Industrial Revolution', Part I, *London Journal*, 7:2 (1981), pp. 144–60.

Humphries, J., '"...The Most Free from Objection..." The Sexual Division of Labor and Women's Work in Nineteenth-Century England', *Journal of Economic History*, 47:4 (December 1987), pp. 929–49.

—, *Childhood and Child Labour in the British Industrial Revolution* (Cambridge: Cambridge University Press, 2010).

Hunt, T., *Building Jerusalem* (London: Pheonix, 2004).

Inwood, S., 'Policing London's Morals: The Metropolitan Police and Popular Culture, 1829–1850', *London Journal*, 15:2 (1990), pp. 129–46.

Jenner, M., 'Circulation and Disorder: London Streets and Hackney Coaches, c. 1640–1740', in T. Hitchcock and H. Shore (eds), *The Streets of London* (London: Rivers Oram Press, 2003), pp. 40–53.

Johnstone, A., *Johnstone's London Commercial Guide & Street Directory* (London: Barnard and Farley, 1817).

Kent, D. A., 'Ubiquitous but Invisible: Female Domestic Servants in Mid-Eighteenth Century London', *History Workshop Journal*, 28 (Autumn 1989), pp. 111–28.

Kidd, A., 'Philanthropy and the "Social History Paradigm"', *Social History*, 21:2 (May 1996), pp. 180–92.

—, *State, Society and the Poor in Nineteenth-Century England* (Basingstoke: Macmillan Press, 1999).

—, 'The "Liberal State": Civil Society and Social Welfare in Nineteenth-Century England', *Journal of Historical Sociology*, 15:1 (March 2002), pp. 114–19.

King, S., '"I Fear You Will Think Me Too Presumptuous in My Demands but Necessity Has No Law": Clothing in English Pauper Letters 1800–1834', *International Review of Social History*, 54:2 (2009), pp. 207–36.

—, 'Negotiating the Law of Poor Relief in England, 1800–1840', *History*, 96:324 (2011), pp. 410–35.

Kirby, P., *Child Labour in Britain, 1750–1870* (Basingstoke: Palgrave Macmillan, 2003).

—, 'A Brief Statistical Sketch of the Child Labour Market in Mid-Nineteenth-Century London', *Continuity and Change*, 20:2 (2005), pp. 229–45.

—, 'Debate: How Many Children Were "Unemployed" in Eighteenth- and Nineteenth-Century England?', *Past and Present*, 187 (May 2005), pp. 187–202.

Kirk, N., *The Growth of Working Class Reformism in Mid-Victorian England* (Urbana, IL: University of Illinois Press, 1985).

Klein, L., 'Gender and the Public/Private Distinction in the Eighteenth Century: Some Questions about Evidence and Analytic Procedure', *Eighteenth-Century Studies*, 29:1 (1995), pp. 97–109.

Knight, C., *London*, Vol. 6 (London: Charles Knight and Co., 1851).

Kok, J., K. Mandemakers and H. Wals, 'City Nomads: Changing Residence as a Coping Strategy, Amsterdam, 1890–1940', *Social Science History*, 29:1 (Spring 2005), pp. 15–43.

Lambert, H., 'The British Lying In Hospital', *Origins*, 18 (1994), pp. 91–3.

Landau, N., 'The Laws of Settlement and the Surveillance of Immigration in Eighteenth-Century Kent', *Continuity and Change*, 3 (1988), pp. 391–420.

Lawrence, J., 'Review', *Journal of Victorian Culture*, 11:2 (Autumn 2006), pp. 376–81.

Lefebvre, H., *The Production of Space* (Oxford: Blackwell, 1991).

Lemire, B., 'Peddling Fashion: Salesmen, Pawnbrokers, Taylors, Thieves and the Second-hand Clothes Trade in England, c. 1700–1800', *Textile History*, 22:1 (1991), pp. 67–82.

—, 'Petty Pawns and Informal Lending: Gender and the Transformation of Small-Scale Credit in England, circa 1600–1800', in K. Bruland and P. K. O'Brien (eds), *From Family Firms to Corporate Capitalism* (Oxford: Clarendon Press, 1998), pp. 112–38.

Lindhert, P., and J. Williamson, 'English Workers' Living Standards during the Industrial Revolution: A New Look', *Economic History Review*, 2nd ser., 36 (February 1983), pp. 1–25.

Lin, P. Y. C. E., 'Citizenship, Military Families, and the Creation of a New Definition of "Deserving Poor" in Britain, 1793–1815', *Social Politics*, 7:1 (2000), pp. 5–46.

Lis, C., *Social Change and the Labouring Poor: Antwerp, 1770–1860* (New Haven, CT: Yale University Press, 1986).

Lis, C., and H. Soly, 'Neighbourhood and Social Change in West European Cities: Sixteenth to Nineteenth Centuries', *International Review of Social History*, 38 (1993), pp. 1–30.

Litton Fox, G., '"Nice Girl": Social Control of Women through a Value Construct', *Signs*, 2:4 (1977), pp. 805–17.

[Lushington, C. R.], *The Practice of the Mendicity Society* (London: John Murray, 1847).

Macfarlane, S., 'Social Policy and the Poor in the Later Seventeenth Century', in A. L. Beier and R. Finlay (eds), *London 1500–1700* (Harlow: Longman, 1986), pp. 252–77.

MacKay, L., 'A Culture of Poverty? The St. Martin in the Fields Workhouse, 1817', *Journal of Interdisciplinary History*, 26:2 (Autumn 1995), pp. 209–31.

—, 'The Mendicity Society and its Clients: A Cautionary Tale', *Left History*, 5:1 (1997), pp. 39–64.

—, 'Moral Paupers: The Poor Men of St. Martin's, 1815–1819', *histoire sociale/Social History*, 67 (2001), pp. 115–31.

—, 'Respectability: A Useful Sort of Weapon', in National Academy of Sciences of Ukraine, *Silva Rerum* (Lviv: Literary Agency Piramida, 2007), pp. 242–58.

MacMichael, J. H., *Charing Cross and its Immediate Neighbourhood* (London: Chatto and Windus, 1906).

Marriott, J., 'The Spatiality of the Poor in Eighteenth-Century London', in T. Hitchcock and H. Shore (eds), *The Streets of London* (London: Rivers Oram Press, 2003). pp. 119–34.

Martin, M., *Substance of a Letter, Dated Poet's Corner, Westminster, 3 March, 1803, to the Rt. Hon. Lord Pelham, on the State of Mendicity in the Metropolis* (London: Society for Bettering the Condition of the Poor, 1811).

Matossian, M. K., 'Death in London', *Journal of Interdisciplinary History*, 16:2 (Autumn 1985), pp. 183–97.

Mayhew, H., *London Labour and the London Poor*, 4 vols (New York: Dover, 1968).

—, 'The Boot and Shoemakers', in E. P. Thompson and E. Yeo (eds), *The Unknown Mayhew* (Harmondsworth: Penguin, 1978).

—, *The Morning Chronicle Survey of Labour and the Poor: The Metropolitan Districts*, 6 vols (Firle: Caliban Books, 1980).

Maynes, M. J., 'Autobiography and Class Formation in Nineteenth-Century Europe: Methodological Considerations', *Social Science History*, 16:3 (Fall 1992), pp. 517–37.

McCalman, I., 'Unrespectable Radicalism: Infidels and Pornography in Early Nineteenth-Century London', *Past and Present*, 104 (1984), pp. 74–110.

McEwan, J., 'The Lodging Exchange: Space, Authority and Knowledge in Eighteenth-Century London', in J. McEwan and P. Sharpe (eds), *Accommodating Poverty* (Basingstoke: Palgrave Macmillan, 2011), pp. 50–68.

McEwan, J., and P. Sharpe, *Accommodating Poverty* (Basingstoke: Palgrave Macmillan, 2011).

McMaster, J., *A Short History of the Royal Parish of St. Martin in the Fields* (London: G. Holder and Sons, 1916).

Medick, H., 'Plebeian Culture in the Transition to Capitalism', in R. Samuel and G. Stedman Jones (eds), *Culture, Ideology and Politics* (London: Routledge and Kegan Paul, 1982), pp. 84–113.

Miller, P., and N. Rose, 'Governing Economic Life', in M. Gane and T. Johnson (eds), *Foucault's New Domains* (London: Routledge, 1993).

Miller, T., *Picturesque Sketches of London* (London: Office of the National Illustrated Library, 1852).

Moritz, C. P., *Journeys of a German in England in 1782*, trans. and ed. R. Nettel (New York: Holt, Rinehart and Winston, 1965).

Morris, S., 'Market Solutions for Social Problems: Working-Class Housing in Nineteenth-Century London', *Economic History Review*, 54:3 (2001), pp. 525–45.

Mort, F., and M. Ogborn, 'Transforming Metropolitan London, 1750–1960', *Journal of British Studies*, 43:1 (January 2004), pp. 1–14.

Mosley, S., 'Fresh Air and Foul: The Role of the Open Fireplace in Ventilating the British Home, 1837–1910', *Planning Perspectives*, 18 (2003), pp. 1–21.

Mui, H., and L. H. Mui, *Shops and Shopkeeping in Eighteenth Century England* (London: Routledge, 1989).

Muldrew, C., and S. King, 'Cash, Wages and the Economy of Makeshifts in the Economy of England, 1650–1800', in P. Scholliers and L. Schwarz, (eds), *Experiencing Wages* (New York: Berghahn Books, 2003), pp. 155–82.

Murphy, E., 'The Metropolitan Pauper Farms', *London Journal*, 27:1 (2002), pp. 1–18.

Neate, A. R., *St. Marylebone Workhouse* (Westminster: St Marylebone Society, 2003).

O'Byrne, A., 'The Art of Walking in London: Representing Urban Pedestrianism in the Early Nineteenth Century', *Romanticism*, 14:2 (2008), pp. 94–107.

Ogborn, M., *Spaces of Modernity: London's Geographies 1680–1780* (New York: Guildford Press, 1998).

Ogilvy, A., 'Poor Brother Jack', *Once a Week* (7 December 1867), pp. 668–72.

Olsen, D., *The Growth of Victorian London* (London: Batsford, 1976).

Otter, C., 'Making Liberalism Durable: Vision and Civility in the Late Victorian City', *Social History* 27:1 (January 2002), pp. 1–15.

Owen, D., *English Philanthropy, 1660–1960* (Cambridge, MA: Belknap Press, 1964).

Paine, R., 'What is Gossip About? An Alternative Hypothesis', *Man*, new ser., 2 (1967), pp. 278–85.

Pascoe, C. E., 'About London XI Seven Dials', *Appleton's Journal*, 15 (1876), pp. 816–18.

Peller Malcolm, J., *Anecdotes of the Manners and Customs of London during the Eighteenth Century* (London: Longman, Hurst, Rees and Orme, 1808).

Phillips, H., *Mid Georgian London* (London: Collins, 1964).

Phillips, R., *Modern London* (London: C. Mercier, 1804).

Pinchbeck, I., *Women Workers and the Industrial Revolution, 1750–1850* (London: Virago, 1981).

Pitt-Rivers, J., 'Honour and Social Status', in J. G. Peristiany (ed.), *Honour and Shame* (Chicago, IL: University of Chicago Press, 1966), pp. 19–77.

Place, F., *The Autobiography of Francis Place*, ed. M. Thale (Cambridge: Cambridge University Press, 1972).

Pollock, L., 'Living on the Stage of the World: The Concept of Privacy among the Elite of Early Modern England', in A. Wilson (ed.), *Rethinking Social History* (Manchester: Manchester University Press, 1993), pp. 78–96.

Poynter, J. R., *Society and Pauperism* (London: Routledge and Kegan Paul, 1969).

Prothero, I., *Artisans and Politics* (Folkestone: Dawson, 1979).

Rendall, J., 'Displaying Sexuality: Gendered Identities and the Early Nineteenth-Century Street', in N. Fyfe (ed.), *Images of the Street* (London: Routledge, 1998), pp. 74–91.

Revest, D., 'Street Trading *versus* Street Traffic in Victorian and Edwardian London', *Cycnos*, 19:1 (June 2008), at http://revel.unice.fr/cycnos/index.html?id=1263 [accessed 17 July 2012].

Robey, A., '"All Asmear with Filth and Fat and Blood and Foam": The Social and Architectural Reformation of Smithfield Market during the 19th Century', *Transactions of the Ancient Monuments Society*, 42 (1998), pp. 1–12.

Robinson, R. J., '"The Civilizing Process": Some Remarks on Elias's Social History', *Sociology*, 21:1 (February 1987), pp. 1–17.

Rogers, N., 'London's Marginal Histories', *Labour/Le Travail*, 60 (Fall 2007), pp. 217–34.

Rodger, R., *Housing in Urban Britain 1780–1914* (Basingstoke: Macmillan, 1989).

Ross, E., 'Survival Networks: Women's Neighbourhood Sharing in London before World War One', *History Workshop Journal*, 15 (Spring 1983), pp. 4–27.

—, '"Not the Sort that Would Sit on the Doorstep": Respectability in Pre-World War I London Neighbourhoods', *International Labour and Working-Class History*, 27 (Spring 1985), pp. 39–59.

Rudé, G., *Paris and London in the Eighteenth Century* (Harmondsworth: Penguin, 1973).

Rule, J., *The Experience of Labour in Eighteenth Century English Industry* (New York: St Martin's Press, 1981).

St Martin in the Fields, *Report on the Subject of the Casual Poor Admitted by Relief Tickets into the Workhouse of the Parish of St. Martin in the Fields* (London: J. Smith, 1839).

Sala, G., *Twice Round the Clock* (New York: Humanities Press, 1971).

Schwarz, L. D., 'Occupations and Incomes in Late Eighteenth-Century London', *East End Papers*, 14:2 (December 1972), pp. 87–100.

—, 'Conditions of Life and Work in London, c. 1770–1820, with Special Reference to East London' (unpublished D.Phil. thesis, University of Oxford, 1976).

—, 'Income Distribution and Social Structure in London in the Late Eighteenth Century', *Economic History Review*, 2nd ser., 32:2 (1979), pp. 250–9.

—, 'The Standard of Living in the Long Run: London 1700–1860', *Economic History Review*, 2nd ser., 38:1 (1985), pp. 24–41.

—, *London in the Age of Industrialisation* (Cambridge: Cambridge University Press, 1992).

—, 'Review', *Journal of Historical Geography*, 23:1 (January 1997), pp. 81–2

—, 'London 1700–1840', in P. Clark (ed.), *The Cambridge Urban History of Britain*, Vol. 2 (Cambridge: Cambridge University Press, 2000), pp. 641–72.

—, 'Hanoverian London: The Making of a Service Town', in P. Clark and R. Gillespie (eds), *Two Capitals: London and Dublin 1500–1840* (Oxford: Oxford University Press, 2001), pp. 93–110.

Scott, J. C., *Weapons of the Weak: Everyday Forms of Peasant Resistance* (New Haven, CT: Yale University Press, 1987).

—, *Domination and the Arts of Resistance* (New Haven, CT: Yale University Press, 1990).

—, *Seeing Like a State: How Certain Schemes to Improve the Human Condition Have Failed* (New Haven, CT: Yale University Press, 1999).

Sharpe, J. A., *Defamation and Sexual Slander in Early Modern England: The Church Courts at York*, Borthwick Papers No. 58 (York: University of York, 1980).

—, *Remember Remember the Fifth of November: Guy Fawkes and the Gunpowder Plot* (London: Profile, 2006).

Shesgreen, S., *Images of the Outcast: The Urban Poor in the Cries of London* (New Brunswick, NJ: Rutgers University Press, 2002).

Shoemaker, R., 'Decline of the Public Insult in London, 1660–1800', *Past and Present*, 169 (2000), pp. 97–131.

—, 'Male Honour and the Decline of Public Violence in Eighteenth-Century London', *Social History*, 26:2 (May 2001), pp. 190–208.

—, 'The Taming of the Duel: Masculinity, Honour and Ritual Violence in London, 1660–1800', *Historical Journal*, 45:3 (2002), pp. 525–45.

—, 'Public Spaces, Private Disputes? Fights and Insults on London's Streets, 1660–1800', in T. Hitchcock and H. Shore (eds), *The Streets of London* (London: Rivers Oram Press, 2003), pp. 54–68.

—, 'Streets of Shame? The Crowd and Public Punishments in London 1700–1820', in S. Devereux and P. Griffiths (eds), *Penal Practice and Culture* (Basingstoke: Palgrave Macmillan, 2004), pp. 232–57.

—, *The London Mob* (London: Hambledon and London, 2004).

Simond, L., *Journal of a Tour and Residence in Great Britain during the Years 1810 and 1811* (London: Archibald Constable and Co., 1815).

Sims, G., *How the Poor Live* (London: Chatto and Windus, 1883).

Smith, G., 'Civilized People Don't Want to See That Kind of Thing: The Decline of Public Physical Punishment in London, 1760–1840', in C. Strange (ed.), *Qualities of Mercy* (Vancouver: University of British Columbia Press, 1996), pp. 21–51.

Smith, W., *Consumption and the Making of Respectability 1600–1800* (New York: Routledge, 2002).

Soja, E. W., *Postmodern Geographies: The Reassertion of Space in Critical Social Theory* (London: Verso, 1989).

—, 'Author's Response', *Progress in Human Geography*, 30 (December 2006), pp. 817–20.

Sokoll, T., *Essex Pauper Letters, 1731–1837* (Oxford: Oxford University Press, 2001).

Spierenburg, P. (ed.), *Men and Violence: Gender, Honor, and Rituals in Modern Europe and America* (Columbus, OH: Ohio State University Press, 1998).

Stedman Jones, G., *Outcast London* (Harmondsworth: Penguin, 1971).

—, 'The Cockney and the Nation, 1780–1988', in D. Feldman and G. Stedman Jones (eds), *Metropolis London: Histories and Representations since 1800* (London: Routledge, 1989), pp. 301–28.

Steinberg, M., 'The Dialogue of Struggle: The Contest over Ideological Boundaries in the Case of the London Silk Weavers in the Early Nineteenth Century', *Social Science History*, 18:4 (Winter 1994), pp. 505–42.

—, 'The Roar of the Crowd: Repertoires of Discourse and Collective Action among the Spitalfields Silk Weavers in Nineteenth-Century London', in M. Traugott (ed.), *Repertoires and Cycles of Collective Action* (Durham, NC: Duke University Press, 1995), pp. 57–87.

—, '"The Labour of the Country is the Wealth of the Country": Class Identity, Consciousness, and the Role of Discourse in the Making of the English Working Class', *International and Working-Class History*, 49 (Spring 1996), pp. 1–25.

—, *Fighting Words: Working-Class Formation, Collective Action and Discourse in Early Nineteenth-Century England* (Ithaca, NY: Cornell University Press, 1999).

—, 'The Talk and Back Talk of Collective Action: A Dialogic Analysis of Repertoires of Discourse among Nineteenth-Century English Cotton Spinners', *American Journal of Sociology*, 105:3 (November 1999), pp. 736–80.

Stewart, F. H., *Honor* (Chicago, IL: University of Chicago Press, 1994).

Storch, R., '"Please to Remember the Fifth of November": Conflict, Solidarity and Public Order in Southern England, 1815–1900', in R. Storch (ed.), *Popular Culture and Custom in Nineteenth-Century England* (London: Croom Helm, 1982), pp. 71–99.

Tanner, A., 'The Casual Poor and the City of London Poor Law Union, 1837–1869', *Historical Journal*, 42 (1999), pp. 183–206.

—, 'Dust-O! Rubbish in Victorian London, 1860–1900', *London Journal*, 31:2 (November 2006), pp. 157–78.

Taylor, B., *Eve and the New Jerusalem* (London: Virago, 1983).

Taylor, J. S., *Poverty, Migration and Settlement in the Industrial Revolution* (Palo Alto, CA: Society for the Promotion of Science and Scholarship, 1989).

Tebbutt, M., *Making Ends Meet: Pawnbroking and Working-Class Credit* (Leicester: Leicester University Press, 1983).

—, *Women's Talk: A Social History of 'Gossip' in Working Class Neighbourhoods, 1880–1960* (Aldershot: Scolar Press, 1997).

Thomas, K., *The Ends of Life* (Oxford: Oxford University Press, 2009).

Thompson, E. P., and E. Yeo (eds), *The Unknown Mayhew* (Harmondsworth: Penguin, 1974).

Thompson, F. M. L., *The Rise of Respectable Society* (Cambridge, MA: Harvard University Press, 1988).

Thompson, V., 'Telling "Spatial Stories": Urban Space and Bourgeois Identity in Early Nineteenth-Century Paris', *Journal of Modern History*, 75 (September 2003), pp. 523–56.

Tomkins, A., 'Pawnbroking and the Survival Strategies of the Urban Poor in 1770s York', in S. King and A. Tomkins (eds), *The Poor in England, 1700–1850* (Manchester: Manchester University Press, 2003), pp. 166–98.

—, *The Experience of Urban Poverty, 1723–82: Parish, Charity and Credit* (Manchester and New York: Manchester University Press, 2006).

Treble, J. H., *Urban Poverty in Britain* (New York: St Martin's Press, 1979).

Tristan, F., *The London Journal of Flora Tristan 1842: The Aristocracy and the Working Class of England* (London: Virago, 1989).

Turvey, R., 'Street Mud, Dust and Noise', *London Journal*, 21:2 (1996), pp. 131–48.

Twells, A., *The Civilising Mission and the English Middle Class, 1792–1850* (Basingstoke: Palgrave Macmillan, 2009).

Van Krieken, R., 'Violence, Self-Discipline and Modernity: Beyond the "Civilizing Process"', *Sociological Review*, 37 (1989), pp. 193–218.

Vickery, A., 'An Englishman's Home is his Castle? Thresholds, Boundaries and Privacies in the Eighteenth-Century London House', *Past and Present*, 199 (May 2008), pp. 147–73.

—, *Behind Closed Doors* (New Haven, CT: Yale University Press, 2009).

Vincent, D., *Bread, Knowledge and Freedom* (London: Europa, 1981).

Waddams, S. M., *Sexual Slander in Nineteenth-Century England: Defamation in the Ecclesiastical Courts, 1815–1855* (Toronto: University of Toronto Press, 2000).

Walker, G., *Gatherings from Graveyards* (London: Longman and Co., 1839).

W. C., 'Costers and their Donkeys', *Chambers's Journal*, 727 (1 December 1877), pp. 753–5.

Wegs, R. J., 'Working-Class Respectability: The Viennese Experience', *Journal of Social History*, 15:4 (1982), pp. 621–35.

Weld, C. R., 'On the Condition of the Working Classes in the Inner Ward of St. George's Parish, Hanover Square', *Royal Statistical Society, London Journal*, ser. A, 6:1 (April 1843), pp. 17–23.

Weinreb, B., and C. Hibbert, *The London Encyclopaedia* (London: Macmillan, 1987).

White, J., *London in the Nineteenth Century* (London: Vintage, 2008).

White, M., '"Rogues of the Meaner Sort"? Old Bailey Executions and the Crowd in the Early Nineteenth Century', *London Journal*, 33:2 (July 2008), pp. 135–53.

Wiener, M., *Men of Blood: Violence, Manliness, and Criminal Justice in Victorian England* (Cambridge: Cambridge University Press, 2006).

Williamson, J., *Did British Capitalism Breed Inequality?* (Boston, MA: Allen and Unwin, 1985).

Willmott, P., and M. Young, *Family and Kinship East London* (London: Routledge and Kegan Paul, 1963).

Wilson, P., 'Filcher of Good Names: An Enquiry into Anthropology and Gossip', *Man*, new ser., 9 (1974), pp. 93–102.

Winter, J., *London's Teeming Streets, 1830-1914* (London: Routledge, 1993).

Wohl, A., *The Eternal Slum* (New Brunswick, NJ: Transaction Publishers, 2009).

Wrightson, K., 'Mutualities and Obligations: Changing Social Relationships in Early Modern England', *Proceedings of the British Academy*, 139 (2006), pp. 157–94.

Zukin, S., 'Postmodern Urban Landscapes: Mapping Culture and Power', in S. Lash and J. Friedman (eds), *Modernity and Identity* (Oxford: Blackwell, 1992), pp. 221–47.

INDEX

Abrams, Philip, 3
Adelaide, Queen (wife of William IV), 142
adultery, 22
Alexander, Sally, 93, 94, 95
Amer, Catherine (in court records), 38
Anderson, Michael, 87, 88
animals, cruelty to, 4, 148
    dog fights, 153
anti-Semitism, 92
apprenticeships, 85, 96–7
    see also employment patterns
armed forces, 84, 111
Armstrong, W. A., 82
Ashford, Mary Ann
    as a domestic servant, 91–2, 135–6, 137,
        139, 140, 143
    family, 135–8, 140–1, 142
    financial position, 137, 138, 140–2
    Life of a Licenced Victualler's Daughter,
        91, 135–44
    pregnancies, 11–12
    as a respectable woman, 135, 137–44,
        154
August, Andrew, *Poor Women's Lives*, 87, 88
autobiographies/biographies, 29, 34, 35–7,
        41–2, 43, 55, 88, 91–2, 97, 100, 101,
        111–12, 113, 119, 135–44
    accuracy/value, 9

Babbage, Charles, 59
Badcock, John, 53
Bailey, Joanne, 62–3
Bailey, Peter, 9
bakers, 101
Bakhtin group, 10
Ball, Michael and David Sunderland, *An
    Economic History of London*, 79

banking/financial markets, 12, 13, 79, 81
    bank failures, 12, 81
    personal banking, 136
Barber, Jane (in court records), 40
BBC, 3
Beames, Thomas, *The Rookeries of London*,
    48
beggars, 16, 32, 108–10
    Mendicity Society for assistance to, 100,
        108–9, 110
    women/children as, 109, 110
behaviour, 1–4, 16, 139–40, 155–6
    civilizing of *see* social change
    as compartmentalized/variable, 9
    deference, 3, 47, 139–41, 142
    at hangings, 29
    individual responsibility, 2, 4, 7, 8, 37
    marital, 24–5
    resistance/accommodation, 9–11, 138,
        142
    respectable *see* respectability
    as situational, 9
    street disputes, 5–6, 57–61, 131–2
    visual surveillance of, 47
    of women, 22–33
        control over, 25–6, 92
        sexual, 21–7, 171n18
Benson, John, *The Penny Capitalists*, 149
Best, Geoffrey, *Mid-Victorian Britain*, 7
Bland, Elizabeth (in court records), 39, 40
Booth, Charles, 81, 82
borrowing *see* credit; mutual support
Boulton, J., *Neighbourhood and Society*,
    183n19
Bower, William (in court records), 26, 31
Bradley, Ann (in court records), 42

For Product Safety Concerns and Information please contact our EU
representative GPSR@taylorandfrancis.com
Taylor & Francis Verlag GmbH, Kaufingerstraße 24, 80331 München, Germany

www.ingramcontent.com/pod-product-compliance
Ingram Content Group UK Ltd.
Pitfield, Milton Keynes, MK11 3LW, UK
UKHW021614240425
457818UK00018B/559